Got Murder?

The Shocking Story of
Wisconsin's Notorious Killers

Martin Hintz

Trails Books
Madison, Wisconsin

Library of Congress Control Number: 2007932369
ISBN 13: 978-1-931599-96-2

Editor: Mark Knickelbine
Designer: Mark Porter

Printed in the United States of America.
12 11 10 09 08 07   6 5 4 3 2 1

Trails Books, a division of Big Earth Publishing
923 Williamson Street • Madison, WI 53703
(800) 258-5830 • www.trailsbooks.com

CONTENTS

Acknowledgments

The author wishes to thank all those who provided background on *Got Murder? The Shocking Story of Wisconsin's Notorious Killers*. Their insights and assistance were invaluable in researching and writing this compendium of Wisconsin's baddest of the bad. Extra thanks go to Maureen Doll, Mario Raspanti, Elizabeth Altman, Rebecca Russell, Beth Jamnek, and Kate Grande who jump-started the digging on several cases.

A nod must be given to all the reporters, editors, and photographers who covered and shaped these complex stories as they broke, meeting deadlines and demonstrating that a vibrant press always provides the rough draft of history. Thanks especially to all the authors whose books on the criminal mind were always fascinating, albeit sometimes frightening.

Thanks also to Lt. Kurt Barthel, jail administrator, Sawyer County Jail; Steven Beck, assistant warden, Redgranite Correctional Institution; attorney Jerry Boyle; attorney Michael Bowen, president, Council for Wisconsin Writers; Ryan Bronson, supervisor, Southeast Asian Outreach Program, Minnesota Department of Natural Resources; Dale G. Burke, assistant chief, University of Wisconsin-Madison police department; Dennis Chaptman, University Communications, University of Wisconsin-Madison; John Dipko, Wisconsin Department of Corrections; Brian Downes, *The Chicago Tribune*; Ron Glensor, assistant chief of police, Reno, Nevada, independent learning instructor in criminal justice, University of Nevada, Reno; Mike Hanson, City of Madison Police Department; Sergeant Ken Henning, Milwaukee Police Department; Craig Jacobsen, Taliesen Preservation; Philip Kingston, warden, Waupun Correctional Institution; Richard Leonard, retired editor, *The Milwaukee Journal*; E. Michael McCann, retired Milwaukee County district attorney; Dennis P. McCormick, assistant library director, *The Capital Times/Wisconsin State Journal*; Frank Meyers, retired director, Division of Criminal Investigation, Wisconsin Department of Justice; Doug Moe, *The Capital Times*.

Plus, Dale Mueller, retired special agent and coordinator of the polygraph exam unit, FBI Milwaukee Field Office; Dick Otto, operations director, natural resources office, U.S. Army Corps of

Engineers; Martha Rolli, MD, co-director, in-patient psychiatric care, University of Wisconsin Hospital and Clinics; Barry Slagle, Milwaukee court commissioner; John Stanley, Dane County coroner; Kevin Strum, Bureau of Justice Statistics, U.S. Department of Justice; Ryan Sugden, Wisconsin Office of Justice Assistance; historian Bobby Tanzilo; Mark D. Thibodeau, Adams County district attorney, and the office staff of the Adams County Clerk of Circuit Courts; Officer Richard Thompson, Open Records Division, Milwaukee Police Department; Sauk County district attorney staff; Wisconsin Department of Justice; Wisconsin Attorney General's Office; the Frank Lloyd Wright Foundation; and Chief Deputy Tim Zeigle, Sawyer County Sheriff's Department.

And all the others . . .

To the victims and their families

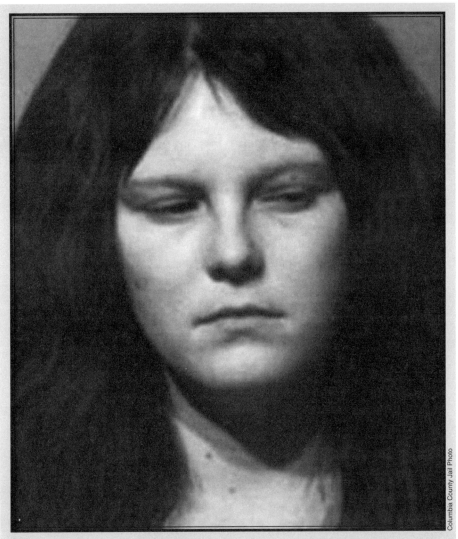

Candace Clark was charged with participating in the murder of a woman and the torture of an 11-year-old boy.

Introduction

Cesspool of the Human Soul

Was that a noise outside your window?
What's that shadow on the blind?
As you lie there naked
Like a body in a tomb
Suspended animation
As I slip into your room . . .

—AC/DC, "Night Prowler," *Highway to Hell* [1]

It happened again. In the early summer of 2007, headlines about a bizarre murder in the Wisconsin heartland shocked the world.

On June 14, Portage police received a request from investigators in Florida to visit an a house on Oneida Street; the Florida cops had a tip that a 2-year-old girl, abducted by her mother from her foster parents, might be there.

At the home, police and investigators discovered three young girls between the ages of 3 months and 2 years old, a 15-year-old girl, and two adult women. The older suspects at first gave false names, but further questioning revealed that one of the women was the mother police were seeking, Candace Clark, and that the two youngest girls were her daughters, including the one taken from Florida.

But that wasn't all. The suspects also revealed that there was an 11-year-old boy being held in a closet of the Oneida Street house. And a body buried in the backyard.

Police returned to the home the next day and found the boy

cowering in a closet, malnourished and covered with burns that looked like they were made with boiling water. A cadaver dog alerted them to a spot of fresh landscaping in the yard; later that afternoon, police dug up the remains of Tammie Garlin, 36, the mother of the boy and the 15-year-old girl.

A case of kidnapping, child torture, and apparent murder would have been horrifying enough for the people of Portage, a quiet community in the rolling hills along the Wisconsin River that bills itself as "Where the North Begins." But the story that unfolded over the next several days was almost unbelievably grotesque.

On June 20, police charged the 15-year-old, Felicia Mae Garlin, along with three adults—Candace Clark, 23, Michaela Clerc, 20, and Michael Sisk, 25, who had been captured at the Greyhound bus station the day the body was found. All were charged with first-degree intentional homicide, abuse of a child, mutilation, hiding a corpse, false imprisonment, aggravated battery, three other felonies and a misdemeanor. The adults were also each charged with contributing to the delinquency of a child.

According to police, the group was a band of grifters that had financed its activities through fraud and identity theft. Garlin and Clerc had been lesbian lovers, and Sisk was Clark's boyfriend. The group had wandered from Florida to Portage in the fall of 2006 after stops in Maine and Wisconsin Dells, with Garlin and Clark's children in tow; they told police they came north because they wanted to see the snow.

Over the next few months, life in the household became increasingly violent, possibly due to tension that erupted when Tammie Garlin expressed a sexual interest in Clark. According to the criminal complaint, the boy said that on at least 10 occasions, the group tied him up, placed him in a bathtub and poured scalding water over his body. The torture mutilated the boy's hands, feet and head.

As the *Milwaukee Journal Sentinel* reported, "The adults also whipped the boy with belts and extension cords, [he told a medical investigator], hog-tied him, choked him until his eyes would close and forced him to drink gallons of water until he passed out. He said he got one meal a day and often had to stay in a cramped space under the stairway."

The boy told the investigator that his mother had joined in the torture—until she herself became a victim of the deranged "family."

Clark and Felicia Garlin told police that Tammie Garlin was kicked and abused by the others after she became incapacitated sometime shortly before her death. After Sisk reportedly bashed Tammie Garlin in the head with a folding chair, Clark stitched up the wound herself.

Clark said that Sisk went into the bathroom with the unresponsive Garlin, emerged a few minutes later, and announced, "She's dead." The report of Garlin's autopsy later identified the cause of her death as strangulation.

Felicia Garlin told police that she then helped the adults remove her mother's body through the bathroom window, and later helped Sisk bury the dead woman in the back yard, according to the criminal complaint. [2]

At the time of this writing, the facts in the confusing case were still emerging, and the trials of the suspects were yet to be scheduled. But one thing was starkly, terrifyingly clear: Yet another shocking homicide had been added to the annals of crime in Badgerland.

For all its bucolic Dairy State iconography, Wisconsin has never been immune to murderous tragedy, whether a single death, the heinous crimes of serial killers, or a mass catastrophe. Since the days of early statehood, this land of cow pasture, northern forest, and urban pavement has witnessed incidents of notorious mayhem. After John McCaffary drowned his wife, Bridget, on July 23, 1850, he earned the distinction of being the last man executed under Wisconsin law. The arm and leg restraints that bound him are in the collection of the Wisconsin Historical Society; ask to look at museum objects #1976.249.1–.2.

As the home of terror superstars like Ed Gein and Jeffrey Dahmer—and with a notoriety for unsolved murders—Wisconsin may seem like America's Mayhem-land. But is the Badger State really any more prone to whack-'n'-blast rampages than anywhere else?

"If we could understand them, we could catch them," said Frank

Got Murder?

Meyers, retired director of the Division of Criminal Investigation, Wisconsin Department of Justice. Meyers, a law enforcement veteran with thirty-four years of service, added that sometimes, however, you just can't fathom why people do what they do. Yet Meyers asserted that Wisconsin is actually no better or worse than many other states when it comes to violent crime.[3]

His assessment meshed with that of Dale Mueller, a special agent from 1971 to 2003 and polygraph specialist in Milwaukee from 1986 until his retirement. During his investigative career, Mueller provided polygraph and crime scene analysis assistance to law enforcement agencies on hundreds of violent crime cases in Wisconsin and the Midwest. Many of Mueller's examinees were violent-crime suspects.[4]

According to both law enforcement experts, despite the lurid headlines and newscasts used to attract readers and listeners, violent crime has not risen much in Wisconsin over the past four decades. In 1960, Wisconsin had a population of 3,951,777, with a murder rate of 1.3 per 100,000 people or 50 deaths. In 2005, there were 5,536,201 Wisconsinites, with a homicide rate of 3.5 per 100,000 people, with 207 reported killings.[5]

In fact, Wisconsin has shared in the national trend toward fewer violent crimes in the past decade.

According to the FBI, in 2004 compared to ten years prior, there were more than 40,000 fewer total index offenses (–20.2% change), a 15% reduction in violent crime (12,704 to 11,645) and a 32.3% drop in the number of homicides in the state (227 to 154). Using the rate of offense per 100,000 residents to adjust for population growth, the rate of total index crimes was down 27.2%, violent crime down 22.4%, and homicides down 37.8%. In Wisconsin in 2004, there were 2.8 murders per 100,000 Wisconsin residents—more than 50% less than the 2003 national rate of 5.7 murders per 100,000—and homicides made up only 0.1% of all index crime.[6]

Even in Milwaukee, Wisconsin's only metropolis and a place some out-state folks think of as a cross between Chicago and Sodom, crime also dropped significantly between 1994 and 2004. Total index crimes were down 26.74%, violent crime down 27.74%, and murders down

37.4%. In Madison and Green Bay, Wisconsin's other urban areas with populations currently at more than 100,000, overall crime rates dropped over the same period, with slight increases of homicide in Green Bay and violent crime in Madison.[7]

Early analysis of 2005 and 2006 crime data showed a rise in violent crime in the nation and the state. In Wisconsin, murders were up in 2005 but dropped again in 2006. According to a semiannual report recently issued by the FBI, violent crime in the United States is up nearly 3.7% in the first half of 2006 compared to the first six months of 2005. The FBI stated that in the violent crime category, the number of robbery offenses increased 9.7%, murders increased 1.4%, and aggravated assault offenses rose 1.2%. Forcible rape decreased less than 0.1%. Cities with populations of 500,000 to 999,999 had the largest increase in reported murders, up 8.4%. In metropolitan communities, reported murder offense increased 3.1%. While overall, violent crime increased throughout the country during the reporting period, at this writing, it is difficult to definitively tell if this recent surge of violent crime is or is not the beginning of an upward trend.[8]

Homicides in Milwaukee plummeted 16% in 2006, compared with the previous year. The drop was attributed to the decrease in fatal robberies. There were 88 people killed in 2004, 122 in 2005, and 103 in 2006. Of the 2006 toll, the median age of the murdered was twenty-four, with thirty-six being twenty-one and under. Most were males; 84.5% of the former and 80.6% of the latter were black. Guns were the major death-dealing instruments of choice, at 75.7%.[9]

* * * *

While single homicides of individuals are terror enough, Wisconsinites are shocked by mass murders, a relatively rare occurrence in which numerous victims are killed in one horrific incident. Often the perpetrator then commits suicide or is killed by the authorities. On the next deadly step up the heinous ladder are serial killers, who kill three or more people over an extended period of time (some authorities lower the threshold to two murders).

Criminals who commit a string of murders are often psychopaths, who at first glance can seem normal and charming . . . until they kill. The common conception of the "psycho killer" includes the sexual overtone that often seems associated with their actions. However, University of Wisconsin–Madison psychologist Joseph Newman warns that the "psychopath" label is too often applied to ordinary criminals and sex offenders whose "behavior may reflect primarily social factors or other emotional problems that are more amenable to treatment than to psychopathy." His research shows that psychopathy is similar to a learning disability. A psychopath seems to be characterized by the interaction of information-processing deficits with violent inclinations influenced by social climate, aggressive personality traits, and related factors. Without such circumstances, Newman does not believe that the common deviant is significantly prone to violence or killing.[10]

However mysterious the motivation of a serial killer, there is one safe bet: the perpetrator is probably a white man. White males are much more likely to be serial killers than male African Americans or male Hispanics. There are female serial killers, who usually murder people they know or participate in the crimes of husbands or boyfriends. Women number barely 8% of American serial killers. African Americans make up 12% percent of the American population but only 5% of serial killers; Hispanics account for approximately the same percentages. Whites comprise 75% of the population but 90% of serial killers, according to Eric Hickey, a criminal psychology professor at California State University in Fresno. [11]

It doesn't take a psychologist to realize that people who kill for fun are criminally insane individuals, their minds twisted because of a mental illness. Tragically, their crimes might have been prevented if their diseases were caught and treated in time. The trend toward deinstitutionalizing the mentally ill, along with declining resources to meet the growing demand for treatment, and our general social stigma against mental illness may mean that the disease of psychopathy—the disease that kills others—is one of the least treated of all.[12]

Given the terrible nature of their crimes, murderers might be expected to plead not guilty by reason of insanity—and they often do. Making that plea stand up in court, however, hinges upon whether the defendant knew the difference between right and wrong when committing the crime. Even a diagnosis of mental illness will not get a defendant off if the jury is convinced that the killer knew he was doing wrong. And even when a defendant is found not guilty because of a mental deficit, the murderer is not allowed to go free, as some in the public perceive. The state has had two primary care facilities for such individuals, each offering a range of security levels from minimum through moderate to high risk. The latter comes complete with the bars and all the other trappings of a full-blown jail, making them distinctly unpleasant places in which to live.

The FBI has two general categorizes of serial killers. The first are the organized types, usually highly intelligent. They plan their murders carefully, often kidnapping their victims and getting rid of their bodies in another place. Then there are the disorganized ones, people usually of low intelligence who use whatever weapons are close at hand. They don't plan their assaults or make an effort to hide their murderous acts. Police seek signatures, or psychological markers, that might link one crime to the next. The killer might perform an act that is beyond what is necessary to commit murder, such as posing the body, or he may rely on a characteristic modus operandi such as a particular method of strangulation.[13]

Chicago forensic psychiatrist Helen Morrison, who keeps the brain of Windy City murderer John Wayne Gacy in a plastic bag in her basement for further study, believes serial killers are often hypochondriac men who talk a lot. Remorseless, they stab, strangle, and rape, looking at their unfortunate victims as inanimate objects. "You say to yourself, 'How could anybody do this to another human being?'" Morrison said. "Then you realize they don't see them as humans. To the killer, it's like pulling the wings off a fly or the legs off a daddy long legs. You just want to see what happens. It's the most base experiment."[14]

Often footloose vagrants or employed in jobs that allow them to travel, serial killers pop up around the country. One well-traveled example is Alabama-born white supremacist Joseph Paul Franklin. In a three-year span, Franklin is thought to have killed between thirteen and twenty victims, many of whom were interracial couples. Disguised as a cowboy, Franklin held up a bank in Madison on August 7, 1977. While fleeing, Franklin shot and killed a black man and a white woman, Alphonse Manning and Toni Schwenn, apparently angered by the slow pace of Manning's driving. He murdered the motorist when Manning eventually stopped and got out of his auto, and then shot Schwenn.[15]

Franklin continued his shooting spree in Georgia, West Virginia, Utah, and other states, returning to Wisconsin in the spring of 1980. He allegedly shot hitchhiker Rebecca Bergstrom with a handgun near Tomah on May 2. Franklin was arrested in September 1980, and finally confessed to Bergstrom's murder in 1984. During a myriad of trials, he was convicted in the Manning and Schwenn deaths and received two life sentences in 1985 for the murders.[16]

Serial killers often target their victims among the community's most vulnerable members. Hookers, drug addicts, and others who live on the fringes of society are often unprotected and little missed or mourned. In fact, the outcast status of their victims may help killers rationalize their behavior through a twisted sense of self-righteousness.

Throughout the 1990s, one or more killers stalked and murdered at least twelve women and dumped their bodies throughout Milwaukee's North Side. The dead were black prostitutes and addicts who, despite their ragged lives, certainly did not deserve to be killed and flung into garbage bins. Some authorities thought that another serial killer was again ravaging the community, since the memory of Jeffrey Dahmer's methodical mayhem was still fresh. Forensic psychiatrist George Palermo, who worked at the Milwaukee County Jail, believed that such a murderer was afoot.[17]

But the FBI's Dale Mueller believes any large city with a population of prostitutes will have a serial killer, one who kills either on a self-proclaimed mission to rid the community of such women or because he is high on drugs, possibly needing money for a fix.[18]

In that string of deaths, a fifty-two-year-old crack addict, George L. "Mule" Jones eventually was charged and convicted for the murder of one victim, Shameika Carter, and was sent to prison for life without parole. Jones was also considered a prime suspect in several other mysterious murders during that time. Authorities believed he dope-dated the victims, exchanging sex for drugs. Apparently, Jones strangled Carter when she laughed at his inability to perform sexually. Jones was also later convicted of stabbing a woman to death in Mississippi in the early 1970s.[19]

Most serial killers come from dysfunctional backgrounds and often were physically, sexually, or psychologically abused as children. As such, there is usually a link between the crime and what happened to them while they were growing up. Often the killers display at least three warning signs as youngsters: starting fires, cruelty to animals, and bed-wetting. They can turn into thrill seekers, viewing both the hunt and murder as a game. They enjoy the media attention and evading the police. Their thirst for power and control over the victims is related to the powerlessness they felt as a young person.[20]

Wisconsin author August Derleth, who described sixteen killings in his 1968 book, *Wisconsin Murders*, had little tolerance for such psychological appeals. Of the insanity defense, he railed, "It helps…if you are possessed of a split personality, or if you can prove that your mother hated you when you were young, or if you can set forth with moderate conviction that your little ego was painfully wounded by society when you were only three weeks old…Judges are always impressed with the plea that you should have another (and another and another) chance, even if you didn't give your victim a snowball's chance in hell."[21]

If Derleth didn't buy psychological excuses for murder, he trusted the notion of rehabilitation even less. "The sociologists and the psychiatrists have a quaint credo which holds that if a murderer can be rehabilitated (whether or not he has ever been habilated) it is a mark of social progress, even if it costs the lives of several of the murderer's victims in order to bring about this happy state," Derleth wrote.[22]

He then railed on about the "mob of demented yokels" who can always weep copiously for murderers and shed nary a tear for their victims. Yet Derleth agreed that murderers were "interesting characters" and that their ingenuity in dealing death "has a fascination all its own." His stories, he asserted, were not morality tales but simply studies in murder, "rather of character and circumstances than of suspense and gore. They are primarily inquiries into states of mind which, but for the grace of God, might be our own."[23]

* * * *

One of the difficulties of establishing whether a string of serial murders is in progress is knowing who is dead and who is merely missing. Without evidence of foul play, there is little the authorities can do. At the time of the Dahmer murders, 882 Wisconsinites were considered missing persons, as reported by the National Crime Information Center.[24] "We didn't know we had a serial killer in Milwaukee," Milwaukee County District Attorney E. Michael McCann recalled fifteen years after the tragedies. He pointed out that cases of missing males are viewed differently by police than those of missing women or children. "So many men and older boys up and go and then come back," he said, adding that unless there is foul play involved, there is not much the police can do. Often, cases remain open because families never report when a man returns home.[25]

"If you are over the age of emancipation, you have the right to be missing," FBI spokesman Bill Carter said in a 1991 interview around the time of the Dahmer murders. "If you decide you no longer want to live where you live . . . it's a free country," he pointed out.[26]

In order to determine whether or not any given murder was part of a serial string, you have to first solve the case—and a disturbing number of murder cases in Wisconsin are simply never solved. It's a phenomenon that amazed FBI agent Dale Mueller when he was first assigned to Wisconsin in 1976. Since the statute of limitations never runs out on such cases, both the FBI and the Wisconsin Department of Justice are always ready to help with any such "cold cases" if requested by a local jurisdiction.[27]

In 2005, the Milwaukee Police Department clearance rate on the year's 122 murder cases was 71%; for the 103 murders in 2006, the clearance was 72%. The department points out that it has one of the highest rates in the nation for a city its size due to the round-the-clock work by its Criminal Investigation Bureau. Unlike some departments elsewhere, the incoming shift of homicide detectives in Milwaukee is briefed by the outgoing shift for a seamless transition in the investigation. Although it is always a challenge in cases when witnesses do not come forward, the department's high clearance rate is also attributed to the fact that most often witnesses do come forward.[28]

It was August Derleth's feeling that the unlikelihood of being caught contributed to Wisconsin's prominence as a murder hotspot. As he wrote in the introduction to his volume on Wisconsin homicides, "The accounts which go to make up this book are inquiries into the curious states of mind of some citizens of Wisconsin, and an examination of all the trouble they went to in order to commit murder in a state where murder can be done with at worst no more than an inconvience."[29]

* * * *

The image of the killer has been a fixture of American popular culture even before nineteenth-century author Edgar Allan Poe began transcribing his chilling stories. A popular sociology class at the University of Wisconsin–Whitewater in 2004 explored this interest in serial murder cases, discussing Ted Bundy, Charles Manson, John Wayne Gacy, David Berkowitz, and other killers. Speakers included defense attorney Gerald Boyle and Milwaukee County District Attorney E. Michael McCann, central figures involved in the Jeffrey Dahmer case. In the class, instructor Wayne Youngquist traced the sociological causes of serial murderers, saying that his students were fascinated with the simple notion of good versus evil, "white hat vs. black hat—good guy, bad guy."[30]

At other times, interest in murder may not be so educational or benign. In 1991, one company began turning out trading cards featuring prominent murderers, including Wisconsin's own Ed Gein and Jeffrey Dahmer, while another company manufactures serial killer action figures. Comic books have celebrated murderers' exploits, again with Dahmer among the offerings. Even *People* listed the former chocolate company employee as one of the hundred most intriguing personalities of the twentieth century.[31] This material is fascinating because it's so bizarre to most people.[32]

Got Murder?

Popular television shows trace the crimes of other killers, complemented by dozens of Web sites devoted to murder and massacre. Actors such as Oscar-winning Charlize Theron, who played serial killer Aileen Wuornos in the 2003 film, *Monster,* sometimes are called on to portray their characters in a sympathetic light. Dozens of films fictionalize the actions of killers, including the terrifying *The Silence of the Lambs* (1991) and *The Red Dragon* (2002), along with other such scary titles like *Copycat* (1995) and *Natural Born Killers* (1994).[33]

Music stores peddle discs that play up the macabre, including songs by a band of that same name. New York-based punkers in the group Ed Gein's Car were barely glints in their grandparents' eyes when the Plainfield handyman performed his handiwork.[34] Gein and the Graverobbers was a notable Boston "instrumental horror surf band," whose 2001 debut album included a lively rendition of "Hang Ten with Gein and the Graverobbers."[35] The California alternative metal band Marilyn Manson is happy to promote its own brand of shock rock , with each musician member taking the name of a serial killer in memory of cult leader Charles Manson.[36]

Lively lyrics such as the following from Church of Misery's "Room 213"—which are certainly not from your mother's "Kumbaya"—refer to Jeffrey Dahmer's home apartment number:

> *You can smell someone's rotting*
> *Death comes behind you*
> *There's nowhere to run*
> *Dismembered your remains and nobody cares*
> *Factory of murder is this Room 213.*[37]

Perhaps attempting to subconsciously mask the horrible reality of these vicious murders, puns and jokes abound about killers. Yucks about Gein were so popular that they actually earned the sobriquet "Geiners."

Q: What did Ed Gein have for dessert?
A: Lady fingers.

Introduction

Q: Why did they have to keep the heat on in Ed Gein's house?
A: So the furniture wouldn't get goose bumps.

Q: Why did Ed Gein's girlfriend stop going out with him?
A: Because he was such a cut-up.[38]

Even though it has been years since Dahmer's murders, his name keeps popping up in contemporary jokes, such as "They've added a new charge to those against Jeffrey Dahmer. Apparently, he was selling arms to Saddam Hussein." Then there are the old favorites: "Did you know the Milwaukee cannibal was let out on bail today? I heard it cost him an arm and a leg." And "A neighbor comes over to Dahmer's apartment, asking to borrow some lettuce. His response, 'Look in the fridge, I'm sure there must be a head in there somewhere.'"[39]

Even if crime statistics don't bear out the myth that the Dairy State produces as much homicide as cheese, the iconic infamy of killers like Gein and Dahmer keep the idea alive. Could Wisconsin cheese be a factor in manslaughter? Can the state food result in mental aberrations? An intensive British Cheese Guild study in 2005 showed that munching cheese a half hour before going to bed resulted in weird dreams, particularly for women. The research showed that 85% of the women studied who ate Stilton, called the King of Cheeses, were most affected. This variety of flavorful blue cheese is the only British cheese with its own trademark. Yet recorded visions induced after eating this cheese included those of a vegetarian crocodile angry because it could not devour children, party guests being exchanged for camels, and a riotous soiree in a lunatic asylum.[40]

Apparently, say the Brits, selecting the type of cheese one eats before bedtime may "help determine the very nature of often colorful and vivid cheese-induced dreams." Remember also that author Charles Dickens's Ebenezer Scrooge blamed "a crumb of cheese" for seeing his late-night apparitions. The jury, as wags say, is still out on whether or not eating certain kinds of cheese leads to murder. Obviously, to be on the safe side, one should stick with quality Wisconsin Colby before retiring to the boudoir.[41]

Got Murder?

With all the off-beat humor and morbid interest in these sensational crimes, it is often easy to forget the victim. Not nameless and faceless, each was an individual with a personality, grieving survivors, and law enforcement personnel determined to track down the killers. There has been a lot of tragedy within Wisconsin's compact 65,503 square miles of land and water.[42] As an example, zeroing in on the Madison area alone, an incomplete list of unsolved murders by victim, year, and county remains long:

Georgia Jean Weckler, 1947, Jefferson
Christine Rothschild, 1968, Dane
Charles Mumford, 1969, Dane
Albert Buehl, 1969, Rock
Thomas Speer, 1971, Dane
Mark Justl, 1972, Dane
Kathy Sjoberg, 1974, Jefferson
Debra Bennett, 1976, Dane
Julie Ann Hall, 1978, Dane
Susan LeMahieu, 1979, Dane
Shirley Stewart, 1980, Dane
Timothy Hack/Kelly Drew, 1980, Jefferson
Julie Speerschneider, 1981, Dane
Donna Mraz, 1982, Dane
Barbara J. Nelson, 1982, Rock
Barbara Blackstone, 1987, Juneau
Virginia Hendrickson, 1988, Rock
Chad Maurer, 1990, Dane
Terryl Stanford, 1994, Rock
Alfred Kunz, 1998, Dane
Gregory Bray, 2003, Dane[43]

Even in Wisconsin, the happy land of Packer mania, bowling leagues, and Friday night fish fries, of North Woods serenity and Wisconsin Dells escapism, sometimes the thin barricade is torn down between society and those who have stirred the darkest cesspool of the human soul.[44] The cases in this book tell of some who fell, were pushed, or leapt into the abyss.

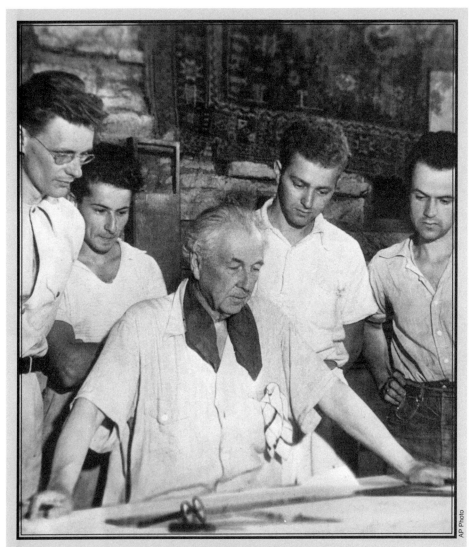

Frank Lloyd Wright and his students at Taliesin.

AP Photo

Chapter 1

The Hatchet Man of Taliesin

Spring Green, Wisconsin
August 15, 1914
Death toll: 7
Wounded: 2

With the frenzy of a fiend, sunk a shingler's
hatchet into their skulls.

—reporter, *Wisconsin State Journal*[1]

Along with its more prosaic treasures—such as cheese, football, and beer—many noted personalities claim Wisconsin as their home. Among them is Frank Lloyd Wright, one of the nation's most noted architects of the twentieth century. But even Wright's legacy was not immune from the murderous macabre. The killing of seven members of his household by a servant on August 15, 1914, remains one of the state's worst mass murders. It ranks in horror to the deaths of ten in a Milwaukee police station bombing in 1917 and the massacre of seven persons during a Brookfield church service in 2005.

The notorious Taliesin case grabbed headlines around the country, not only for the tragic death toll but also because it involved people closest to the famed architect. The sordid details of the incident included an illicit love affair, an abandoned family, and lots of lingerie, making the story ripe newspaper fodder.

Only weeks before the murders, Europe had exploded, as the assassination of Austrian Archduke Franz Ferdinand in Sarajevo

Got Murder?

heralded the onslaught of World War I.

But all that horror was far away from the quiet hills and glens along the brown-black waters of the Wisconsin River. Wright had returned here to his boyhood home after establishing his reputation as one of the country's greatest architects. "I turned to this hill in the Valley as my Grandfather before me had turned to America—as a hope and haven," he wrote in his autobiography. "There must be some kind of house that would belong to that hill, as trees and the ledges of rock did; as Grandfather and Mother had belonged to it in their sense of it all."[2]

But Wright was not merely seeking a site for a new home or the opportunity to design his own house. He also felt that, to keep his self-respect, he had to move away from his home in Oak Park, Illinois, as a "voluntary exile into the uncharted and unknown."[3] Actually, Wright had abandoned his wife, Catherine "Kitty," and their six children in 1905 to take up with Martha "Mamah" Borthwick Cheney, a feminist writer and free love advocate. Cheney, born in Boone, Iowa, in 1869 was two years younger than Wright. The mother of two young children, she was the estranged wife of electrical engineer Edwin Cheney, for whom Wright had designed and built a house in 1903.

Wright and Cheney had already spent 1909 in Europe, leaving behind a public outcry where newspaper editorials and ministers condemned them. Feeling that his professional back was against the wall because of the resulting scandal, Wright still attempted to sugarcoat the situation, saying the move back to his home state was "to test faith in Freedom. Test my faith in life, as I had already proved faith in work."[4]

Wright first returned briefly to Oak Park; he was running out of money and wanted to reunite with his children. Cheney stayed in Europe. Kitty Wright hoped for a reconciliation and restricted Wright's visits with the children to only times when his mistress was not around. But Wright would not change his mind about "the other woman." He subsequently began designing his Wisconsin masterpiece, calling it Taliesin, Welsh for "shining brow." He wanted to share the complex of studios and living quarters with Cheney as soon as she was divorced, and felt this home needed to be an emotional fortress, protecting himself and his lover.

Taliesin was a long, low structure cut into the brow of a hill. On three sides, the $50,000 building framed an oblong court; the fourth side was a terrace joining the building to the slope. At one end of another adjoining court were a granary, stables, and men's sleeping rooms. At right angles and connecting the two ends were offices, a studio, and an open loggia. A portion of the structure was being used temporarily as a dining room by the workmen and draftsmen. Despite the grandeur and innovation of Taliesin, *The Chicago Examiner,* learning of its construction in 1911, insisted on referring to Wright's masterpiece as the architect's "love nest."[5]

Cheney, retaking her maiden name of Borthwick, finally left her marriage in the summer of 1911 and moved into Taliesin. One reporter from the *Chicago Tribune* wrote that Wright had been seen carrying Borthwick across an icy brook and that she had displayed "a good deal of lingerie of a quality not often on display in that part of Wisconsin."[6]

The two lived happily together at Taliesin for three years, with Borthwick working on her writing. She also published a translation of Swedish feminist Ellen Key's writings on free love, *The Woman Movement*, and enjoyed visits from her children. Wright spent his time organizing an exhibition of his works to be showcased in San Francisco. Several of his employees moved to Taliesin to help. Wright tried to patch up the situation with his own young brood back in Illinois, attempted to get Kitty to agree to a divorce, and slowly rebuilt his practice. He had also landed a commission for blocklong Midway Gardens, a center for concerts, dancing, and restaurants on Chicago's South Side. He was assisted in the project by one of his sons, John, and commuted regularly between Wisconsin and Chicago.[7]

In 1914, Wright hired Julian Carlton, a thirty-year-old workman to act as a butler and handyman at Taliesin. Carlton's wife, Gertrude, was to be the cook. Claiming to originally come from Barbados, the Carltons were recommended by John Vogelsan, a noted Chicago restaurateur and developer of the Midway Gardens project. Carlton was of medium height, thin, and well educated. But despite the quality of his references, he soon ran afoul of the other workers around the Wright place, who distrusted him and called him hotheaded. Supposedly, a heated argument took place between Carlton and Emil Brodelle, a thirty-year-old draftsman from Milwaukee. Allegedly, Brodelle called Carlton "a black son-of-a-bitch" when he refused to saddle Brodelle's horse. Carlton soon complained to Wright that others in the household work crew were picking on him.[8]

On the fateful day of August 15, Wright, forty-seven, was again in Chicago and Borthwick was entertaining her children and handling the affairs at Taliesin. It is not known precisely what happened to set the terrible events of that day in motion. Perhaps Borthwick fired the Carltons or had some other altercation with the servants. Or perhaps Carlton considered the live-in situation between Borthwick and Wright as immoral. Some accounts say that the Carltons gave notice because Gertrude was homesick for Chicago. Several others indicated that Carlton said he committed the murders out of revenge. But regardless of the reason, their last day on the job was to be that Saturday.

The household ate lunch as usual that day, served by Carlton in his white jacket. Several workmen were in the smaller room, which was about twelve feet square. Down a hallway, Borthwick and her two children were in an enclosed porch, with its wide view of the Wisconsin River.[9]

Apparently, Carlton asked for and was given permission from Wright's foreman and master carpenter, William H. "Billy" Weston of Spring Green, to clean several carpets with gasoline. However, the handyman then took the volatile liquid and warned his wife to escape before pouring the gasoline, possibly lighting the fire by tossing a match through the kitchen door.[10]

However the exact sequence of events unfolded, the tragedy happened quickly. When those inside tried to escape, Carlton, whom the newspapers described as "the death-dealing maniac," hacked them to death with an ax. Many accounts indicate that the first victim was Borthwick, whose skull was almost split in two by the blow; she died instantly. It is believed that her son, John, eleven, was killed next. His charred bones were found later. It was theorized that Carlton poured extra gas on their bodies and set off another blaze. Borthwick's daughter,

Martha, nine, must have tried to escape because she was found dead in the courtyard. Her clothes had been burned off and there were severe burns on her arms and legs. Martha had been hit by at least three blows behind her right ear, each above the other. One had penetrated her skull.[11]

Herbert Fritz, nineteen, a draftsman from Chicago, survived the attack. He later recalled that Carlton had just left the men's dining area when the workers noticed a liquid flowing under a screen door leading outside. Realizing it was gasoline, the workmen jumped up just as one side of the room burst into flames. His clothes on fire, Fritz managed to smash through a window and tumbled to the rocky ground. Although he broke his arm, was wrapped in flames, and cut by the shattered glass, Fritz was able to roll around and extinguish the fire. He was the first out and could see Carlton running around the house with the hatchet.[12]

Fritz was followed through the window by Brodelle. As the second man struggled to get out, Carlton attacked him. Fritz watched in horror as Carlton buried his hatchet in Brodelle's head, splitting it to the hairline. The injured man staggered around the courtyard before collapsing to his knees and keeling over. He would die later in the day in the home of Andrew Porter, one of Wright's relatives who lived nearby.

Weston and the others in the dining room were trying to get out through the door beside the window. Hostler Thomas Brunker, sixty-eight, of Ridgeway, was attacked just as he made it outside. A blow smashed his brains and he lived only for a few hours. Weston's badly burned thirteen-year-old son, Ernest, was also hit, his skull collapsing under repeated blows. The boy had been visiting his father that day, helping around the compound.[13]

The elder Weston, who survived the attack, told police that Carlton struck him with the flat end of the hatchet. But the foreman was able to struggle to his feet and tried to run across the courtyard. Carlton followed him for about seventy-five feet and struck him a second time, hitting him in the neck and knocking him down again. Most likely thinking the man dead, the servant went back to the burning house. Weston crawled away, finding the moaning, severely burned David

Got Murder?

Lindblom, thirty-eight, Wright's gardener and landscape artist. The two men then made their way to a nearby home a half-mile away and telephoned the marshal in Spring Green for assistance. He, in turn, alerted the sheriffs in Sauk and Iowa counties.[14]

After calling in the alarm, Weston staggered back to the burning house and attempted to douse the fire with a garden hose. He refused to stop until rescuers forced him to leave. Among the first on the scene were Frank Sliter, who lived the closest to the Wright complex, along with other neighbors Jack Farries, Albert Beckly, and Fred Hanke. Farries found the dead Martha Cheney and Ernest Weston, who had managed to walk a short distance before collapsing. The farmer carried the youth's limp, bloodied body to the shade of a nearby tree before running back to the house where he then discovered Borthwick's charred body. The Weston boy subsequently died around 9 p.m.[15]

The Spring Green Fire Department as well as teachers and workers from the nearby Hillside Home School and the Tower Hill School of Religion and Ethics were joined by threshers working in nearby fields. They organized a bucket brigade to quench the flames. Their efforts limited the fire to Taliesin's living quarters, with two-thirds of the main building heavily damaged. Nurses Margaret Rathbun and Jennie Thompson also rushed to help. With their medical supplies, the pair arrived in Spring Green on the 4 p.m. train from Madison. Many neighbors, including women and children and Wright's uncle, the Unitarian preacher Jenkin Lloyd Jones, were among the ninety or so people on the scene.[16]

As soon as they arrived, Iowa County Sheriff John T. Williams and Sauk County Undersheriff George Peck organized a posse to hunt for the killer. Bloodhounds were brought from Richland Center. Several hundred persons fanned out across the countryside. Carlton was found by one of the searchers, Charles Burdell, who alerted Williams at about 5:30 p.m.; the killer was hiding inside the firebox of the house's unlit furnace where he was safe from the blaze upstairs. However, he had swallowed muriatic acid used to clean masonry surfaces and was in agony. Carlton stuck his head out of the furnace, crying, "Help, give me a drink." Telling the sheriff he had taken poison, he supposedly said, "Ah's gwine to die, ah is. Ah's done took poison. Ah's dying right now. You all doan' need ter kill me." The patois was probably a fiction concocted by a newspaper reporter.[17]

The sheriff grabbed the murderer by the collar and hauled him from his hiding spot, wrestling the bloody hatchet away from the man. Williams called for assistance and took Carlton out of the basement.[18]

The crowd in front of the ruins wanted to lynch Carlton on the spot, forcing Williams and a few deputies to retreat with their prisoner and exit out a back way and into an automobile. Just as they were about to drive off, three carloads of men drove up and two of them jumped out, brandishing ropes. The officers needed to draw their guns to hold off the mob before they could haul Carlton off safely to the jail in Dodgeville, eighteen miles away in the Iowa County seat.[19]

Wright learned about the disaster by telephone while at work on the Midway Gardens project in Chicago. His face ashen, the stricken architect asked his son John to call a taxi so they could get the next train to Wisconsin. While on the station platform, the Wrights encountered Edwin Cheney, Borthwick's ex-husband who was also waiting for the sad train ride north. Meeting the trio to Madison were several of Wright's aunts and his cousin, *Wisconsin State Journal* reporter Richard Lloyd Jones, son of preacher Jenkin Lloyd Jones. Jones urged Wright to get a grip on himself despite his sorrow. When he arrived at Taliesin around midnight, Wright described what he saw as a "devastating scene of horror."[20]

Cheney returned to Chicago on Sunday via the Chicago, Milwaukee and St. Paul railroad, the train carrying a single casket holding the remains of his two children. Resting in a simple wooden casket hand built by Wright's craftsmen and filled with flowers from her garden, Cheney's former wife was buried the next day near Taliesin in the Unity Chapel cemetery, where many of Wright's family were interned. Accompanying the architect were his son John and two of his nephews, Orrin Lloyd Jones and Ralph Lloyd Jones. Borthwick's body was carried on a farm wagon from the Porter home. Orrin Lloyd Jones led the sorrel horses as Wright and his son followed, their heads down. After lowering the coffin into the grave, Wright asked the others to leave. He stood alone before filling in the deep grave. Wright returned to the remains of the Taliesin complex, to sleep on a cot in a studio workshop spared by the blaze. "The dark was friendly," Wright wrote in his autobiography.[21]

Also on that Sunday, Sheriff Williams stationed six men armed with Winchester rifles around the ruins of the Wright home to drive off the sightseers who had flocked to Taliesin hoping to snare souvenirs from the site. Extra guards also ringed the Dodgeville jail; it was feared that another lynching attempt was imminent.[22]

One of those allowed on the grounds was Alvina Boettcher, Emil Brodelle's fiancée, who arrived from Milwaukee with her brother Clarence and undertaker William C. Feerick. When he came to the city to attend school as a fourteen-year-old orphan from Richland Center, Brodelle roomed for a time with the Boettchers' parents. Clarence Boettcher was able to speak with Wright and Edwin Cheney. "Both were broken up over the affair and each took care of the bodies dear to them and removed them from the gaze of those who were thronging the premises," he said.[23]

A *Milwaukee Journal* reporter and several others returning to Spring Green came across Gertrude Carlton on the road about a half-mile from the Wright estate. The journalist said her dress "was torn, her waist soiled, her hair disheveled and she appeared extremely nervous and almost hysterical," fearing being lynched. When she was turned over to the authorities, Gertrude claimed she had no knowledge of her husband's motive. She was first held in Spring Green and then sent to the Dodgeville lockup until she was released on August 29. The woman quickly left the area and disappeared into history.[24]

Monday, August 17, was partly cloudy; the anticipated rain seemed to mirror the sorrow of the scene. Young Weston was buried that afternoon but his mourning father was not able to attend the funeral because of his wounds. The badly burned Brunker, a widower, paralyzed and barely able to talk, passed away in the evening. Before he died, the workman managed to gasp out a few words telling of the weekend horror and how he had lain wounded on the lawn outside the burning building, unable to aid anyone.

He was interred at Wanderer's Rest Cemetery in Milwaukee on Tuesday, August 18.[25]

Lindblom, a native of Denmark with no known relatives in America, also was buried on Tuesday near Borthwick's grave in the Unity Chapel cemetery. An earlier graveside service was delayed until after 6 p.m. by the rainstorm foretold the previous day. Wright himself attended the rites.[26]

The murderer eventually died of starvation weeks later on Wednesday, October 7. At the time of his death, Carlton had lost almost sixty pounds, wasting away despite initially receiving liberal doses of milk and whiskey in the hope of flushing out his system. His weakened condition didn't lessen his aggression, however; he tossed a drinking glass and bucket at Sheriff Williams and grabbed the lawman's leg during one incident. Carlton made two court appearances but never stood trial, and his motive for the attack was never explained. Later, Gertrude Carlton did say her husband was acting strangely several days before they were to leave Taliesin and that she was afraid of him. Gertrude indicated that her husband had begun sleeping with a hatchet tied up in a sack near their bed. After his death, Carlton's body was shipped to the University of Wisconsin. There it was dissected and his brain studied for abnormalities that might have explained his actions. His remains were cremated.[27]

In a letter to his neighbors, published in the *Wisconsin State Journal*, Wright mourned his lover:

"She is dead. I have buried her in the little Chapel burying ground of my people—beside the little son of my sister, a beautiful boy of ten, who loved her and whom she loved much—and while the place where she lived with me is a charred and blackened ruin, the little things of our daily life gone, I shall replace it all little by little as nearly as it may be done. I shall set it all up again for the spirit of the mortals that lived in it and loved it—will live in it still. My home will still be there."[28]

True to this promise, Wright eventually built a second Taliesin, even grander than the original structure. He lived there on and off until his death in 1959 at ninety-two. Herb Fritz Jr., son of Wright's apprentice who had survived the massacre, visited Wright at Taliesin the year before his aging mentor died, gifting him with a loaf of homemade bread. The younger Fritz was a noted architect by then, designer of Hilltop, now a major conference center on Highway 23 in Spring Green. The building, which often hosts programs on the environment and global warming, is part of Wright's Wisconsin legacy. Taliesin itself remains a major tourist destination in Wisconsin, offering regular tours and programs.[29]

The fascinating, tragic story of Frank Lloyd Wright, his lover, Mamah Borthwick Cheney, and his treasured Taliesin has been retold in many formats. A critically acclaimed opera entitled *Shining Brow* was composed by Daron Aric Hagen and Paul Muldoon; the Madison Opera premiered the piece in April 1993. *Taliesin: Choruses from Shining Brow,* a suite based on the original opera, was commissioned in 1995 by the Madison Symphony Orchestra. In the production, an orchestral "Fire Interlude" represented the conflagration and murders at Taliesin.[30]

As Reaper in Summer Grain, by Keith Byron Kirk, is another opera relating the story of the tragedy through Julian Carlton's eyes and how he stumbled into madness and murder. The piece also drew from the work by Hagen and Muldoon and was presented at the Immigrants' Theatre Project in New York, the Eugene O'Neill Theater Center in Waterford, Connecticut, and other venues throughout the first decade of the twenty-first century.[31]

The murders are also the subject of a book by Professor William Drennan of the University of Wisconsin–Baraboo/Sauk County. *Death in a Prairie House* was released by the University of Wisconsin Press in 2007.

With each retelling, the "birds of prey" that Wright imagined were let loose upon Borthwick's death seem as alive today as the turkey vultures circling over that peaceful but still sad valley.

Ironically enough, those "birds" released in 1914 appear to have roosted in the village of Plainfield. During that year, a stern, formidable woman named Augusta Gein moved her family there, refugees from the "depravity" of La Crosse. On the family farm outside of that north-central Wisconsin village, Mrs. Gein expected her youngest son, Eddie, to grow up safe from the allure and enticements of the outside world.

August Giuliani, whose fiery sermons provoked carnage.

Chapter 2

The Deadly Big Bang

Milwaukee, Wisconsin
November 24, 1917
Death toll: 10
Wounded: dozens

"This is a bomb, I found it under the church."

—Sam Mazzone[1]

For immigrants of all nationalities, Wisconsin has always been a land of dreams and opportunity. Located over the proverbial rainbow on the western shore of Lake Michigan, the region's lush pastureland, abundant fresh water, mineral resources, and open spaces were attractive to those seeking a new life in a new place. But for some, those dreams turned to deadly nightmares.

In September 1917, Italian immigrant pastor August Giuliani, a Methodist evangelist, was actively preaching in Milwaukee. He had set his sights on converting the Catholics of the largely Sicilian Third Ward and the smaller northern Italian enclave of Bay View on the city's south side. On the corner of Bishop and Potter streets, the former priest and his entourage, including coronetists Sam Mazzone and Angelo Germanotta and Maude Richter with her portable organ, regularly sang patriotic songs. They encouraged the neighborhood to back the American effort in World War I.

Giuliani was usually met with resistance from the area's numerous

Got Murder?

antiwar activists, recent European immigrants who knew firsthand what war was like. The preacher, an ex-priest, was also unwelcome because, it was said, he defamed Catholicism while attempting his conversions. He subsequently sought security help from the police, who assigned four officers to watch over one of his prayer sessions on Sunday, September 9, 1917.

A crowd gathered to jeer Giuliani and his supporters. Approaching the hecklers, several of whom were armed, police drew their guns. As the crowd scampered to get out of the way, shots rang out. Police returned the fire, killing two protesters and injuring two others. One of the victims was shot in the back. Two officers were also slightly wounded.

Two months later, a bomb was found at Giuliani's Third Ward church. The incident was linked to the Bay View fracas by the clergyman, city authorities, and newspapers like the city's rabidly antianarchist *Milwaukee Sentinel*. The bomb, carried to the central police station by one of Giuliani's parishioners, exploded and killed nine policemen and a civilian. The thunderous blast killed more policemen than any other single incident in the United States until the Oklahoma City bombing on April 19, 1995.

Barely a week after the deadly Milwaukee blast, a trial of several Italians arrested in the initial Bay View fracas began. It wasn't long before nationally recognized figures such as attorney Clarence Darrow and radical activist Emma Goldman became involved, concerned whether the defendants were receiving a fair trial in the wake of the bombing. What led up to the bombing is still cause for speculation.

* * * *

During the ensuing trial, the details of Giuliani's history and the events that led to two deadly outbreaks of violence in the wake of his ministry came to light. The affair was a tragedy, a story woven from threads of fear and ethnic hatred.

Rev. Giuliani was not like most of the city's Italian immigrants. His light brown hair, blue eyes, and fair complexion showed that he was a northerner.[2] He was born on January 28, 1881, in Vignanello, a small town in Italy's Lazio region, northwest of Rome. His father, Serafino, was a colonel in the Papal Army and died when his son was twelve. His mother was said to have been from a distinguished Milanese family. Giuliani was ordained in 1901 by an uncle who had close ties to the Vatican.[3]

Despite serving in the parish of Taranto, becoming secretary to a bishop, and teaching in a seminary, Giuliani became a Protestant. One reason for the switch in denominations might have been his encounter with an injured American engineer whose strong faith inspired the young priest. Whatever the reason, Giuliani formally became a Methodist on November 13, 1909.[4]

After graduating from the Methodist University in Rome, he met his future wife, Katherine Eyerick, an American missionary on a three-month pilgrimage through Italy. Eyerick was six years older than Giuliani and had long been preaching in Italian neighborhoods in Wellsville, Ohio, and Chicago. She was also active in Milwaukee evangelical circles in 1908, struggling to convert the city's Catholic Sicilians. In 1910, Eyerick convinced Giuliani that Milwaukee was the place to win souls, so he sailed to America that year. The two were married on July 17, 1911, and Giuliani formally declared his intent to become a United States citizen.[5]

By 1914, Giuliani had become an elder in the new Italian Evangelical Church in Milwaukee's increasingly Sicilian Third Ward. The church helped newly arrived immigrants to secure jobs, housing, and medical care. He also served as an interpreter for the local courts in addition to holding church services, vacation Bible school, and evangelical trips to Waukesha. His street meetings attracted the curious, both pro and con, mostly because of his speaking style and the upbeat music.[6] Giuliani became a citizen on June 14, 1916. A month later, on July 23, his son was born. His wife died of complications two days later.

The fiery pastor ardently supported the Americanization of immigrants and was a strong foe of political dissenters of any kind. He denounced anyone who disagreed with the war effort. This attitude endeared him to nativists who considered Milwaukee's Italian colony to be a festering nest of anarchism and Black Hand activity. Assistant

Got Murder?

District Attorney Arthur H. Bartelt praised Giuliani and Milwaukee's Italian Evangelical Church, congratulating the pastor for "making Christians out of Italians with IWW [International Workers of the World] and Bolsheviki tendencies."[7]

During World War I, Bay View centered around the Illinois Steel Company rolling mill, where many of the neighborhood's residents were employed. The community was home to émigrés from Italy's northern Piedmont and central Marches regions. By 1910, Bay View had a vibrant Italian community of 100 to 150 families. These 300 people accounted for 8.5% of the population in the Seventeenth Ward.[8]

After establishing himself in the Third Ward community, Giuliani figured it was time to preach in Bay View. With police permission, he began his open-air meetings on August 26, 1917. Displaying the American flag and singing patriotic songs, he urged Italian American men to report for the draft. A group of dissenters appeared immediately, among them Mary Nardini, brothers Adolph and Vincent Fratesi, Amedeo Lilli, Bartolo Testolin, and Gavina Denurra. They stood away from the other spectators.[9] When the meeting ended, twelve or so activists told Giuliani they didn't believe in any form of government or religion and suggested that he visit their social club.

In the trial of the Bay View protesters after the police station bombing, Giuliani testified that Lilli had said, "You came here because you want to preach about a war."[10] According to the pastor's testimony, Denurra said, "I don't believe in God, I don't believe in priests, I don't believe in government, I don't believe what you are saying." In response, Giuliani offered to buy steamship tickets back to Italy for anyone who did not approve of the United States and proclaimed he would return to the neighborhood to preach again.

The next Sunday, the evangelicals returned. Nardini and about fifteen others stood close to the pastor. The anarchists began singing their own songs.[11]

Giuliani said the dissenters threatened him, warning him, "You must not come down here any more. We have a lake here and we throw you down in the lake and we cut your heads off."[12]

After belligerent posturing from both sides, Giuliani sent Maude

Richter to get the police.[13] Guliani testified that Nardini then yelled, "Go and take a gun and some rotten tomatoes and onions and potatoes and we will have a show here." The police arrived and broke up the meeting.

Fearing for his safety but unwilling to back down, Giuliani asked John T. Janssen, Milwaukee's chief of police, and the U.S. Department of Justice for protection prior to his third Bay View street meeting.[14]

On September 9, a cloudy Sunday, Giuliani met with Detectives Albert H. Templin and Paul J. Weiler at the Central Police Station on Oneida (now Wells) and Broadway and walked with them a block west to city hall. There, they met about forty supporters, including six or seven women.[15] Riding a streetcar to Bay View, the contingent linked up with John Wesolowski and Joseph Rydlewicz, patrolmen from the Bay View squad. The two officers were already staked out on the northwest corner of the intersection of Bishop and Potter where more than two dozen protesters had already gathered. The two groups immediately began shouting at each other and singing songs.[16]

Patrolman Wesolowski approached Lilli and grabbed him, warning, "If you don't like the meeting, get a move on or keep quiet." Another officer began patting down some demonstrators. Wesolowski later testified, "I seen guns coming out of their pockets and didn't wait a moment and shots were fired and I drew my gun and fired into the crowd."

Officer Rydlewicz saw another of the "anarchists," twenty-three-year-old Antonio Fornasier, draw a pistol and fire. Rydlewicz and Detective Weiler returned the gunshots, knocking Fornasier to the ground. Augusto Marinelli shot at Detective Weiler and Wesolowski fired back, the bullets making chunking sounds as they hit the man.[17] Even as the gunfire rang out and bodies tumbled to the bloodied pavement, Giuliani continued to sing, organist Richter frenziedly pounding out "America" on her organ's small keyboard.[18]

After the shooting ceased, Fornasier was dead, face down on the curb, and Marinelli was slowly bleeding to death. Several others were wounded. Screaming and crying, the rest of the crowd had scattered.

When police later raided homes of the protesters, no other weapons were found.[19] Yet the searches of houses, saloons, and a meeting hall uncovered evidence just as damning in the eyes of the authorities: anarchist and communist literature, books on the Russian Revolution published in Italy, and volumes on free love and agnosticism.[20] In addition to eleven people arrested at the shooting scene, at least fifteen more Milwaukeeans of Italian descent were taken into custody the next day.

On September 12, Socialist District Attorney Winfred Zabel ordered defendants Peter Bianchi, Amedeo Lilli, Angelo Pantaleoni, the Fratesi brothers, and Pasquale Nardini to his office. They shuffled in, chained by heavy shackles that clanked as they walked. Each was sworn in and cross-examined individually. In a strange twist, Giuliani served as a court interpreter, translating for the defendants. However, Vincenzo Fratesi and Nardini objected, claiming that Giuliani lied and misinterpreted their statements.[21]

Milwaukee was divided over the shootings, just as they were about American involvement in the war. Some were sympathetic toward the anarchists and launched a fund drive to help pay for their lawyers. Many blamed Giuliani for mishandling the situation, saying that his fiery speeches and attitude only made matters worse. Comments and letters supportive of the defendants appeared in the *Milwaukee Leader*, the city's daily Socialist newspaper. However, the *Milwaukee Sentinel* did not waste any time in making its position known. It suggested, "It is a good opportunity, now that the federal authorities may take hold, to put permanently out of business the anarchic and predatory elements that have long been pestering and terrorizing peaceable and law abiding Italian-American citizens in this community."[22]

On November 24, a week before the trial of eleven arrested anarchists, Erminia Spicciati, forty-seven, and her eleven-year-old daughter, Josie, were cleaning the Italian Evangelical Church. The elder Spicciati found a package wrapped in brown paper and tied with string near the church. She wondered what it was, but left the bundle where it lay beside a fence outside the building.[23]

Giuliani was out of town that day, so Spicciati sent her daughter to tell Richter about the package and later went to talk with her about it. The musician visited the church and brought the package into the basement. Suspicious, she phoned the central police station at 5:30 p.m. and spoke with the chief of detectives, who said an officer would be sent to pick up the mysterious package.

About 6:20 p.m., Sam Mazzone arrived at the church to stoke the furnace. Richter asked him to take the package the half-dozen or so blocks to the police station. The young man hoisted the package, estimated at about thirty-five to forty pounds and the size of a half-gallon jar, and trudged over to the station.[24]

Within ten minutes after Mazzone dropped off the package, as the officers were descending the stairs after roll call, the police station was rocked by a blast that shook the neighborhood. The package was indeed a bomb, the explosion of which was heard throughout downtown Milwaukee. Among the dead were seven detectives, Sergeant Henry Deckert, and a civilian woman. Edward Spindler, a police alarm operator on the floor above the explosion was also killed, maimed by shrapnel that shot through the floor and passed between the seat and arm of his chair. The burning metal slashed into his body at the waist and exited through his head. His co-workers on either side were unharmed.[25]

In addition to Deckert and Spindler, officers killed included Frank Caswin, Fred Kaiser, David O'Brien, Stephen Stecker, Charles Seehawer, Al Templin, and Paul Weiler. The woman who died, Catherine Walker, had come to the station to file a complaint against a boyfriend. Eighteen prisoners in the city jail were spared.

In lurid detail, newspaper reports described the glass, plaster, shredded clothing, shattered torsos, arms, legs, and burned papers that littered the floor. One story told how "a cap from an officer's head hung on a broken bit of glass in a side window. Through the gaping windows, the faint light of a street lamp flickered on the scene . . . from the ceiling swung loosened planks and the two blackened chandeliers."[26]

What puzzled subsequent investigators was why the officers had not checked whether or not the package was actually a bomb, especially given Mazzone's concerns regarding what he thought he was carrying. The police had at least two hours from the receipt of Richter's phone call to potentially disarm or dispose of the bomb. The reason for the delay remains a mystery.

After the catastrophe, Milwaukee police rounded up about thirty Italians and other "usual suspects" for intense interrogations. Dragnets of immigrant and anarchist communities in Seattle and Omaha were also launched, seeking some link with the Milwaukee tragedy. Despite these efforts by federal and local authorities, no one was ever charged in the bloody massacre.

In addition to the popular notion that the bombing was revenge for the Bay View shootings that September, it was also suggested that the neighborhood's northern Italians might have been influenced by the fighting raging along Italy's Alpine frontier where the Allied and Austro-German armies were locked in combat.[27]

In December, the trials of the Bay View rioters began. Judge A. C. Backus consolidated the first eleven cases to speed up the proceedings. In the initial complaints, District Attorney Winfred C. Zabel named all the defendants as principals to a charge of assault with intent to kill.

In his testimony, Giuliani stressed that his Bay View street preachings were patriotic in nature and not religious. He objected to the charge that the riots occurred because he insulted the Roman Catholic religion. Six of the defendants readily admitted they were anarchists. The proceedings were halted several times when Zabel accused Italians in the courtroom of taunting witnesses. He claimed that some of the defendants were biting on their thumbs, which he said was considered a symbolic threat among Italians.[28]

On December 12, the state rested its case and the defense began trying to prove that anarchy did not equal violence and that the defendants were only attempting to educate themselves by reading philosophical and political literature.

Several Italians attending the trial were arrested when they appeared at the court sessions, allegedly for their role in the police station bombing. Three were picked up when they attempted to bail defendant Angelo Pantaleoni's brother, Enrico, out of jail. Federal authorities requested the men be taken into custody as suspects in the police deaths.[29]

The Deadly Big Bang

At 8:20 p.m., Thursday, December 20, after deliberating seventeen minutes, the jury found all eleven riot defendants guilty of conspiracy to "assault with the intent to kill and murder." Each was sentenced to serve twenty-five years at the state prison in Waupun. Areno Nardini, the infant son of Pasquale and Mary Nardini, was sent to the detention home in Wauwatosa. A few days later, the judge sentenced the boy to spend the next twenty-five years in an orphanage, ignoring pleas from other family members who offered to care for the baby.[30]

On December 28, an inquest was launched into the police station bombing. Among those called to the witness stand were Mazzone, Erminia Spicciati, and some of the police officers at the station the night of the bombing. Giuliani served as translator.[31]

Fearing that the Italians were not receiving a fair trial, noted political activist Emma Goldman recruited famed Chicago lawyer Clarence Darrow to appeal the case to the Wisconsin Supreme Court in Madison. Concerned by the severity of the sentences, Darrow wrote a brief and argued orally at the court in March 1919.[32]

It didn't matter to Darrow that the defendants were aliens who spoke no English, or even that, as his biographer Irving Stone put it, their "public conduct proved them to be emotionally unbalanced." Darrow believed that anyone allowed to live in the United States should be afforded the same rights.[33]

After reviewing the evidence, including the fact that women and children were present at the Bay View incident and hence a conspiracy was unlikely, the Wisconsin Supreme Court overturned all of the convictions except those of Vincent Fratesi and Amedeo Lilli. They had been armed at the public meeting and failed to leave the scene when trouble started.[34]

All the defendants were returned to Milwaukee on Thursday, April 3, and were held in the county jail while the Department of Justice initiated deportation proceedings against them. But on Monday, April 21, all were released from custody by Judge Backus, who granted District Attorney Zabel's motion. Zabel said he felt justice had been served since the men had already been imprisoned fifteen months and the expense of another trial would be too much for the county. Before granting the motion, the judge asked each of the Italians if they planned to become American citizens after their release. Many decided to leave the city.[35]

Giuliani continued his missionary work in Milwaukee and always claimed he was doing God's work. Up until his death in 1929, he maintained that "the Bay View Italians hate me and my church because in addition to regular services we often had meetings at which we advocated patriotism and true Americanism."[36]

In February 1922, Governor John J. Blaine commuted the sentences of Vincent Fratesi and Amedeo Lilli, the two defendants in the Bay View incident still serving time in Waupun. The police never solved the bombing case despite continued assertions by principals such as Maude Richter that the culprits were the anarchists, all of whom had been deported in the wake of the Bay View shootings.

The xenophobia exibited during those tumultuous days continues to echo in America a generation afterwards, augmented by misplaced patriotric fervor, overzealous authorities, and a fearful populace. Outsiders, whether immigrant Italians of 1914, Muslims in the wake of 9/11, or illegal aliens in 2007 often become easily targeted "bogeymen" in an uncertain world.

Yet we must keep in mind Darrow's argument, "There is no such crime as a crime of thought; there are only crimes of action. . . . If we wish to keep speech free, to keep criticism open and alive, we have to tolerate even such criticisms as these, distasteful as they may be to us."[37]

Ed Gein, right, a quiet Wisconsin farm boy whose crimes shocked the nation.

Chapter 3

Homegrown Body Snatcher

Plainfield, Wisconsin
1950s
Death toll: 2
Graves desecrated: 12

Being mother's little boy had its drawbacks.[1]

—Robert Bloch, *Psycho*

In the mid-1950s, a strange little Wisconsin man with his twisted smile—and an even more twisted mind—put the state on the murder map and earned many names for himself: the Backyard Bogeyman, the Plainfield Butcher, the Cheeseland Flayer, The Plainfield Ghoul, Slicin' Ed, the Badger State Skinner.

But by any name, he's one of the most famous serial killers in history: Ed "Chop 'n' Dice" Gein.

Ed Gein was more than a murderer; his story is one of unspeakable horrors so terrible they inspired uncounted articles, dozens of books, and many movies. The latter include Alfred Hitchcock's trend-setting danse macabre entitled *Psycho* (1960); the consummate fright film, *The Silence of the Lambs* (1991); and Tobe Harris's classic death-by-machinery romp, *The Texas Chainsaw Massacre* (1974).

There were such oddball genre spin-offs as the gory psychic downer, *Maniac* (1980), the shtick-flick *Three on a Meathook* (1972), and the ultimate carry-your-dead-mummy-until-she-rots-away cliffhanger, *Deranged* (1974). Of course, there eventually had to be a film entitled *Ed Gein, The Movie* (2000). Also known as *In the Light of the Moon*, the movie was a box office hit among Gein cultists. The new media are not immune to the craze, either. A half century after his crimes came to light, almost a hundred thousand Web sites focus on this mild-mannered rural man, whose fetishes still shiver the spine.

But Edward (a.k.a. Ed or Eddie) Theodore Gein was not actually a serial killer in the strict sense of the term. Why? Basically, he only murdered twice—a far cry from Ted Bundy serialists and Charles Whitman mass murderers who do in many more victims. Yet Wisconsin's own Man of Murder was far from being a run-of-the-mill killer. The fact that Gein tended toward necrophilia and was a deranged transvestite added to his weird mystique. Gein's mind was a psychotic cocktail, one that frightened the bejeebers out of people throughout Wisconsin and everywhere else.

Born on August 27, 1906, in La Crosse, Gein was probably behind the eight ball from Day One. Augusta Gein, his mother, was a domineering and fanatically religious woman who ran a grocery store. At the time, the riverboat town was a rough-and-tumble city on Wisconsin's western rim. It was already a commercial hub along the Mississippi River, reveling in its prime location midway between the Twin Cities in Minnesota and Milwaukee, the Dairy State's largest community. According to those who knew him, Gein's father, George, was a timid soul, an alcoholic farmer loathed by a wife who ran the family home with a puritanical fist.[2]

George Gein's parents and older sister drowned in a flash flood near their farm in Coon Valley in 1879; he was raised by strict Scottish grandparents. As a result, Ed's father became a brooding young man most comfortable alone. Although he was trained as a blacksmith and had the size to match, George was fond of drink and a regular patron at area taverns. He met his future wife when he was twenty-four and she was nineteen. Even as a young woman, Augusta was considered a formidable creature, with her thick body, fierce determination, and stern looks. Of German heritage, Augusta was brought up in a dour Lutheran family, with a father who believed that regular beatings were necessary to enforce discipline within his large brood.[3]

What the two saw in each other will never be known. Perhaps George, who had a hard time getting and keeping jobs, needed a base of support and saw Augusta's expansive family and its hard-working ways as a gravy train. Augusta, on the other hand, might have seen her future husband's demeanor as malleable, figuring she could straighten him out—or at least reshape him to her vision of what a man should be like. Augusta certainly wasn't high on any most-sought-after list among area bachelors; she may have been glad to have found a man who showed any interest at all in her. Whatever their reasons, George and Augusta were married on December 4, 1899.[4]

After the nuptials, George continued to drink. He grew more reclusive, usually remaining silent in the face of frequent verbal attacks from the increasingly frustrated Augusta. The sullen man and his vociferous wife regularly quarreled, often coming to blows. What sex they had was probably perfunctory, since Augusta was known to have felt that making love was a loathsome duty, one to be tolerated only to sire offspring. However, this union of mismatched souls produced a son, Henry, on January 17, 1902. He was a robust little fellow with a good set of lungs. Then, on August 27, 1907, Augusta gave birth to second son, Edward Theodore.[5]

Two of Augusta's brothers ran successful grocery stores in La Crosse and they helped George open his own place in 1909. It wasn't long, however, before Augusta needed to step in and run the business, located at 914 Caledonia Street. Apparently, George just didn't have the business sense to keep the shop viable. Years later, Ed Gein recalled sneaking through a back door of the store when he was young and seeing his parents butchering a hog. He remembered the entrails spilling into a tub at their feet and their leather aprons slimy with blood, his mother holding a long-bladed butcher knife.[6]

In 1914, evidently disgusted by what she called the "depravity" of La Crosse, Augusta moved the family to Plainfield, a town she believed was a more righteous location. However, this small, God-fearing village turned out to be no better than the city, at least in Augusta's eyes. She considered the place to be a "hellhole" and kept young Henry and Ed on a remote farm, seven miles southwest of Plainfield. She wanted them well away from anything she considered dangerous, tempting, or a sinful influence. Augusta was especially concerned about what she imagined were legions of whores lurking beyond the fringes of the family fields. She worried about the wickedness of carnal love that could be the downfall of her sons, particularly the mild-mannered youngest.[7]

The boys' father finally escaped his wife's constant carping when he died of a heart attack in 1940 at age sixty-six. By the time he passed away, the poor wretch was crippled, unhappy, and unloved. George's funeral was held on April 4, 1940, in Plainfield's combination furniture store and mortuary. Neither Augusta nor her two sons seemed to miss the deceased paterfamilias. It was tough enough to eke out a living on the sandy, hardscrabble west-central Wisconsin farm. It was said that Augusta kept a clean home, even without electricity or plumbing.[8]

Henry proved to be more independent minded than either his father or his younger brother. He often bad-mouthed Augusta for her puritanical ways, complaining to Ed, who regularly defended her honor. Apparently, Henry wanted a family and longed to be free of his mother's tight domestic reins. His meek brother Ed, on the other hand, exhibited no inclination to escape to the wider world.[9]

When World War II broke out, Henry was too old to be called into service and Ed was excused because of a growth on his left eyelid that blurred his vision. They continued to work the farm, but Henry began getting more jobs that freed him from the clutches of his mother. He regularly worked with a road contractor and even managed a gang of Jamaican contract farm laborers in Wisconsin to help the war effort.[10]

In May of 1944, at age forty-three, Henry died in a suspicious brush fire on the family's 195-acre spread. According to the story Ed told the authorities, he put out part of the fire as it approached a grove of pines but lost his brother in the encroaching darkness. Seeking help, the younger man called in the sheriff who rounded up a search party. The authorities were subsequently surprised when Ed led them directly to his older brother's body, which was untouched by the flames although the area around him was scorched.[11] No one suspected foul play, even though the back of Henry's head showed numerous bruises. It was surmised that he had bumped his head when falling after being overcome by smoke.[12]

Son and mother continued to live reclusive lives after Henry's death. Augusta helped on the farm, lifting hay bales and running tractors as well as any man. So when she collapsed in the spring of 1945 and needed to be taken to the hospital in nearby Wild Rose, Ed was beside himself. According to doctors, she had suffered a stroke. Augusta eventually recovered enough to be sent home, but she never fully recuperated, needing to be tended to day and night by Ed. Even in her illness, Augusta kept warning her son to be careful of women and saying that only she loved him. Ed took the admonitions to heart and was never known to have dated anyone. On December 29, 1945, at age sixty-seven, Augusta finally died. Other than her weeping son, the only mourners at the funeral were several of her siblings.[13]

Ed returned home from the cemetery, truly alone and huddling in increasing squalor. He had lost any interest in keeping up his personal appearance, much less dusting the furniture or weeding the front yard. Ed did manage to maintain his arsenal—several rifles, a shotgun, and a pistol—much like any other farmer in the region. For income, he depended on federal farm subsidies and odd jobs as Plainfield's resident handyman and part-time babysitter. Despite his unkempt looks and lack of regular bathing, Ed was always polite, hard working and dependable, according to the townsfolk and farmers who hired him.[14]

He rarely went out to socialize, instead staying home to read girlie magazines and pulp fiction, building a library of medical encyclopedias, anatomy books, and histories of Nazi experiments. The one place Ed visited regularly, however, was Mary Hogan's tavern in Pine Grove, seven miles from his home. A tiny cinder-block building, Hank's Place looked more like a warehouse than a bar. But it was cozy inside. Hogan was a well-known character in the community, weighing almost two hundred pounds. Originally from Chicago, it was rumored that she was divorced twice, had mob connections, and ran a Windy City whorehouse before journeying north to Wisconsin.[15] Whether any of that was true or not, Ed was apparently interested in the tavern keeper, despite the fact that Mary Hogan was obviously the exact opposite of the sainted Augusta Gein—or perhaps because of it.

Over the next few years, authorities were puzzled by the disappearance of several people in western and central Wisconsin. On May 1, 1947, eight-year-old Georgia Weckler of Jefferson vanished. On October 24, 1953, Evelyn Hartley, fifteen, disappeared in La Crosse. While those two incidents were miles from Plainfield, others were in Waushara County. Deer hunters Victor Travis and Ray Burgess were never heard from or seen again after leaving Mac's Bar in Plainfield on November 1, 1952. The latter's car was found abandoned on the farm adjoining the Gein place. Mary Hogan was next to go, leaving only a pool of blood on the floor of her pub on December 8, 1954.[16]

Occasionally, men who hired Ed Gein joked with him about finding a wife or girlfriend. Gein would only reply with his lopsided grin. As in any small town confronted with a tragic mystery, the conversations sometimes came around Hogan's disappearance. Gein was regularly quoted as saying, "She's not missing. She's down at the house now," or "I went and got her in my pickup truck and took her home." Nobody questioned his comments, figuring it was just oddball chattering, especially since Gein always smiled as he talked about Hogan.[17]

Yet there was a gathering darkness around Gein's persona. Stories circulated about strange things seen in the recluse's house. Several neighborhood youths used to hunt with Gein, dropping by to pick him up or play cards. They recalled seeing what seemed to be shrunken heads hanging in various places in the cluttered rooms. When asked, Gein replied that the artifacts were war trophies sent by friends in the military during the war, or told some other story. None of the young men thought much of the incidents until the real story of Ed Gein emerged years later. Instead, the tales became something of a joke around town although neighborhood kids began referring to Gein's rundown place as "the haunted house." It was easy to see why.[18]

* * * *

Deer season in Wisconsin is a time of ritual, mostly a male-bonding ceremony complete with guns, orange vests, games of poker, bottles of brandy, and the occasional trophy rack. Sometimes, hunters themselves are victims, either accidentally shooting themselves or being nailed by others. Holsteins are hidden in barns and canines have "dog" spray-painted on their sides when eager out-of-towners flock to the woods with their artillery pieces. Local men also empty the small towns and head for the timber, leaving behind their "hunting widows" to tend the home fires.

It was no different when the annual shooting season began in 1957. The chill November wind growled through Waushara County's thick woodlots and made the few remaining dry cornstalks shiver in the desolate fields. Three inches of snow covered the ground on November 16, when Ed Gein left his farm and drove into Plainfield. He stopped at a gas station to fill a can with kerosene and then pulled up to Worden's Hardware and Implement Store on the east end of town. The store, in a building dating to the early 1890s, was managed by Bernice Worden, widow of the late owner and daughter of her husband's business partner. The fifty-eight-year-old grandmother was respected in Plainfield for her business sense, civic consciousness, and her churchgoing ways. She was often helped by her son Frank, who also acted as village constable, town fire marshal, and deputy sheriff. Like many of Plainfield's other male residents, Frank Worden was hunting that morning.[19]

Gein had been visiting the hardware store regularly, and had even boldly suggested to Mrs. Worden that the two of them go roller-skating in Hancock, about ten miles south of Plainfield. This was a surprise to all in town who heard about the invitation because Gein wasn't known to ever even look twice at a woman. Neither Worden appreciated his attentions. But since the Gein family had long been customers, the mother and son were good retailers and polite to everyone—even Ed Gein.

What transpired after Gein visited Mrs. Worden, who was alone in her store, came out during his trial and in reams of newspaper reports.

Other shopkeepers had noticed that a man drove away in the hardware store's delivery van early in the morning. A hunter returning from the field met Gein speeding toward his home—a surprising factor considering the little man usually drove very slowly. Later, young neighbor Bob Hill, who regularly hunted with Gein, dropped by the older man's farm with his sister Darlene to ask for help in starting the family car. Gein obliged when they asked him to drive them into town to purchase a new car battery. The Hills recalled that Gein said, "Just let me wash up," then noticed that his hands were bloody. Gein said he was dressing out a deer. After returning from town, Gein was invited to the family's home for supper, prepared by the teens' mother, Irene. He happily accepted.[20]

Frank Worden came back to town empty-handed after a day of hunting. He checked in at the Phillips 66 filling station, an official state deer kill registration site. The station owner, Bernard Muschinski, mentioned that he had seen the Wordens' truck drive off and noticed the store was locked and the lights burning. Knowing that his mother planned on working that day, Worden became worried and went to investigate. Upon entering the hardware store, he immediately saw that the cash register was gone and that a trail of blood led out the back door. He called Sheriff Art Schley in Wautoma, the Waushara County seat, about fifteen miles southeast of Plainfield. Schley was new to the job, having been in office for about a month. Schley called Arnie Fritz, his chief deputy, and the two men hightailed it to Plainfield, siren screaming.[21]

They met Worden who, as an experienced deputy, had already secured the scene. When the two officers got out of their squad car, the storekeeper's son said, "He's done something to her." Puzzled, the sheriff asked whom Worden was referring to. "Eddie Gein," Worden replied quickly, pointing out that Gein had taken to hanging around the store and had asked when he would be hunting. Several days earlier, Gein had also been in the store, asking about the price of antifreeze. A link between Gein and the missing woman was secured when Worden showed the other officers a receipt for antifreeze that his mother had written out to the farmer that same morning.[22]

Schley called for help in locating Gein, rounding up authorities from surrounding communities and counties, including Captain Lloyd

Schoephoerster of the Green Lake County Sheriff's Department. The hunt was on. Over at the Hills' house, where Gein was finishing dinner, another family member came in to tell of Mrs. Worden's disappearance and the arrival of the authorities. Gein seemed nonplussed, remarking, "Must have been somebody pretty cold-blooded." Bob Hill then asked Gein for a ride downtown to see all the commotion and Gein agreed.[23]

The Hills operated a small grocery near their home and Irene needed to relieve her husband, Lester. She had barely sent him home to eat when two policemen arrived at the store asking about Gein, knowing that Bob had hunted with Gein and that the bachelor often ate with the family. Irene indicated that her son and Gein had planned to head into town to find out more about Mrs. Worden. The two officers—Dan Chase and Arden "Poke" Spees—immediately ran out and found Gein sitting in his car in front of the Hills' home.[24]

Placing him in the back of the squad car, the police officers asked Gein what he'd done that day and questioned him about his visits to the Wordens' hardware store. They then encouraged him to repeat the tale. Confronted with several discrepancies between versions, Gein said, "Somebody framed me." Officer Chase asked, "For what?" Gein replied, "Mrs. Worden." The police listened intently as the little man added, "She's dead, ain't she?" Surprised, the officers asked how Gein would have known that. He smiled his off-center grin and muttered that he had merely heard the Hills talking about the case.[25]

Since facts about Mrs. Worden's disappearance were not yet common knowledge, Chase and Spees figured Gein knew more than he was admitting. They reported to Sheriff Schley that they had a suspect in custody. In the meantime, around 8 p.m., Schley and Captain Schoephoerster were on their way to Gein's home, figuring it would be a prime place to begin a search for Mrs. Worden. The November night wind was freezing and the snow crunched under their car tires as they headed out to the rundown farm.[26]

All the doors on Gein's house were locked except for the summer kitchen, which was merely an attached shed. Schoephoerster pushed open the door with his boot and the policemen entered the ramshackle structure. Stepping around piles of junk, they shined their flashlights around the room. Schley bumped into something in the darkness and turned the beam toward the object. The glare spotlighted the gutted, headless body of Mrs. Worden suspended from the ceiling. Stumbling out of the house, both men vomited into the snow.[27]

Still reeling from the shock, Schoephoerster called for help. Within the hour, dozens of lawmen were on the scene along with state crime lab investigators. They were stunned into silence as they observed the body, dressed out like a butchered heifer. Cautiously, the police moved into the main house. Stepping around and over the filthy clutter, the police began a thorough search. By the light of flickering kerosene lamps and probing flashlights, it was obvious that only a couple of the rooms appeared lived in.[28]

To their horror, the men began finding odd and terrible examples of Gein's insanity. Tops of skulls used as bowls, a belt dressed out with nipples, one box of female genitalia and another holding four noses, four chairs with seats of skin, skulls on his bedposts, a shade pull made of a woman's lips, and other grotesque items. A generator was brought in and a dozen years of Gein's squalid life were exposed in the glare of floodlights. By now, a horde of journalists had descended on the scene and were kept at bay by the police, who only said that Mrs. Worden's body had been found and that the situation inside the house was "horrible beyond belief."[29]

As the search of the building and adjoining land continued, the remains of several female bodies were found. Scariest of all the discoveries were masks made of the facial skin of at least nine women. One deputy found a brown paper bag and lifted up its contents to the light. It was the head of missing tavern keeper Mary Hogan. Other authorities found Mrs. Worden's still warm intestines and located her head in a burlap bag, stuffed between two rotting mattresses. Her ears had been punctured by nails connected by twine, ready to be hung up as Gein's latest trophy.[30] Other police officers found the blood-soaked Worden delivery truck, abandoned near Plainfield on a narrow back lane.[31]

Almost as surprising was the discovery of another bedroom and the house parlor, which, unlike the rest of Gein's home, were tidy. Dust on the furniture indicated that the rooms hadn't been disturbed for years—probably since Augusta Gein's death. For more than a decade, the peaceable, always smiling Ed Gein had maintained his own hidden shrine to his beloved mother.[32]

An agitated Sheriff Schley confronted Gein in his cell about 2:30 a.m., slammed the little man up against the wall, and needed to be restrained by other deputies. Ed Gein refused to talk, not admitting anything. By 5 a.m., Sunday, November 17, the police had removed numerous human parts and Mrs. Worden's body from the house. Only twelve hours had elapsed since a distraught Frank Worden began searching for his mother. But in that short time, a homegrown monster had been uncovered.[33]

The autopsy report on Mrs. Worden related the details of the woman's mutilation, describing the extent of dissection and the effects of a .22-caliber bullet to the back of her head that was the cause of death. Unlike the dispassionate medical report, rumors became headlines. As if the reality of the situation were insufficiently grotesque, the story was endlessly embroidered: It was said that quart jars of human blood were found in Gein's cellar; that he was about to eat her entrails; that the body parts were carefully wrapped in butcher paper for storage. The myth of Ed Gein as a cannibal was already receiving wide play.[34]

The police continued to search Gein's acreage, a task that took a week. The police later found bodies exhumed from local graveyards and carved up by Gein.[35]

For thirty hours, Gein was closemouthed with police interrogators. But on late Monday morning, he finally cracked, admitting to killing Mrs. Worden. He claimed it was all done in a daze and that he could not remember the particulars of the murder. He could only recall dragging her body to the panel truck and returning to town to get his own car and take the store's cash register. Gein was, however, able to talk about how he hung up the body and drained its blood, taking the still-warm fluids to bury near his outhouse. According to investigators, the real surprise in Gein's revelations was that he was not a true serial killer, saying that Mrs. Worden's death was a fluke. He procured the other body parts from cemeteries over a five-year period starting in 1947.[36]

All the "victims" were recently deceased middle-aged women, many of whom Gein had known in Plainfield. An avid obituary reader, he would then venture to the new graves, unearth the bodies, and take what he wanted. Again, he claimed this nocturnal aberration was done in his self-described daze.[37]

By Sunday, the media was already on the story. The early edition of that day's *Milwaukee Journal* was dispassionately headlined, "Missing From Store, Widow Found Dead." The *Milwaukee Sentinel's* six-star final edition only had "Woman Store Owner Dead; Suspect Held" for its front-page story below the fold.[38] But on Monday, the banner headline screamed, "Murder 'Factory' on Farm! Find Remains of 5 Slain Women; Plainfield Widow Cut Up, Hanged by Heels in Shed."[39]

Dick Leonard, retired editor of the *Milwaukee Journal*, recalled that on Sunday, November 17, 1957, he was working on the state desk, the only staffer in the newsroom other than a sportswriter. An Associated Press writer from an adjoining office burst in to report that a killer had been apprehended in Plainfield and that there were odd things found in the suspect's house.

"I finished what I was doing, then got in my car and drove up there as fast as I could. I knew it would be a good story," said Leonard. But it was getting dark and he wondered if he could find the rural site. "I finally made it, but couldn't get into the house because it had been secured by that time." Leonard filed his front-page story from a motel room later that night, with "Plainfield Farmer Admits Grisly Act" as its headline.

Leonard remained in the area for several days, covering the story and attending Gein's arraignment. "I went into the courtroom and sat on one of the long wooden benches. They brought in Gein and put him down right next to me. He was nervous, not too bright. Gein turned to me and grabbed my hand, asking, 'What are they going to do to me. What are they going to do?'" Leonard said. The surprised reporter tried to settle down the little farmer, saying that everything would be all right.

"That was an historic moment for me, my hand being held by a killer," Leonard recalled with a laugh. Ever the reporter, however, he lamented that he never had the chance to directly ask Gein any questions because the court proceedings started and the accused killer was then whisked away.[40]

On that Monday, Gein was taken to the Waushara County Courthouse and arraigned on charges of armed robbery, because of the cash register theft and the $41 it contained. The state wanted to delay any murder charges until it could wade through all the evidence. Saying he could afford his own attorney, bail was set at $10,000 and Gein was sent back to his cell. Despite ongoing questioning, the bachelor handyman still denied anything to do with Mary Hogan's death, despite the fact that the police literally had evidence of her murder "in the bag."

Also that day, Detective Lieutenant Vern Weber of the La Crosse Police Department spoke twice with Gein about the disappearance of little Evelyn Hartley four years earlier. Weber concluded there was no connection between the Plainfield man and the Hartley case, although Gein was born in La Crosse and lived there as a child. As with many others who interviewed Gein, Weber was almost sympathetic, saying that the prisoner was very meek. He did not appear to be the person portrayed by the press as a crazed sex killer. He said Gein implied that his interest in the cadavers was only to learn more about human anatomy.[41]

On Tuesday, the pack of eager journalists and photographers were finally allowed to tour Gein's house, all the skulls, skins, bones and entrails having been removed to the state crime lab. A horde representing the *Chicago Tribune*, the *Milwaukee Sentinel*, the *Milwaukee Journal*, the Associated Press, the *Minneapolis Star*, the *Capital Times*, *St. Paul Pioneer Press*, the *Chicago Sun-Times*, *Life* magazine, and dozens of others waded through the mess that made up Ed Gein's sad, solitary life.[42]

Milwaukee Journal reporter Bob Wells described the scene in vivid detail under the headline: "Incredibly Dirty House Was Home of Slayer." *The Milwaukee Sentinel* told it all with "Plainfield Butcher's Story! Ghoul Stole 10 Female Corpses; 'Moon-Mad' Gein Robbed Graves, Mutilated Bodies."[43]

Got Murder?

Also visiting the house amid the storm of journalists was attorney William Belter. The thirty-year-old former state assemblyman, a sole practitioner from Wautoma, had been retained by Gein to be his defense lawyer. The next day, after an hour-long conference with a quiet, composed Gein, Belter said that he got the impression that the man realized his condition "is such that he needs the sort of help that an institution can provide."[44]

Belter would eventually enter a plea that his client was not guilty by reason of insanity. Two Chicago detectives also showed up to question Gein about several murders in the Windy City but determined that he was not involved. The Plainfield man claimed never to have traveled any farther from home than his trip to Milwaukee for his army physical in 1942.[45]

With all the stories flying around town ripe for picking by deadline-desperate out-of-town media, Ed Marolla, publisher and editor of the *Plainfield Sun*, subsequently spent an inordinate amount of space and ink refuting many of the exaggerations and rumors printed as fact. One story concerned a local woman, Adeline Watkins, who allegedly had been Gein's sweetheart. A *Minneapolis Tribune* piece headlined "I Loved Kind, Sweet Man, Still Do, Says Confessed Killer's 'Fiancée.'" The distraught Watkins came to Marolla saying that many of her comments were exaggerated and taken out of context, although she and Gein occasionally went to a movie. Many other Plainfield residents seemed happy to embellish their knowledge of Gein, with a number describing alleged close calls with the man of the hour.[46]

In an interview with a *Milwaukee Sentinel* reporter, Gein's friend Ira Turner was asked if Gein had ever gone out with girls. Turner replied, "Never. Ed was shy. The most bashful man I have ever seen. If a girl talked to him, Ed would look down at the ground. Very bashful." According to Turner, "Gein was the best friend I ever had," saying that as a young man, the Gein farm "was practically my second home" where he stopped regularly after school and ate dinner many times. Turner claimed that they hunted together regularly and that Gein taught him to play the accordion and the flute.[47]

Sheriff Schley grew increasingly upset with the hordes of reporters following him everywhere, demanding interviews. Sometimes up to sixty writers and broadcasters tailed the officer as he attempted to go about his business in what was once a sleepy backwater of Wisconsin. On one occasion, Belter had secured permission from his client to allow interviews with the accused killer. More than two dozen reporters packed into a small room and waited endlessly for their subject to appear. The journalists became more upset and angry at the delays, figuring there was some hidden motive on the part of the authorities that prevented their meeting with Gein. It turned out that Schley—who had to make do with two deputies to patrol his county and an annual department budget of barely $11,000 —was in the jail basement trying to repair a leaky water pipe. Belter, who doubled as a justice of the peace, had also gotten caught up reviewing game-law violations.[48]

Even after working out a pool approach whereby several reporters would relay the story to the others, Schley was still pursued by the entire Fourth Estate mob attempting to cover the Gein story. Confronted with the shouting, jostling group, the burly sheriff called off the interview and stepped back inside his jail, banging its door behind him.[49]

However, there was "no statutory or case law of which I am aware" that prohibited interviews of Gein by the press, declared Wisconsin Attorney General Stewart Honeck on Thursday, November 21. Honeck issued his opinion after being asked to do so by Wisconsin Governor Vernon Thomson. The governor was pressured to secure a ruling by *Milwaukee Sentinel* police reporter Floyd J. Gonyea. Thomson was phoned by Gonyea from Wautoma where he was covering the case, asking if it "was lawful for a 'panel' of reporters to interview Gein in the Waushara County Jail."[50]

Journalists weren't the only ones flooding the community's streets in the weeks after Gein's arrest. Sightseers by the hundreds also drove around, seeking out Gein's now-boarded up home and other places that figured in the crimes. Among the curious were groups of University of Wisconsin–Madison fraternity boys determined to hold beer parties on Gein's porch. Portage and Waushara county deputies were posted at the house to keep these thrill seekers away.[51]

Through it all, Plainfield tried gamely to continue with its small-town way of life. Frank Worden would reopen the hardware store two weeks after the discovery of his mother's body, saying that it was necessary to "carry on as before." But there remained an undercurrent of guilt that, somehow, someone somewhere should have been putting together all the shreds of evidence that showed Gein's long, slow slide into murderous insanity.[52]

There were those who doubted Gein's grave-robbing stories, including several police officers, the Plainfield cemetery caretaker, and the city's mortician. They pointed out that the graveyard was regularly patrolled and maintained and the sandy soil was difficult to dig in a short amount of time without someone discovering the desecrations.[53]

Graveyard sexton Pat Danna, who lived at the cemetery, contended that he would have noticed a prowler and seen any disturbance of the freshly turned soil. He indicated that each grave was mounded, then carpeted with sod. "All of this would have to be spaded up and the drift around the casket removed before anybody could get to the body," he said. Danna went on to explain that the caskets were closed with screws and enclosed in wooden boxes or concrete vaults. "You can't tell me one man could get to the body in a night, and cover things back up so I wouldn't have noticed it."[54]

On Tuesday, November 19, Gein was in Madison for a lie detector test and more questioning by assistant crime lab superintendent Joseph Wilimovsky. Gein was very cooperative and calmly answered every question he was asked. He even admitted wearing masks made of skin and a mammary vest, according to Wilimovsky, who Gein would later fondly call Joe. Not only did Gein prance around his house in his macabre getup, he said he also danced in the moonlight. Under intense questioning, Gein finally admitted to killing Mary Hogan and burning her body parts in a stove. But he steadfastly denied murdering Bernice Worden. Throughout his life, he kept saying that her shooting was accidental. He described in detail how he looted graves, first testing the earth with a metal rod to see if it could easily be dug up. Gein pointed out that he only took parts that he wanted and then would put the cadaver back in the coffin and rebury it.[55]

Charles Wilson, director of the state crime lab, said the lie detector test eliminated Gein as the person responsible for the disappearances of Hartley, Weckler, and Travis. But they were inclusive in the disappearance of another woman, Irene Johnson of Fort Atkinson, on August 20, 1956.[56] No ties were ever established between Gein and that crime, however. Based on a Wednesday lie detector test, Attorney General Honeck said that it was "established that Gein operated alone in the nine grave thefts he has admitted."[57]

During his interrogation about using skulls for bowls and skinning heads, Gein asked for something to eat. He was given a piece of apple pie with a slice of cheddar cheese, but complained that the Wisconsin cheese was dry.[58]

Speculation on Gein's motive for the grave robbing mutilations were endlessly analyzed by the media. Sources claimed that Gein's Oedipal complex led him to act out his perverse inclinations. Apparently, Gein had even thought about changing his sex and supposedly considered doing the operation on himself.[59] This revelation, naturally, resulted in an uproar among the police and medical communities, with psychiatrists, psychologists, sociologists, and other -ists offering their opinions. All sorts of reasons for Gein's behavior were subsequently tossed around by armchair evaluators, none of whom had ever spoken with Gein or reviewed what he said. In fact, not a single professional psychiatrist had interviewed Gein to that point.[60] It wasn't until November 29 that doctors learned they could review transcripts and recordings of Gein's two interviews at the Wisconsin State Crime Laboratory.[61]

Gein's arraignment in front of Waushara County Judge Boyd Clark lasted three minutes. A preliminary hearing was waved after the not guilty pleas were entered into the record. According to the charges, Edward Gein "did on the 16th day of November, 1957, at the village of Plainfield in said county feloniously and with intent to kill, murder Bernice Worden, a human being, contrary to section 940.01 of the Wisconsin statutes against the peace and dignity of the state of Wisconsin."

Bernice Worden's funeral on Wednesday, November 20, was attended by 250 of the 680 residents of Plainfield, as well as the media.

Got Murder?

The Methodist church she attended overflowed with mourners who included her son, Frank, and daughter, Miriam Worden Walker. The Reverend Gerard Tanquist used the Twenty-Third Psalm, "the Lord is my shepherd," as the basis for his sermon. He called for continued faith in God, saying, "In face of the horrible incidents of the past few days, the Lord has not abandoned us."[62]

Before the service, the congregation and the dead woman's friends silently filed past the gold-colored casket. Six sturdy pallbearers carried the casket from the church to the hearse. Mrs. Worden was buried in the tiny local cemetery.[63]

In his Thursday issue, editor Marolla of the *Plainfield Sun* commented, "Those of the outside world will remember of her just what they read. We here in our community will remember her as she was. . . a pleasant person, a very good businesswoman when widowed and kept it going. . . . We remember selling her an ad on each Monday, the discussion of public affairs and her pointed comments; her fondness for her first-born grandson and her hopes that 'little Frankie' (now quite a big boy) would someday join her and his dad in the business."[64]

Also on Thursday morning, in an odd twist, the Reverend Kenneth Engleman, the thirty-three-year-old pastor of the Wautoma Methodist Church, gained access to Gein and prayed for him. That afternoon, Engleman told the press corps, "Boys, I'm here to correct an erroneous impression which the newspapers have been printing about this fellow. He is truly remorseful. In fact, he cried twice while I was talking to him." Engleman said he decided to meet with the killer because "I am a Christian minister and here is a man who needs help." Engleman would then accompany Gein to his initial court appearance.[65]

According to Sheriff Schley, it would be up to relatives of the women whose graves Gein robbed to decide whether they should be reopened. Schley indicated anyone whose relative might be in a desecrated grave would be notified as soon as the state crime lab completed its investigation.[66]

On Friday, November 22, Gein appeared before Circuit Judge Herbert A. Bunde, who committed the grave robber to Central State

Hospital in Waupun for mental testing. The judge found "it advisable under the circumstances as related by both the counsel for the state and the counsel for the defendant that expert determination be had whether he [Gein] is now competent to stand trial" and whether he was sane when Mrs. Worden was killed.[67]

If Gein was found to be sane, he would stand trial. If not, his trial would have to wait until he regained his competency—if indeed he ever did. The state would have then needed to prove Gein was sane at the time he murdered Mrs. Worden.[68]

Saturday morning, Gein was scheduled to be transferred to the state hospital. The day's first order of business, however, was to take Gein back to his home to show officers where he burned Mary Hogan's body. That accomplished, Gein left for Waupun around 2 p.m. For the trip, he wore his now-infamous wool jacket, plaid hunting cap, and rubber boots.[69]

On Sunday, authorities were drawing up a list of graves to inspect, while hundreds of cars and their gawking occupants clogged Plainfield's Main Street.[70] The police got the jump on the media on Monday, heading out early to begin their probe. As a plane chartered by the *Milwaukee Journal* circled overhead, a tent was erected over the first grave investigated—that of Mrs. Eleanor Adams, who died on August 1, 1951. Gein said Mrs. Adams had been one of those used for his experiments, so investigators were not surprised to find the wooden box cover had been hacked open and the casket was empty.[71]

The next grave opened was that of Mrs. Mabel Everson, who died on April 15, 1951. Only a few of her bones were found interred in the broken casket. They had been returned by Gein, who said he occasionally had pangs of conscience and replaced pieces of bodies he didn't need for his fantasies.[72] Returning to the farm on November 30, police found a set of bones they originally thought might have been those of missing hunter Ray Burgess. The skeleton turned out to be that of another woman.[73]

Through the crime lab's efforts, it was established that Gein had desecrated the corpses of at least twelve women whose bodies were taken from a graveyard in Hancock and from the Spiritland Cemetery in Almond in addition to the Plainfield cemetery.[74]

In the first weeks of December, the lead stories in *Life* and *Time* magazines brought the Gein story to the nation. As his story began to take its place in American culture, Gein himself was undergoing psychological and psychiatric tests at Central State. The massive report that resulted was given to Judge Bunde the week before Christmas. One of its insights was that Gein was bitter toward his neighbors, claiming that he wouldn't have turned out the way he did if they had shown more interest in him. He also continued to praise his mother, saying she "was good in every way."[75]

One part of the lengthy missive concluded, "There is ample reason to believe that his violation of the graves was in response to the demands of his fantasy life, which was motivated by his abnormally magnified attachment to his mother." Other sections described his loneliness and his rigid code of perceived morality that nevertheless had allowed him to kill Mary Hogan. A board of specialists reviewed the data on December 19, concluding, "This man, in the opinion of the staff, is legally insane and not competent to stand trial at this time."[76] After reading the medical team's report, Judge Bunde agreed to hold Gein at Central State indefinitely; he, too, believed that the frail Plainfield man was not mentally able to stand trial.[77] This angered some of the town's residents who had known and worked with Gein. They figured he was pulling a fast one on the judge.

As the year ended, the Associated Press called the Gein saga Wisconsin's story of the year, beating out the Milwaukee Braves winning the World Series, the death of Wisconsin Senator Joseph McCarthy, the election of William Proxmire to replace the not-so-dearly-departed legislator, an outbreak of Asian flu, and a federal court action in which seven food companies sought to block return of windfall profits on cheese sales to the government.[78]

The courtroom was packed on Monday morning, January 6, the date of Gein's sanity hearing. The 140-pound handyman was dressed in a suit, flanked by Waushara County Sheriff Schley and Wood County Sheriff Tom Forsyth. At the conclusion of the proceedings, Judge Bunde agreed with the experts' testimony and recommitted Gein to Central

State Hospital. "I think it is adequate for me to say that it does not appear that he will ever be at liberty again. Perhaps that is a desirable conclusion. That closes the hearing, and the court is adjourned."[79]

By 8:02 p.m. that evening, Edward Theodore Gein entered the barred doors of the hospital, and that was the last the public saw of the Plainfield Butcher for years. That wasn't enough for Gein's neighbors, many of whom felt he had gotten off too easy, even with the promise of a potential trial if Gein ever was found sane.

Gein's house, its remaining contents, and his land were to be auctioned on March 30, the Palm Sunday of 1958, to satisfy claims filed by several families whose mothers or grandmothers were mutilated. An inspection fee of fifty cents was to be charged to go through the house, a fact that inflamed Plainfield's citizens who felt that the place would become a sordid museum. It took a judge's action to halt that plan.[80]

But on the night of March 20, 1958, Gein's home mysteriously burned down. Arson was suspected but nothing was ever proved. Regardless of the reason for the fire, Plainfield residents were happy to be rid of the eyesore. When told of the blaze, the incarcerated madman only said, "Just as well."[81] The Plainfield fire marshal who summoned his fifteen-member volunteer department to fight the blaze was none other than Frank Worden. Sheriff Schley requested that John Hassler, deputy state fire marshal, investigate the possibility of arson, especially since the building did not have any electrical wiring that could have caused a problem. Hassler indicated the blaze may have been caused by sparks from a nearby bonfire.[82]

On March 23, more than twenty thousand people showed up for the pre-auction site inspection, looking at the cordoned-off, smoldering ruins of Gein's former home and poking around the outbuildings. The procession lasted from noon until dark. About two thousand attended the auction itself, picking up rusted farm equipment, an old stove, a keg of nails, and other household items not connected to the murders—all at bargain prices. The event netted about $5,000, to be held in trust.[83]

The farmland itself went for $3,883 to Sun Prairie developer Emden Schley, who eventually tore down Gein's remaining outbuildings and planted sixty thousand trees over the site. Fourteen bid for Gein's 1949 maroon Ford. The auto, which sold for $760, had been used by Gein to haul Bernice Worden's body to his home. The winner was Bunny Gibbons of Rockford, Illinois, who took the vehicle on the carnival circuit. A 1938 Chevrolet pickup, which Gein used to haul Mary Hogan's corpse, went for $215 to Chet's Auto Wreckers of Highland to be used for hauling scrap iron.[84]

Ed Gein's life as a free man was over, but his legend had only begun. In 1960, Robert Bloch's fictionalized takeoff on the story was immortalized in Alfred Hitchcock's *Psycho*. It was probably fitting that in May of that year, workmen planting trees came across a pile of human bones buried near where Gein's barn once stood. And in December 1962, at the request of Madison Bishop William O'Connor, the crime lab's human relics from the investigation were buried instead of cremated.[85]

Ten long years after he had been institutionalized, Gein was considered to finally be able to understand the charges against him and a hearing was ordered. On January 22, 1968, Gein entered the Waushara County courtroom in Wautoma. The proceedings were presided over by the genteel Judge Robert H. Gollmar, who would write *Edward Gein: America's Most Bizarre Murderer* in 1981. In addition to a general recounting of Gein's life and crimes, the book was notable for its inclusion of many Gein-related jokes as well as for extensive court testimony, a posttrial interview with the Plainfield killer, and eight pages of gruesome police photographs of his body parts collection. At his trial, Gein was dressed well and had put on weight. His appearance demonstrated that hospital living apparently agreed with him.

Art Schley, the Waushara County sheriff who found Bernice Worden dressed out like a deer in Ed Gein's house, died of a stroke on March 22, 1968. He was only forty-three. Friends thought that stress over being subpoenaed for the upcoming Gein trial might have contributed to his death. Many said the popular Schley was Gein's last victim.[86]

Legal complexities delayed Gein's trial until late autumn. On Thursday, November 7, 1968, Gein was finally back in the courtroom.[87]

The trial was conducted without a jury at the request of the defense, which again had entered a plea of not guilty by reason of insanity. There were two parts of the judicial process: one trial for the murder of Mrs. Worden and a second to determine if Gein was sane at the time. Assistant Attorney General Robert Sutton served as special state prosecutor, with attorney Dominic Frinzi acting for the defense in what Sutton called a "battle of legal wits." Gein took the stand, claiming that his rifle had discharged accidentally, resulting in Mrs. Worden's death. He claimed he couldn't remember what happened next, including her butchering.[88]

On Thursday, November 14, almost exactly eleven years after her murder, Ed Gein was found guilty of killing Bernice Worden. The second part of the trial was concluded quickly on the same afternoon. The court found Gein insane when he shot and subsequently carved up the hardware store owner. Gein was sent back to Central State Hospital after a short news conference in which he again blamed many of his troubles on the way he was treated in his hometown. Enjoying a round of "refreshing beverages," Sutton and his team unwound after what he termed "an open and shut case."[89]

Back in the hospital, Gein resumed his prison duties as a mason, medical center aide, and carpenter's helper, making $1.50 a week. He enjoyed watching television and toyed with a shortwave radio in his spare time.[90]

In February 1974, Gein filed a petition with the Waushara County Clerk of Courts, claiming he had recovered and that there was no longer any reason for him to remain imprisoned. During a June 27 hearing, several psychiatrists testified that while Gein appeared docile on the surface, his mental health challenges were still a problem. His petition was rejected and he was returned to Central State.

In 1978, Gein and several other Central State patients were transferred to the confines of the Mendota Mental Health Institute in Madison. Officials cited his "stable condition and low security status." Gein was seventy-two by that time, senile and in poor health.

Afflicted with cancer and respiratory ailments, Gein died six years later, on July 26, 1984. His obituary was a prime newspaper feature around the world. Gein was secretly buried in an unmarked plot next to his mother in the Plainfield cemetery.[91]

If the newspapers got one more round of headlines out of Gein's death, the people of Plainfield were less than happy about their renewed notoriety. *Milwaukee Journal* reporter Alex Dobish was tossed out of a Plainfield cafe for asking about the deceased killer. "Out! Out!" the owner screamed, pointing to the exit. "That's my comment, out! Out! I've already popped one guy today."[92]

Looking back on the case he prosecuted, Sutton remarked, "It was the most fascinating case I've ever been involved in." He added, "Our psychiatrists proved he was not insane but it just couldn't be accepted. If Gein wasn't insane, then nobody was. Of course, I'll admit it's obvious the man was not in his right mind. . . He had some mental problems. Everybody would agree he did things a normal person would not do in the most macabre and darkest side of one's soul, but was he criminally insane?"[93]

Defense attorney Frinzi commented, "I don't think he was a murderer per se. The woman [Bernice Worden] was killed with one shot. To this day, I think the shooting was an accident."[94]

Noted FBI profiler John Douglas was assigned to Milwaukee in the 1970s and wanted to learn about the Gein case. When he initially checked in with the state attorney general's office, he was told the records were closed because of Gein's insanity. However, by using his FBI clout, he got the office to open the files.

"I'll never forget going with the clerk and taking the boxes off the endless shelves and actually having to break a wax seal to get in. But inside, I saw photographs that instantly became seared in my mind," he wrote afterward. "As horrible as these images were to contemplate, I began speculating as to what they said about the person who had created them, and how that knowledge could have aided in his capture. And in a real sense, I've been contemplating that ever since."[95]

Forty acres that had been part of Gein's Plainfield property were put up for sale on eBay in April 2006 by Mike Fisher, grandson of the man who purchased the land at the 1958 auction. In his pitch seeking $250,000 for the real estate, Fisher played up Gein's connection with the site. However, he received only one lowball offer and then eBay halted the online auction after only five days, citing its policy of prohibiting the sale of murder memorabilia.[96]

As of this writing, the property remains for sale.

As a testament to Gein's enduring notoriety, there is even a MySpace site reserved in his name, with his interests listed as "working in my shed" and "grave robbing."[97]

Sterling Hall, where the body of Christine Rothschild was abandoned.

Chapter 4

Murders Most Foul

Madison, Wisconsin
1968–1984
Death toll: 8

I think we might have a psychopath on our hands.

—Clyde F. "Bud" Chamberlain Jr., Dane County coroner[1]

Christine Rothschild, May 25, 1968

Throughout Sunday, May 25, 1968, and into the next day, a steady rain pounded Madison. The University of Wisconsin campus was soaked, with large puddles creating little lakes on every paved space. Umbrellas were plentiful as sleepy-eyed students trudged between their Monday morning classes. Tuesday was to be the last day of classes for the semester, with final exams continuing through June 8. Students had begun cramming for tests, eating their late-night rations of pizza and curtailing, albeit only somewhat, their visits to area pubs.

Fog blanketed Wisconsin, causing flight cancellations at General Mitchell Field airport in Milwaukee as the work week began. Visibility on some highways in Waukesha and Dodge counties was less than one hundred feet. Four people died in Brown County when highway spray from a truck was blamed for blinding a motorist, who then lost control of the vehicle and hit another car.[2]

Not only were driving conditions treacherous that weekend, but

Got Murder?

something more dangerous was about to unfold. A knife-wielding murderer stalked through Madison, using the bad weather as cover.

The university's surrounding neighborhoods had been edgy for weeks because of more than forty vicious muggings, assaults, and armed robberies since early April. As a result, authorities stepped up their patrols on weekdays throughout the area. Yet many of the victims were disdainfully described by police as "hippies." Subsequently, worried that they weren't getting enough police protection, a student defense committee was formed and began patrolling the university a week before classes ended. On May 18, two students reported an attack by six people outside the Wisconsin Center; one of the victims was slashed with a razor. When police responded to their calls for help, an officer allegedly told the students, "The best you can do is cut your hair and get a shave." The police then supposedly left and did not look for the attackers.[3]

But it wasn't only the beads-and-fringe set being attacked. A married couple strolling across campus were among the victims. Adding to university police concerns was the war. The Vietnam conflict was raging, and Madison was already well known as a focal point for opposition to the military mayhem half a world away. South Hall had recently been firebombed and it was surmised that the attacks on students and campus hangers-on could have been committed by alienated Madison youths out to pound anyone who appeared to be antiwar.[4]

Around 4 a.m. on May 25, Gertrude Armstrong, a night supervisor at Ann Emery Hall, saw eighteen-year-old freshman Christine Rothschild on her way to the restroom. The dorm doors were regularly locked at 1 a.m.; a side door was reopened at 4:30 a.m. and the front door of the building was unlocked at 5:30 a.m. The blond coed was still in her nightclothes, but she may have been preparing for her regular early morning walk. That stroll to the facilities in the dim predawn hours was the last time anyone saw the girl alive.[5]

Rothschild had a private room, number 119, on the second floor of the dorm and did not have much contact with other residents and was not known to have a boyfriend. The comely five-foot-seven,

120-pound young woman was planning a journalism career and was a part-time model in her hometown, Chicago. She was considered "classy" and "preppy," not fitting in with the campus flower child movement. Rothschild's sister, Roxanne, was already a top fashion designer in the Windy City, and her father was an inventor, developing a parking gate used at airports. The elder Rothschild was also president of two Chicago corporations.[6]

On Monday, around 7:30 p.m., twenty-two-year-old Phillip Van Valkenberg was in search of a friend who worked in the student machine shop in Sterling Hall, the university's physics building two blocks south of Bascom Hall. Finding the doors locked due to tighter campus security, the part-time maintenance man in the university's primate lab pushed his way through the high bushes fronting the building. He intended to knock on the window of his pal's office.[7]

Looking down to avoid the mud, Van Valkenberg stumbled across Rothschild's body lying on its left side in a rain-diluted pool of blood. Her head lay against a basement window. Rothschild was wearing a blue cotton minidress, three-quarter-length beige coat, and knee-high black boots. Rothschild's large black umbrella, with several broken stays, was angled deep into the mud. There was no sign of a struggle, nor was Rothschild sexually assaulted. Expensive rings were on both hands.[8]

The coed's murder was the first in the university's long history.[9] Rothschild's death made the early editions of the Monday morning newspapers. The scrambling reporters only laid out sketchy details of the crime and what little initial information was known about her and her family.[10]

She had been stabbed fourteen times in the neck and chest. The force was so great that several ribs were shattered and her heart punctured. Rothschild's upper and lower jaws were also broken and she had been strangled by a strip of lining apparently torn from her raincoat. Her gloves were jammed down her throat.[11] The woman had been dead for four to ten hours before being discovered, placing the time of death between 9:30 a.m. and 3:30 p.m. on Sunday. A Waukesha couple touring campus around 3 p.m., Sunday, later told police that their children had spotted what they thought was a dummy tossed into the bushes as a student hoax. They did not call authorities until they read of the murder in the newspaper.[12]

It was an ignominious end of life for Rothschild, described as "a sweet girl, always with a smile, one of the nicest girls around here. She always had a nice 'hello' for everybody," said Ruth Toussiant, Emery Hall business director. Her comments were echoed by other university officials, high school administrators, and classmates.[13] Rothschild was known to take regular Sunday morning walks around campus, starting when she began school that previous September. She did not show up for the regular 8:30 a.m. breakfast in Emery Hall that morning, but a pathologist's report indicated that she had eaten later. Her purse, makeup, and identification were found in her room. Rothschild's cigarette lighter, with her room key attached by a thin gold chain, was discovered next to her body. A name tag on her blouse aided in her identification. No motive was known for the slaying.[14]

With the discovery of the battered body, concerned coeds hunkered in the safety of their dorm rooms and apartments that Monday night as extra police roamed the campus. Women talked about using umbrellas for defense since they were not allowed to carry weapons on campus. Others said they would scream if attacked.[15]

The sixty-three officers on the university's force were commanded by Ralph E. Hanson, chief of UW security, who coordinated efforts between his staff, state troopers, and Madison police officers. Among Dane County officials called to the scene were Undersheriff Vernon "Jack" Leslie, Chief Deputy Reynold Abrahams, Captain Earl Sorenson, Dane County Coroner Clyde "Bud" Chamberlain Jr., and two deputy coroners: John W. Stevenson and A.E. Ferchland. Assistant District Attorney Dave Mebane also helped. The state crime lab analyzed the evidence.[16]

Chancellor William H. Seward said that no connection had been determined between the spate of other attacks and Rothschild's murder. But he warned students to be vigilant. His suggestions including keeping to lighted areas, not walking alone, and being careful about riding with strangers.[17]

The Madison newspapers pleaded for any witnesses to contact police, especially since the murder apparently took place during daylight hours. An editorial feared that someone who might have seen what transpired had not come forward because they "don't want to get involved."[18]

Asked by police to draw up a psychological profile of the killer, UW psychiatrist Seymour Halleck pointed out that the murderer probably selected Rothschild at random. He admitted that in such cases, psychiatry along with "any other behavioral science has little to contribute in this area." After studying the report, which was not released to the press on the advice of the district attorney, UW Police Chief Hanson agreed that Halleck's study had limited value. While they agreed that the perpetrator probably did not know Rothschild, officials admitted that anyone could have committed the murder and so they could not even narrow their search to a student or a man with mental problems.[19]

Madison's Eighth Ward Alderman Paul Soglin—the city's future mayor was a university graduate student in 1968—took the lead in complaining about what many students felt was lack of police concern about campus crime. Speaking on Wednesday, May 29, at a meeting called by Mayor Otto Festge to "bridge the gap between the university community and the city," Soglin claimed that many additional assaults on students went unreported. He said that the Madison press fostered the image that the university was full of "weirdoes, freaks and Communists and that it was all right to beat them up." Wilbur Emery, Madison's police chief, maintained that his officers were doing what they could, assigning extra squads and beefing up patrols.[20]

Hanson said he wouldn't argue with Soglin on the crime issue, noting that some students got more publicity because they were the loudest complainers. "The hippie group is more vocal. Whether it opposes Dow Chemical or Vietnam, it is magnified out of proportion," the university police chief claimed, implying they were doing the same with the security challenges.[21]

In 1968, Madison's population of 180,000 included 33,000 students and 2,000 faculty and staff. Once largely clustered in the 700-acre campus area, the growing student population had spread throughout the greater Madison area. Many now lived in what were described as "tough neighborhoods," especially south of Regent and east of Francis streets. Police officers emphasized that those not living in dorms often placed themselves in jeopardy by their own actions, especially by walking alone in unlit areas, drinking too much, and not being cautious around strangers.[22]

Robert Hanson, a sophomore leading the student patrol unit, said that his group would continue its work, though school would soon to be out for the semester. Using autos and motorcycles, students kept watch around the community. Some were posted on house porches on streets surrounding the campus. Hanson claimed at least one attack was thwarted by their presence.[23]

The murder soon became political fodder for Wisconsin politicians, particularly such Republicans as Robert Warren, the state senator from Green Bay, then running for attorney general. Shortly after the murder, he warned that "society was in danger unless we abandon the over-permissiveness which has eroded respect for law and order, unless we emphatically reject civil disobedience and physical violence as instruments of social change." He had previously announced that he was suspicious of "foreigners" from other states at the university, free-thinking students whose views did not conform to that of the GOP platform. A Madison newspaper rapped the senator for his "loathsome performance" and the "lust for votes" that led him to try to capitalize on the tragedy.[24]

On Friday, May 31, responding to rumors flying around campus, police denied holding a suspect in Rothschild's death. But UW Police Chief Hanson did say that his staff had questioned more than one hundred people and were awaiting forensic tests on material forwarded to the FBI in Washington.[25]

The number interrogated rose by another fifty within a few days. Among them was a forty-three-year-old former Madison hospital worker who was questioned in New York because he had been in the Ann Emery dormitory area around 4 a.m. the morning of the murder, walking a friend back to her residence. After speaking with Madison detectives, the man was released.[26]

Police also searched Sterling Hall three times. Evidence included a man's blood-stained handkerchief found under the woman's head. It was neatly folded and of quality linen, but police thought it might have been tugged from the murderer's coat pocket. Later on the day of the murder, a pair of wet, bloody, gray trousers was discovered in a trash barrel at a shopping center a mile from the scene. But analysis showed they were not connected to the crime.[27]

As students left campus for the semester, the immediate fear that followed Rothschild's death dissipated. Yet UW Police Chief Hanson kept up the pressure, requesting that the university offer a $5,000 reward for tips in the case that would lead to an arrest and conviction.[28] A gift from an anonymous donor boosted the reward to $6,000.[29]

Early in June, a citizen's advisory committee to Mayor Festge recommended establishing an eight-member city–university safety council. Encouraging students to report all assaults was among its proposed goals.[30] Police also hoped to conduct a shoulder-to-shoulder search of a wooded area on campus, in the hope of finding the weapon that killed Rothschild. Yet a heavy rain on Wednesday, June 12, postponed the quest, which was resumed on that Friday to no avail.[31]

By June 5, no new leads in the case were forthcoming despite a confession by a former mental patient who called police from a pay phone to say that he killed Rothschild. The unemployed twenty-nine-year-old had been released from an Illinois institution in 1964 and was being treated at the UW hospitals as an outpatient. He even told authorities where to find a knife he claimed was the murder weapon, hidden in a bookcase at a local co-op. The knife was not the same as that used in the killing, based on a study of Rothschild's wounds. After taking a polygraph test, the man was sent to Mendota Mental Health Institute for observation.[32]

A year later, police were still struggling to find leads in the case. Yet they were no closer to finding the killer than they were at the time of Rothschild's murder. Authorities had interviewed a thousand people. They even sought to find a possible link between the Rothschild case and the murders of five girls in Ypsilanti, Michigan, near the Eastern

Got Murder?

Michigan University campus. While there were similarities, the cases were determined not related.[33] Rothschild's father hired a private detective as well, but he was also stymied by the lack of leads.[34]

Police from several Big Ten universities that had unsolved murders on their campuses compared their investigations with UW–Madison's. No link was found with the beating and slaying of a woman student in January 1968 at the University of Iowa in Iowa City or the stabbing death of a coed at the University of Michigan in Ann Arbor in July 1968. Illinois state police also were in contact with UW authorities, attempting to find connections between Rothschild's death and that of Valerie Percy, daughter of Senator Charles Percy of Illinois. The young woman was murdered in her parents' home in 1966. Both had lived on Chicago's northwest side, about fourteen miles apart. Again, nothing.[35]

Even into the 1970s, Madison authorities were still trying to find the killer. Richard Macek, a twenty-eight-year-old murder suspect being held in Milwaukee, was questioned in December 1975, to check for a possible link with the Rothschild case. The McHenry, Illinois, man was charged in the death of Paula Cupit, twenty-four, a maid killed in 1974 at the Abbey Resort in Fontana, Wisconsin. He also faced charges of sexual perversion and rape in an attack on a maid at a Wauwatosa Holiday Inn in 1974. Macek was returned to Wisconsin from where he was hiding in California. The man had an extended arrest record stretching back to 1966, including battery and window peeping in the Chicago area. However, no link was established between Macek and the murdered coed.[36]

By 1972, University of Wisconsin Police Chief Hanson said his department had checked upward of three thousand leads. University of Wisconsin Detective Paul Radloff traveled to University of Wisconsin–Stevens Point in May of that year to help investigate an attack on a coed there, plus two other assaults on the University of Wisconsin–Green Bay campus.[37]

In September 1972, police were optimistic that they might have found a link in the Rothschild slaying: a man who stabbed a seventeen-year-old woman in Portage thirty times. Since both attacks occurred in early morning rainstorms with the victim being pulled into bushes near a main road, police hoped that a connection could be made. The Portage girl survived and provided a description of her attacker; a police sketch of the man was sent to campus and police departments around the country. Alas, this also was a dead end.[38]

Thirty-eight years later, in 2006, friends and family still mourn Christine Rothschild. "I want to know the details," said Linda Tomaszewski Schulko, a college pal from Fort Worth, Texas. "I want to know how much she suffered, what caused her to get behind the bushes, was she mugged—what happened to her? I think it will give . . . a little more consolation, but there will be no closure."[39]

Rothschild's murder also remained uppermost in the mind of former UW Police Chief Ralph Hanson until his death in 1996. His son, Mike, who became a spokesperson for the Madison Police Department in the first decade of the twenty-first century, said, "He was just so upset by the violence that occurred and how devastating it was for the family. He always felt bad that they were never able to arrest anybody."[40]

There are two bizarre addenda to the Rothschild slaying. In the first, Sterling Hall again figured prominently in the news two years after the coed's body was discovered in front of the building. On August 24, 1970, a bomb exploded there at 3:42 a.m., aimed at destroying the Army Math Research Center housed on the building's upper floors. In addition to damaging Sterling, the explosion killed thirty-three-year-old researcher Robert Fassnacht, working late in his basement lab.

Arrested for the bombings were brothers Karleton and Dwight Armstrong and their friend David Fine. All three served prison terms for their role in the bombing and Fassnacht's death. Another suspect, Leo Burt, was never arrested and remains at large.[41]

In the second incident, the Dane County coroner who investigated the Rothschild murder, Clyde "Bud" Chamberlain Jr., and an office secretary, Eleanor Townsend, were shot to death. The two were killed on January 15, 1988, by nineteen-year-old Aaron Lindh, who carried a .22-caliber rifle into the Madison Police Department detective bureau and began blasting away. Lindh was convicted in the fatal shootings and, in a separate trial, was declared sane. He was sentenced to two consecutive life prison terms and given an additional thirty-five years for the wounding of Erik Erickson, who was in the wrong place at the wrong time, merely paying a parking ticket.[42]

Donna Mraz, July 1–2, 1982

After the bombing at Sterling Hall in 1970, no other murders were reported on or around campus until the night of July 1–2, 1982. Fourteen years, one month, and six days after Rothschild was stabbed to death, twenty-three-year-old Donna Mraz completed her work shift at the Bittersweet Restaurant on State Street. The business administration junior had cleared tables there since 1979. It seemed like the end of an ordinary day when the outgoing, well-liked young woman said good-bye to her co-workers around 11:30 p.m. Hopping on a bus in front of the Bittersweet, Mraz rode silently to a bus stop near her home at 1717 Van Hise Avenue, two blocks from Camp Randall Stadium. She shared the house with two girlfriends.[43]

At approximately midnight, the dean's list student from Delavan left the bus and headed for her house, taking a narrow but lighted pathway between the stadium and a practice field. There she was attacked by a man who repeatedly stuck a knife into her upper torso, face, and arms. A fatal wound ripped open her heart. Mraz was screaming all this time, attempting to fight her assailant. The killer dashed into the darkness, shielded by the looming walls of the stadium. Mraz's money, paycheck, and keys were left at the scene; she was not sexually assaulted.

Her cries roused the neighborhood and two men living across the street looked out their window and saw Mraz attempting to run and then collapse just east of Breese Terrace. One called the police while the other rushed from the apartment in a futile attempt to help. Paramedics quickly arrived to find Mraz in a pool of blood about thirty feet from where she had been stabbed. Without gaining consciousness, Mraz died two hours later at the University of Wisconsin Hospital and Clinics.[44]

UW police immediately set out to determine if Mraz's murder was linked to a spate of assaults against women in Madison that summer, two of which occurred around the time the coed died. In one case, a twenty-five-year-old woman was beaten and raped in a parking lot behind the Shuffle Inn on Thursday evening and, in the second, another was raped in her apartment around 4 a.m. on Friday the same week as Mraz's death.

Forty officers conducted a door-to-door investigation in the neighborhood of Mraz's killing.[45] A drawing of a man seen in the area around the time of her murder was circulated throughout the community but the suspect was never found. Police continued to ask Madisonians for leads and tips that could be passed along to the Major Crimes Unit, comprised of officers from UW, the Dane County Sheriff's Department, and the Madison Police Department. A pair of bloodied jeans, found hanging in a tree on Keyes Avenue, three blocks from the murder site, was analyzed by the Wisconsin State Crime Laboratory. But the pants were discounted as a link to the Mraz murder when the stains were found to be rabbit blood.[46]

A 1980 UW survey made public in 1982 after Mraz's murder indicated that a quarter of all students did not feel safe on campus, especially between dusk and 6 a.m. Another 9% said that their concerns for safety depended on the circumstances. Issues of security had been rising on the campus since a man attacked a woman with an ax in the university's Memorial Library in 1979.[47]

University officials lamented after Mraz's death that numerous safety seminars in dorms over the years had been poorly attended. Students seemed under the impression that "this can't happen to them," said Mary Rouse, assistant dean of students and head of the campus safety committee in 1982. Rouse had ridden to work on her bicycle the morning Mraz's body was found, aiming to take her usual path near the stadium. Instead, she found it blocked because of the police investigation.[48]

Despite the security concerns, there had been no surge in violence on the campus in the late 1970s and early 1980s. From 1976 through 1981, UW police statistics showed that there were no murders, but there were seventeen robberies and thirteen incidents of aggravated assault. From 1976 through 1979, there were six rapes. In 1980, when a new reporting system was developed to reflect various degrees of

Got Murder?

such attacks, there were ten cases of sexual assault; six were reported in 1981. Areas students felt were security risks included State Street, the stadium neighborhood, Capitol Square, and Langdon, Johnson, and Mifflin streets.[49]

Mraz's body was exhumed late in 1982 as part of the ongoing murder investigation. The police wanted to study her teeth and compare them with bite marks on a Madison man arrested after allegedly stalking a woman in the Camp Randall area. Eighteen-year-old suspect Lonnie Taylor was also accused of trying to break into the woman's apartment. Wounds made by teeth were found on one of his arms, but no link was ever established between the cases.[50]

A $5,000 reward was offered for leads in the case three weeks after Mraz's death. The following year, an anonymous donor doubled the reward, hoping for the arrest and conviction of Mraz's murderer. Yet no one ever came forward with substantive tips.[51]

University police admit they continually need to deal with the widely held perception that the campus is an oasis that is somehow insulated from the wider community. When a murder occurs, people are genuinely upset that this protective cocoon has been violated; they want the police to strike back with everything they can throw at the situation, and to return to normalcy as soon as possible.[52]

Unfortunately, in the Mraz case, the likelihood of eyewitnesses was slim. The murder took place late at night in a lightly traveled area on the shadowy north side of the stadium. There certainly wasn't a lot for the police to go on initially; they bemoaned the randomness of the incident, in which there was no connection between the victim and the killer. The most that could be done was to try to make the area safer by cutting some trees down and installing more lights on that side of the stadium.[53] By the time students came back in September 1982, the incident had already slipped from their attention.

Janet M. Raasch, October 1984

The final murder in this horrible trio of UW–Madison deaths occurred in the autumn of 1984. On November 17, hunters on the first day of deer season in the Town of Buena Vista stumbled across the partially clad body of a young woman in a heavily wooded area southeast of Highway 54, at the junction with County Highway J. The body was eventually identified as that of twenty-year-old Janet M. Raasch, a business major in her third year at UW. A hard worker, Raasch was a staffer at the DeBot Dining Center on campus. Friends had reported her missing on October 15, but she was last seen on October 11. A friend picked her up hitchhiking about two miles from her dormitory, Watson Hall, and dropped her off at the Highway 54 site near where her body would be found a month later. The five-foot-one-inch, hundred-pound blond coed was carrying a duffel bag. She had made arrangements for a substitute at work so she could visit her family over the weekend, and was probably trying to get a ride to her hometown of Merrill. She never arrived, and the Raasches alerted police.[54]

Once again, there seemed to be nothing for police to go on. The body's advanced decomposition made it difficult to determine the cause of death, although strangulation was suspected. The coroner was even unable to set the time of death, pointing out that she might have died a week to ten days before her body was discovered.[55] No eyewitnesses stepped forward, and the few leads authorities had led nowhere. Once again, months and then years passed without an arrest.

In 1988, Portage County District Attorney William Murat said the sheriff's department received a tip that was deemed important enough to fly a detective to Pennsylvania and Maryland to interview a number of witnesses. Yet the trip produced nothing conclusive.[56]

In 2002, Raasch's body was exhumed from its resting place at St. Paul's Cemetery in the Marathon County community of Hamburg. Members of the Portage County Sheriff's Department, forensic pathologist Dr. Robert Huntington III, Portage County Coroner Scott Rifleman, Marathon County Sheriff's Department deputies, and the Marathon County coroner were all on hand. The grave site was roped off while the digging took place under the privacy of a tent. Attorney General Jim Doyle told the media nothing more than that Raasch's body was being dug up as part of the investigation of her murder and that DNA samples were collected.[57]

Got Murder?

Whatever authorities thought they were looking for out East or in the chromosomes of the dead girl, it appears they found nothing useful. Almost a quarter century after it occurred, the Raasch murder remains the only open homicide case for the Portage County Sheriff's Department.[58]

* * * *

While these cases grabbed the most public attention, the Madison area was plagued by additional unsolved killings of young women between 1968 and 1984, sandwiched between the murders of Christine Rothschild and Janet Raasch. After Rothschild, the next victim was twenty-year-old Debra Bennett, whose burned body was dumped in a roadside ditch outside of Cross Plains in July 1976. She was last seen walking barefoot in the 1400 block of Loftsgarden Avenue. Three weeks after her body was found on July 21, the key to her room was mailed back to the Cardinal Hotel where she was staying. No other evidence ever turned up and the case was filed as unsolved.[59]

Next was eighteen-year-old Julie Ann Hall, an assistant at the Wisconsin Historical Society Library. In 1978, her body was unearthed in a shallow grave near Waunakee, about fourteen miles north of Madison. Celebrating her new job, the vivacious young woman was last seen at the Main King Tap near Madison's Capitol Square. Hall apparently died from a blow to the head.[60]

Twenty-year-old Julie Speerschneider vanished on March 27, 1978, after leaving the 602 Club, a University Avenue tavern. After her disappearance, a local man told police that he had picked up a hitchhiking male and Speerschneider, whom he recognized from news photos. He said he dropped off the couple at the corner of Johnson and Brearly. Despite having a description of Speerschneider's companion, police were unable to find him. Friends and relatives distributed posters around Madison, offered a $500 reward for information, and consulted psychics for help. Her decomposed body was eventually found by a sixteen-year-old hiker on the banks of the Yahara River in 1981 and had to be identified through her dental records. Initially, Madison police thought the Hall and Speerschneider cases might be linked because each was attractive, had long hair, and lived in the city.[61]

On December 15, 1979, twenty-four-year-old Susan LeMahieu disappeared. Her body was found by two bird-watchers the following spring in the "Lost City" area of the University of Wisconsin–Madison Arboretum. LeMahieu lived at Allen Hall, a treatment facility for physically and mentally challenged adults. At first, authorities figured the young woman had simply wandered off. But an autopsy showed that she died from multiple stab wounds to the chest.[62]

Seventeen-year-old Shirley Stewart dropped from sight in January 1980. She had just left the Dean Clinic; her body was eventually found in July 1981, in a heavily forested area north of Madison. The cause of death could not be verified because of the body's advanced stage of decomposition.

Could the same murderer been involved in any of these cases? In 1984, imprisoned serial killer Henry Lee Lucas confessed that he and his partner, Otis Ellwood Toole, had passed through Madison a number of times on their way to Minnesota. It was believed that the pair was in Wisconsin in 1971, 1972, and 1982. Lucas, a one-eyed drifter who was the thirteenth child of an alcoholic father and a prostitute mother, was at one time considered one of the country's worst serial killers. He claimed to have killed at least 360 people on his wanderings around the country over eight years in the late 1970s and early 1980s. However, it turned out that Lucas was either in jail or not in the area at the time of the killings.[63]

Of dozens of murders noted nationally during that time, forty-three were attributed to Lucas, fourteen to Toole, and thirty-three to the pair acting together. Lucas turned out to be a little too willing to confess, however. In order to catch him in his lies, Texas authorities faked a murder. They showed Lucas a file with photos and other vivid details of the supposed crime. He confessed, elaborating at great length about the slaying. As a result, police who had closed their files on numerous cases that supposedly involved Lucas were cautioned to reopen them.[64]

Despite Lucas' recantations of several crimes, Dane County

Got Murder?

Sheriff Jerome Lacke said he still believed that the man was involved in the killings of Speerschneider and Hall. According to lead Dane County investigator Dave Cochems, the accused killer gave detailed descriptions of the murder scenes during a nine-hour interrogation in Texas by Madison and UW police officers.[65] Yet, when Toole was interviewed later at the Florida State Penitentiary, he was unable to provide any details about either case, which ruled him out as a suspect.[66]

Lucas and Toole were also at first suspected in the 1982 killing of Barbara Nelson, 33, of Edgerton. Nelson was abducted from an Albion convenience store and found dead in Walworth County. It turned out that the two were in Texas at the time of her death. The killers were also considered suspects in the 1978 murder of seventeen-year-old Dawn Schnetzer of Menasha. Her body was found in a Calumet County forest in November of that year, two months after her disappearance. Donald Poppy, the county's district attorney, said that both men readily identified the area on a map and described the clothing Schnetzer had been wearing when she was killed. However, no charges were brought against either man in the case. In addition, Lucas told Jim Gauger, a Milwaukee detective, that he killed Janet Marie Bey in Milwaukee on June 22, 1979, and admitted to slayings near Superior and in West Bend, Madison, Plymouth, Manitowoc, and two undetermined Wisconsin locations near the Illinois border.[67]

In the end, it may have been that Lucas only killed the three individuals whose murders he was convicted of. Texas Attorney General Jim Mattox conducted an intensive year-long probe involving numerous polygraph tests; it showed that Lucas was a "hoaxer" and a "grand fraud." Mattox rapped law enforcement officers who earlier had cleared their files of some two hundred cases due to Lucas's phony confessions, despite mounting evidence of his misstatements. Lucas later recanted his statements on all but the murders of his mother in Michigan in 1961, and two Texas women, Kate Rich and Frieda Powell, in 1982.[68] Lucas and Toole were featured in the indie film *Henry: Portrait of a Serial Killer* in 1986, depicted as the cruel personalities they were.

* * * *

The task of protecting the university area continues. The UW Police Department maintains a Web site that provides links to crime prevention tips; crime prevention education; emergency phone locations; discussion of alcohol abuse and drinking issues on campus; *BADGER Beat*, a monthly newsletter published as an outreach effort to inform the campus community; and downloadable pamphlets on various types of crime. Several satellite police offices have also been established on the far ends of campus to increase visibility of the UW Police Department.[69]

Even with all these precautions, there are still crime challenges on and around the campus. But do they include a serial killer on the loose? It is impossible to say whether Rothschild, Mraz, and the other women were murdered by the same person. Although the victims were young, attractive women, several of whom had links to the university, they may simply have been in the wrong place at the wrong time. Whether a serial monster still roams Madison's generally quiet streets is a matter of conjecture. Just watch your back.

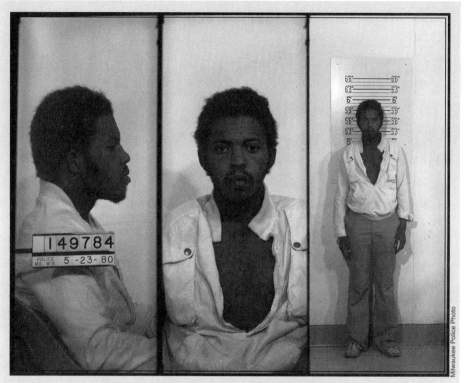

David Allen VanDyke, whose killing spree terrorized Milwaukee for nearly a year.

Chapter 5

Death by Viciousness

Milwaukee, Wisconsin
1979–80
Death toll: at least 6
Escaped death: 1

Mrs. Liggins is laying on the floor, and blood is all over.

—Linda Lowe, neighbor[1]

For nearly a year, the gruesome headlines greeted the people of Milwaukee with a shocking regularity.

Police had no leads on the murder of Della Mae Liggins, a sixty-nine-year-old schoolteacher stabbed to death on Thursday, July 19, 1979.[2]

Authorities said they had no suspects in the stabbing murder of seventy-eight-year-old Florence Burkard, who was terminally ill with cancer. She was killed Friday, August 10, 1979.[3]

Investigators were searching for clues on the city's northeast side after Helen Wronski, seventy-eight, was discovered beaten to death on November 10, 1979. There were no suspects.[4]

Charles Golston, sixty-three, was beaten to death on January 25, 1980. The man was murdered while watching television in his home.[5]

Bernard Herman Fonder, forty-nine, was found beaten and dead on Monday, March 3, 1980. A former roommate was arrested and later released after questioning. There were no other suspects.[6]

Got Murder?

On April 14, 1980, twenty-eight-year-old Sandra Ellis was severely beaten and left for dead by a young man who then stole some money from her house before running away.[7]

A hammer was used to murder Helen Louise Bellamy, a thirty-year-old mother of four, on Friday, April 25, 1980.[8]

These six killings and the one attempted murder eventually attributed to the same individual marked a terrible record for Milwaukee, a horrifying statistic that stood for 17 years until Jeffrey Dahmer was arrested for his criminal dining habits. The May 1980 arrest of vagrant David Allen VanDyke brought a collective sigh of relief to a community on edge. It was the first serial killing case for Milwaukee County District Attorney E. Michael McCann, who would later prosecute Dahmer.

The rash of killings attributed to VanDyke occurred in one neighborhood; the victims' homes, all within a few blocks of each other, overlooked Milwaukee's sprawling downtown skyline. The murder spree started on a sultry day in July. A respected teacher for 23 years, Della Mae Liggins had led classes in kindergarten and first and second grades at Lloyd Street School from 1955 to 1967. Liggins then transferred to the Auer Avenue School from 1967 to 1969; she retired in 1977, while teaching at Garfield Avenue School. Active in the Milwaukee Teachers' Education Association, she spent her vacations studying new techniques in education and once visited England to learn about the open classroom concept. After her husband, James, died in 1977, Liggins had hoped to return to her home state of Oklahoma but could not sell her home at 2341 North Eighth Street.[9]

The personable, always cheerful Liggins was loved by youngsters in the neighborhood. She sometimes even hosted marshmallow roasts in her backyard and former pupils regularly dropped by to say hello.[10]

Friends last saw Liggins on the Monday prior to her death. Concerned that she hadn't been seen for several days, neighbor Linda Lowe entered the unlocked back door and found Liggins about 4:30 p.m. on July 20. The dead woman, stabbed once in the chest, was lying in a pool of blood on her kitchen floor. A bloody butcher knife was discovered by police on top of her refrigerator, and her brown 1972

Pontiac Le Mans was missing. There was no indication that anyone had forced entry to the tidy home.[11]

Next in the deadly string was the stabbing death of Florence Burkard, of 2430 North Hubbard Street. The elderly woman who lived alone was found with forty-three puncture wounds to her chest and back, caused by an ice pick. Slashes on her hands and a broken wrist were attributed to her attempt to fend off the attacker, according to police, who found a bloody pair of scissors at the scene. Her crumpled body was sprawled at the foot of her basement stairwell. Walter J. Baumann, an Eldercare worker who visited her home to deliver a hot meal around noon on August 10, saw a pool of blood under the kitchen sink and contacted authorities. Police surmised that Burkard was murdered sometime between 8 and 10 a.m. She had been released from St. Joseph's Hospital a few days earlier after being treated for lung and liver cancers. Her purse, containing $19, was still in her living room.[12]

Elders obviously made easy prey in this tough neighborhood. Burkard lived a block from Helen Lows, an eighty-six-year-old woman murdered May 5. A suspect, forty-four-year-old Pervan Zeb Smith, was already in custody and charged in that case; Smith was being held for observation in the Central State Hospital in Waupun.[13]

The third murder victim in the series was Helen Wronski, found dead November 10 by her son, David, in her home at 2323-B North Holton Street. He had gone to the house about 10 p.m., worried that he hadn't seen his mother during the day. Wronski, whose face and head had been beaten severely, was under a sheet on her living room floor with signs that the killer may have tried to suffocate her. There was no indication of forced entry and no weapon was found. After her home was burglarized in 1977, a deadbolt had been installed on the front door. Another was on the rear door, which was locked when David Wronski arrived. He then entered the unlocked front.[14]

The next year dawned with the murder of Milwaukee Road retiree Charles Golston, attacked on January 25 in his home at 2216-A North Buffum Street. Youngsters in the neighborhood called him "Uncle Charlie." Attacked with a claw hammer and left in a coma, Golston clung to life, groaning when discovered by a neighbor. He eventually died at County General Hospital on May 10 of head trauma and cardiac arrest.[15]

Golston's death was followed by that of Bernard Herman Fonder, who apparently had a premonition that something might happen to him. The forty-eight-year-old was found beaten to death in his upper flat of the duplex he owned at 2116 North Booth Street on Monday, March 3, 1980. Fonder's body was found on his bed by Michael Harlow, who lived downstairs and entered the unlocked apartment around 5 p.m. The dead man's head with "several gaping wounds" was covered by a towel.[16]

Harlow grew worried about his landlord when the owner of Beckett's Supermarket, where Fonder worked, said he had not seen the man for several days. Harlow said that Fonder had given him a note that he was to pass along to the police in case anything happened to him. Apparently his note tagged a former roommate, who was then arrested at the Antlers Hotel about 10:30 p.m. the day the body was discovered. The suspect had lived with Fonder until December 19, 1979, when he beat the man for no known reason. He was told to leave, and resided with his girlfriend until she also kicked him out. The suspect returned to Fonder's place, and although the former roommate was allowed to spend the night, Fonder was still concerned enough to pass his worries on to Harlow. That suspect, however, was later released.[17]

Sandra Ellis was the fortunate one in this cluster of tragedies. The twenty-eight-year-old woman was badly beaten and robbed Monday, April 14, by a man who came to her home at 2430 North Richards Street. He had visited Ellis previously to look at a car she was selling, so she let him into her home. Once inside, he beat and kicked her, and then left.[18] She later told *Milwaukee Sentinel* reporter Bill Janz she was attacked when she went to get the car title. The assailant hit her with a large ashtray and a wine bottle, both of which cut her severely.[19]

"There was so much blood," Ellis told Janz. "He put his fingers in the cuts and he lifted my head and let it drop back to the floor." He went into another room to look for money, eventually making off with $118; Ellis jumped up and fled. A woman at the first house where she sought help slammed the door in her face, so Ellis ran to a nearby tavern and the patrons contacted police. "In broad daylight, he just didn't care. He didn't give a damn," she said. Yet she felt lucky to escape with her life. "Yes, I do. Yes, I do. I feel that I got all the luck in the world." Ellis later identified her attacker as David Allen VanDyke in a police lineup on May 30. Ellis moved to live with her parents out of state shortly after the attack. "I could never trust no one again, I could never do that," she said.[20]

As Janz pointed out in his article, others in the neighborhood weren't so fortunate. Helen Louise Bellamy was the next to be killed, murdered Friday afternoon, April 25, in her home at 2471 North First Street. Her head was beaten into an unrecognizable state by an auto jack, later found hidden between a mattress and box spring in a bedroom. Sylvester Jr., Bellamy's thirteen-year-old son, found his mother when he returned from school about 3:30 p.m. The savaged body was curled up on the dining room floor under an overturned couch and partially covered by a sheet.[21]

The horror ended only when VanDyke was apprehended May 23 as he attempted to burglarize a house in the 2500 block of North First Street, not far from Bellamy's home. Police were tipped off to the break-in by a witness. At his arrest, VanDyke "made statements that implicated him in all the murders," said Rudolph Will, the Milwaukee Police Department's deputy inspector of detectives. VanDyke was held immediately in the city jail on $315,000 bail set by Circuit Judge Joseph P. Callan.[22] On Saturday, May 31, District Attorney McCann prepared charges against VanDyke for six murders and one charge of attempted murder. The young man was also charged with one count of robbery for taking Ellis's money.[23]

At a press conference, Milwaukee Police Detective Roosevelt Harrell and Lieutenant Carl Ruscitti told how they tracked the case. Harrell noticed similarities in the first four murders, after studying the Golston case. They discussed their theory with Inspector Kenneth Hagopian, who organized a special detail in April to apprehend the killer. Since the murders were conducted during burglaries, the officers scoured the neighborhood, seeking information on break-ins and people peddling stolen goods. Unfortunately, fingerprints at the

Wronski and Fonder homes did not match those of any known thieves. Yet when VanDyke was arrested, his fingerprints were tied immediately to the murder scenes.[24]

The viciousness of the attacks was part of the unifying "signature" of the crimes, police indicated. In addition, VanDyke had the same modus operandi in each case, using whatever weapons were handy in the homes he invaded. He would also pilfer items from the houses, such as a money clip, a clock radio, a television set, or jewelry. Several necklaces found in an attic of an unoccupied house at 2436 North Palmer Street, frequented by VanDyke, were identified by witnesses as those taken from Burkard's house. The fact that the killings occurred between Eighth and Holton and Garfield and Center indicated that the suspect probably lived in the area. When confronted with all the evidence from the various cases, VanDyke broke down and cried in front of the interrogating detectives. He might have confessed to several other murders at the time, but a public defender showed up during a break in the questioning and warned the man to be quiet.[25]

Formal complaints were presented Monday, June 2, to Circuit Judge Rudolph Randa. VanDyke's defense attorney Stephen Glynn requested that electronic media equipment be kept away from courtroom proceedings to avoid adverse publicity that might prevent his client from receiving a fair trial. Randa allowed both reporters and their gear into the trial, but restricted them to one corner of the courtroom. The judge also hiked VanDyke's bond to $400,000, or $50,000 for each of the eight counts. According to the complaint, VanDyke was able to gain entry to the homes by asking to use the phone or the bathroom; his face was probably familiar to a number of the victims since he lived in abandoned cars and basements in the area. For instance, VanDyke occasionally did errands for Liggins, and may even have borrowed her car the day she was killed. He had done some repair work on a car at Golston's house. He once even hit Fonder when the man made sexual comments after meeting him several times in a local tavern.[26]

VanDyke told police he didn't know why he killed his victims, claiming that something inside him "just snapped." He covered his victims, as in the cases of Bellamy and Wronski, because he "couldn't look" at their bodies and "didn't like the sight of blood."[27]

VanDyke was arraigned before Judge Michael Goulee on June 16.[28] A few days later, as VanDyke's trial was progressing, public defender Barry Slagle wound up in the holding tank with his client. In another case that day, prior to VanDyke's appearance, Slagle irritated Goulee with some comment. The lawyer refused to apologize despite being warned of getting slapped with a contempt of court charge. "Bailiff, seize that man," Goulee yelled, sending Slagle out of the courtroom and into the lockup where a well-dressed VanDyke was awaiting his turn to go before the judge. The killer laughed uproariously at the long-haired, sideburned attorney who was unceremoniously tossed into the clink beside him. After three hours of cooling his heels, Slagle was released when his boss, attorney Kevin Dunn, head of the Milwaukee trial division of the Office of the State Public Defender, showed up to spring him.[29]

At the conclusion of his trial, VanDyke was found guilty on all counts and sentenced in 1981 to six consecutive life terms plus forty years. Not eligible for parole until 2050, VanDyke is incarcerated at the high security state correctional facility at Redgranite. After the trial, District Attorney McCann asked the Milwaukee Police Department to form a special homicide unit to better track murder patterns. Such a team was subsequently organized.

* * * *

VanDyke's tale of terror began when he was a young boy. Born January 14, 1959, he quickly exhibited a wild side, and his family grew to fear his violent outbursts. He broke windows, beat smaller children, stole from his brothers, threatened a niece with a knife, and was a chronic truant. A favorite grandmother who helped raise him died in 1965. VanDyke's police and social work paper trail began in 1971 when he was 12. His mother said he was uncontrollable and threatened her regularly. The police were often summoned to the family's home—six straight weekends in one stretch. A hospital social worker indicated that "his relationship with his mother is ambivalent; wanting more affection from her than she is able or willing to give, he is also resentful at not getting it." The social worker went on to say that VanDyke was potentially dangerous and that he should be placed in a residential treatment home.[30]

It took a year, but VanDyke was finally turned over to the welfare department in January 1972. Indicating she thought he had a mental challenge, a sister said, "He wanted to take over the home, so we wouldn't let him stay here." While waiting for placement, VanDyke struck a neighbor because he said she called him "fat boy" and "big fat pig." He dropped out of school when he was fifteen. His mother died in 1974 and the court extended its custody over him until he turned eighteen. As an adult, he was on probation for burglary in 1979 but stopped reporting to his overseeing officer after only a few months. "He was an absconder," according to the division of corrections. "He didn't report to us and we were unable to find him."[31] Perhaps he was too busy to show up. By that July, VanDyke was beginning to kill off his neighbors.

Despite his long history of violence and lawlessness, friends and even foster parents expressed surprise at the murder accusations against VanDyke. "He's a nice boy," was a general comment.[32]

In 1986, Anne Bowe, the wife of public defender Slagle, represented another young Milwaukeean who had earned even more notoriety than the man with whom her husband briefly shared cell time. Her client was Jeffrey Dahmer, arrested for lewd and lascivious behavior because he urinated in front of a group of children. Bowe got the charge reduced to disorderly conduct and Dahmer received one year of probation. He later went on to edge out VanDyke as Milwaukee's most notorious serial killer.[33]

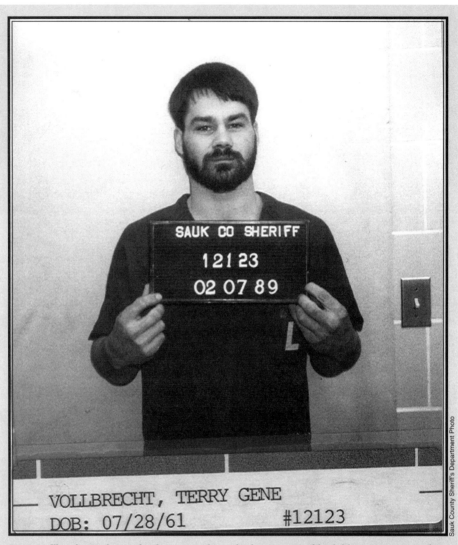

SAUK CO SHERIFF

1 21 23

02 07 89

VOLLBRECHT, TERRY GENE
DOB: 07/28/61   #12123

Terry Vollbrecht tried to make the rape and murder he committed look like a Satanic sacrifice.

Chapter 6

Carnage in the Heartland

Central Wisconsin
1969–87
Death toll: 11

Upon conviction, the defendant shall be
sentenced to life imprisonment.

—criminal complaint, Sauk County Circuit Court[1]

With the deaths of three attractive young women in 1987, central Wisconsin had not been in such a panic since the late 1960s and early 1970s when a spate of gory murders set area residents on edge. Husbands fretted about their home-alone wives, doors were locked, guard dogs purchased, and weapons sales soared as fear swept through the region's isolated communities like an uncontrolled brush fire.

During what seems so long ago, the deadly role call of victims seemed never to end: Luella Hickey, seventy, stabbed repeatedly by an unknown assailant in her Town of Brooks home in 1969; Marvin Collins, forty, and Ervin Schilling, sixty-four, gunned down in their chain-saw repair shop on December 11, 1974; Dedre Hein, seventeen, shot to death on June 10, 1976, in her parents' basement; Sherri Mallezewski, nineteen, and Brenda Erickson, fifteen, murdered in 1976 near Big Flats; Nancy Potts, twenty-one, strangled and her head crushed, October 10, 1978. In some cases, grim-faced suspects were captured and imprisoned. In others, the killer's identity remains frighteningly unknown.[2]

One particularly notorious murder in Central Badgerland during those tense days of the peace-and-love 1970s was that of George Mallason, thirty-four, and his wife, Antoinette "Tony", twenty-seven. On October 3, 1975, this hardworking, back-to-the land couple from Illinois was found dead of numerous .38-caliber gunshot wounds. Their bullet-ridden corpses were wrapped in blood-soaked rugs and buried under cardboard boxes, old furniture, and piles of clothes in the basement of their remote Grand Marsh home in Adams County. Their ten-month-old infant son, Christopher, was strangled by a diaper and found crumpled in his crib. Arriving at night to investigate, the first deputy to the scene needed to crawl through a window into the dark basement. He called for backup and the ensuing search turned up the bodies.[3]

After a nationwide alert, suspects Robert Morgan and Diana Ellen Dirks were finally captured by the FBI on November 23, in the hamlet of Cave Junction, Oregon. Officers had tracked the two to a cabin at the H&H Motel, some eighteen miles north of the California–Oregon state line. Federal agents and local police kicked down the door to their room after the pair refused to come out and surrender. No one was injured in the capture, according to John W. O'Rourke, special agent in charge of the Portland FBI office, and the pair was hustled off to jail.[4]

The two had apparently answered an ad placed by the Mallasons in *Mother Earth News*, a publication devoted to encouraging self-sufficiency and caring use of the land for farming and living. The ad invited others to share in the Mallasons' dream of a back-to-natural-ways lifestyle and sought help working their twenty acres of woods and fields about one and a half miles west of Grand Marsh. Their three-bedroom house was on a dirt road, a quarter mile from the intersection of County E and B. Apparently, the penniless drifters, Morgan and Dirks, saw the ad and hitchhiked to Wisconsin from New Mexico. After the murders, the couple fled to Dirks' home state of Oregon in the Mallasons' off-white club cab Ford pickup truck.[5]

The bodies were uncovered several days later by sheriff's deputies after reports that the family had not been seen or picked up their mail for about a week. At the time, George Mallason had been working at a Wisconsin Dells cheese shop and delicatessen.[6] Morgan and Dirks were eventually convicted of and imprisoned for the crime.

All these deaths in the bucolic Wisconsin heartland attracted the attention of national broadcast and print media, which proclaimed Adams County the murder capital of America. It was said that the county had more killings per capita than anywhere else in the country at the time. NBC aired a three-hour special entitled *Violence in America* on January 5, 1977, in which Adams County was featured prominently. During the show, resident Robert Hein, who had lost a daughter to an unknown killer, remarked, "This is one of the most vicious small communities I've ever seen."[7]

Naturally, this unwelcome notoriety was extremely disconcerting to residents in the area, a sparsely populated part of the state that had been the scene of illegal marijuana growing in the years following World War II. In the first decade of the twenty-first century, that particular law enforcement challenge had evolved into problems involving drug thugs operating methaphetamine labs in the deep woods. There always seem to be places to hide amid the second-growth thickets enveloping the hunting cabins and trailers dotting the wilder, albeit scenic, reaches of the landscape.

This abstract geography north of the broad Wisconsin River figured prominently in the writings of August Derleth (1909–'71), a noted Sauk City author and former parole officer. Derleth holds the title of Wisconsin's most prolific author, with more than 150 books to his credit. A number were mysteries and horror stories, with such titles as *Murder Stalks the Wakely Family* (1934) and *The Lurker at the Threshold* (1945). His 1968 book, *Wisconsin Murders*, was marketed as "an inquiry into mayhem and homicide in the Midwest." In its introduction, Derleth philosophized, "Murder of itself has always had an unholy fascination for those of us who have never gone quite so far ourselves."[8]

Another writer, Madison-based Doug Moe, traveled to Adams County in late 1982 to look behind the grim facts and see what there was about the rural community that made it so infamous. His resulting article, "The Haunting of Adams County," ran in the February 1983, issue of *Madison Magazine*. His observations set plenty of teeth on edge and caused no end of animated conversation in coffee shops, beauty parlors, and grocery store aisles across the county.

In 2006, Moe, by then a full-time columnist for *The Capital Times*, recalled that particular article and its fallout. "The idea for a story just dawned on me that there were a heck of a lot of strange things going on up there," he recalled. Moe, a freelancer at the time, said he talked over a potential assignment on Adams County with magazine editor Jim Selk, a hardened journalist "who was not adverse to a good murder story." Moe thus set out to explore the underbelly of Adams County, armed with plenty of published accounts of at least eight killings there over the few preceding years.[9]

"I went into bars and asked around. I interviewed colorful attorney Jack McManus from Madison for a local angle. He had represented Kenny Ray Eichoff in a double murder case in Adams County a few years previously," Moe said.[10]

When McManus—always good for a provocative, headline-producing quote—offered the observation that "I wouldn't drive through Adams County at night unless I was in a Sherman tank," Moe knew he was onto something. Others, however, including Judge Raymond Gieringer, discounted the suggestion that their county was much different from others. "There's nothing earth-shaking going on up here," Gieringer told Moe.[11]

Yet on a steamy September 4, 1987, Gieringer would be the Adams County jurist hearing a complaint filed against truck driver Kim S. Brown, accused of killing housewife Linda Nachreiner of Dell Prairie. The cheerful, outgoing mother of two daughters was one of three women killed over the course of a few weeks that long, hot summer in central Wisconsin. The cases fueled much-ballyhooed theories that a vicious serial killer was on the loose. Brown eventually would be tried on first-degree murder, first- and second-degree sexual assault, kidnapping, burglary, armed burglary, and arson.[12]

In the Moe article, McManus told the writer he believed that the people of Adams County lived "far from the cultural and economic mainstream" and believed in an "eye for an eye." The writer also found an official in the Wisconsin Department of Justice who said residents there "have a different philosophy of life."[13]

None of this endeared Moe to some Adams County folks, although his former sister-in-law lived in the Town of Adams; Moe had regularly visited the area for family parties and was quite familiar with the community. "They couldn't deny that there were murders there," Moe said with a laugh. Not everyone complained. One *Madison Magazine* reader sent him a T-shirt emblazoned with "Find a Body in Adams County" and another created a tongue-in-cheek permit that allowed Moe to revisit the area, but only if the journalist left by dark. The Adams County Board of Supervisors, however, took plenty of umbrage at Moe's observations; the board issued a proclamation censuring him and the publication. "I've got that framed around here somewhere," Moe said years later.[14]

* * * *

Billboards outside the tiny Badger State community of Lone Rock proclaim the village as the "Coldest Spot in the Nation . . . With the Warmest Heart." The slogan refers to January 30, 1951, when Lone Rock had an icicled temperature of -53°F. That lung-freezing Wisconsin record stood for forty-five years, until February 4, 1996, when the coldest temperature ever officially recorded in the state by the Wisconsin State Climatology Office was -55°F at Couderay.[15] Lone Rock residents don't pay much attention to the newer listing; they've already made their mark.

Lone Rock lies in the southeastern corner of Richland County, where Highway 130 bridges the molasses-dark waters of the Wisconsin River. The 2000 U.S. census pegged the Lone Rock population as 929, with 393 households and 240 families. One dating Web site lists 102 swingers within 100 miles of the crossroads community.[16]

The village was established in 1856 with the arrival of the Milwaukee and Mississippi Railroad, making Lone Rock a nineteenth-century transportation and commercial hub. The community received its name from the majestic 80-foot-high sandstone rock that once reared up like a phallic menhir along the north bank of the roiling river. This was a dangerous passage for early travelers; the river's swift, deadly current made it hard to navigate such treacherous bends as the aptly named Devil's Elbow.[17]

While life along the river, at least on the surface, is as close to a Norman Rockwell vignette as one can find in Wisconsin, catastrophe takes a multitude of shape-shifting forms. Early raftsmen, muscling lengthy log rafts to downriver mills, remembered when a hefty chunk of the landmark rock "fell upon a passing vessel, causing its wreck."[18] Much of the once-mighty stone is gone now, quarried for basements and foundations, thereby lessening any danger of a similar incident. A hummock, all that is left of the pillar, can be found west of Highway 130 across from Brace Park.

The river wasn't the only dealer of death. Pioneer settler Dwight P. Moore recalled in 1933 how "Ed Seaman's mother was killed by the Indians and caused considerable furor among the settlers," at a time when virgin timberlands were alive with bears, timber wolves, and lynxes.[19]

A 1918 tornado cut a swath three hundred feet wide through Lone Rock, then smashed its way along another eighty destructive miles through Wisconsin's soul. The facts still ring harsh: "P. C. Pitkin, aged 40, lawyer, graduate of the University of Wisconsin and editor of *The Tri-County Review*, head crushed. Miss Clara Hatrey, aged 13, killed outright. Donald Hatrey, aged 7, killed outright." Five more persons died and about one hundred were injured in outlying communities as the deadly storm thundered along from the southwest into the far northeast.[20]

There were other quirks of fate, as well. Three large downtown retail buildings were destroyed by the village's first major fire in 1892, started by a burglar trying to blast open a heavy safe in the Fuller and Foster store. Lone Rock's other major fires destroyed the grade school in 1864 and five buildings in the Union Block that burned to the ground in 1942. In 1988, the Franklin Masonic Lodge and an adjacent building were destroyed in a blaze of suspicious origin. Bank robbers hit the Farmers Bank in 1934, escaping with $2,700 in cash. In 1975, another gang hit the State Bank of Lone Rock in a daring raid in which they got away with $3,863.[21]

Yet, those mostly forgotten incidents slipped even further into the mist when a contemporary terror stalked the Wisconsin River shoreline and central Wisconsin in the 1980s.

Lone Rock native Angela Faye Hackl vanished early on June 12, 1987, after leaving Hondo's Bar, a local hangout in nearby Sauk City. The pretty, easygoing eighteen-year-old had graduated from River Valley High School in Spring Green only three weeks earlier. She did not return to her parents' home Thursday night, Richland County Sheriff Fred Schram told a cluster of reporters eager for a story.

Her distraught father, Barney, contacted authorities at 12:41 a.m., Saturday. Hackl told authorities that his daughter had left home Thursday evening with friends Becky Nelson and Joe Wilkinson, driving off in a 1971 Pontiac Le Mans she had borrowed from Ron Lewis, her boyfriend at the time. The elder Hackl learned that Nelson and Wilkinson had returned home but that his daughter's whereabouts were unknown. The man also reported that the Pontiac was found by Angela's brothers, Jeff and Lewis, abandoned along Highway 12 about twenty-seven miles east of Lone Rock. In the car, the two young men found some of her clothing; a .22-caliber Ruger revolver and holster were missing from the glove compartment.[22]

More than a hundred searchers from the sheriff's departments of Sauk and Richland counties and personnel from the Wisconsin Department of Natural Resources, aided by an airplane, swarmed over a two-county grid, moving outward from where the car was found. Sunday, June 14, was one of the hottest June days ever recorded in Wisconsin; temperatures hovered around 101°F, adding to the authorities' discomfort while tromping through back-country brush, pounding across weed-choked ditches, and sloughing around brackish marshland.

Sauk County Detective Kevin J. Fults and Richland County deputy Milin Adams eventually found Hackl's decomposing body the next day.[23] The men were poking along a dirt pathway south of the intersection of Block and Exchange roads and found part of an auto undercarriage and some stirred up sand and pine needles. The auto pieces would later be linked to the Pontiac driven by Hackl the night she disappeared. Exploring the vicinity, they came across a red sleeping bag and then found the body of Hackl, "hanging from a pine tree with a tire chain around her neck, with her body facing the tree."[24]

The corpse was carefully hidden in thick, mosquito-dense stands of pine six miles west of Sauk City. Brush and other vegetation were piled around the body, which was clad only in shoes and a pair of torn pink shorts around the lower part of one of her legs. A white bra was found beneath the sleeping bag. The two officers immediately called for assistance and the victim's body was sealed and taken by Sauk County Sheriff's Deputy Mary Ward to the county morgue.[25]

Initially, authorities refused to comment on how Hackl died, but said the death appeared suspicious and that they were searching for a weapon around the site. Police said the woman's identity would be confirmed after an autopsy on that Tuesday in Madison. On June 16, the body was taken to the Veterans Administration Hospital in Madison for an autopsy led by forensic pathologist Dr. Robert Huntington. Dental records confirmed that the body was that of Hackl. Huntington concluded that Hackl was indeed murdered; her body had three gunshot wounds to the back, including one that penetrated her heart and lungs. She had to have been suspended from the tree after her death, because of the lack of hemorrhage around the neck.[26]

In another chilling incident shortly after Hackl's death, thirty-year-old Barbara Blackstone mysteriously disappeared July 9, 1987. The popular community leader vanished from her home in nearby rural Lyndon Station. The 464-population town is about forty miles northeast of Lone Rock in Juneau County, close to the Wisconsin Dells tourist mecca and just off Interstate 90. Blackstone, a business education teacher at New Lisbon High School, left her purse behind in her house and keys in the ignition of a car parked in its usual place under an open-sided pole shed.[27]

Blackstone was last seen purchasing gas for her riding lawn mower at a Lyndon Station service outlet. She had indicated she was about to clear an area for a family picnic. Her husband, Tom, had come home around 6 p.m. from his lawn care service job in Portage to find his wife missing. Not finding a note, he began calling neighbors and then contacted the Juneau County Sheriff's Department about 9:30 p.m.[28]

A distraught Herbert Fisher, Blackstone's wheelchair-bound father, prophetically proclaimed that "maybe she's lying out in the woods dead or something."[29] Later, the sixty-eight-year-old man said he asked the governor's office to call out the National Guard for assistance with the search. "The sheriff needs more help. We've got to get things done," Fisher pleaded.[30]

Blackstone's nude and decomposing body was finally discovered by a hunter around 1 p.m., Wednesday, August 4, in a wooded area of Lafayette County. It had been dumped some 30 yards off Paulson Road, two miles southwest of Blanchardville. The corpse, sans most of the hair on its head, was in such a deteriorated state that Juneau County Sheriff Thompson said a positive identification could not initially be made.[31]

Blackstone's body was found by David Hendrikson as he scouted locations for deer hunting on the Harold and Bonnie Johnson farm. "I followed a deer trail into the woods, and then I saw the body," the shaken twenty-five-year-old said. "At first, I thought it was a deer, but then I realized it was a person. It makes you feel really weird." He said the nude body was spread-eagled on its back, as if it had been carried into the thicket.[32] The twenty-five-acre tract of woods and glens was cordoned off by police on Thursday, August 6. Even the Johnsons were not allowed into the sealed-off section of their land.

At the time Blackstone's body was found, representatives from the FBI, the state, and five counties—Juneau, La Crosse, Adams, Sauk, and Vernon—were meeting in Mauston at the Juneau County Sheriff's Department. Adding to central Wisconsin's mounting concern, Linda Nachreiner, a part-time office worker from the village of Dell Prairie, had been kidnapped, raped, and gunned to death on July 28. The authorities were discussing the murders of Hackl, Blackstone, and Nachreiner, as well as several other killings and disappearances around Wisconsin. When it was announced that Blackstone's corpse had been found, the meeting broke up. In Madison, Deputy Attorney General

Got Murder?

Mark Musolf told reporters, "We're not speculating on the relationship, if any, of the crimes."[33] Juneau County Sheriff Gervase Thompson, however, noted that Nachreiner and Hackl were killed in the isolated areas, similar to where the body of Terry Dolowy, a twenty-four-year-old woman from La Crosse who had been murdered in February 1985, was discovered.[34]

A three-hour autopsy at the Veterans Administration Hospital by Billy J. Bauman, a University of Wisconsin–Madison pathologist, failed to determine the exact cause of death due to the body's advanced stage of decomposition. Dental records were needed for identification.[35]

Up until his death a couple of years after his daughter's murder, Herbert Fisher always believed that money might have been the motive. He pointed out that Blackstone had a certificate of deposit at a bank in Argyle where she had grown up. Her body was found only eight miles from that town. Fisher theorized that she may have told her abductors about her savings, hoping that they would release her if she led them to the bank.[36] Wisconsin Attorney General Donald Hanaway said the location of the body in Lafayette County raised questions about whether "she went there or was taken there by somebody who knew [about her savings]."[37]

Despite being physically challenged by a stroke in 1976, Fisher also was bitter. "I'd like to get hold of the guy that did it, the dirty dog," he swore. Blackstone's sister, Judy Strutt, also hungered for justice, saying, "I just hope they catch whoever did it, and he suffers. I don't know what else to say."[38]

The body of Linda Nachreiner was found on August 5, just a day after Blackstone's. But on September 3, truck driver Kim S. Brown from Oxford, Wisconsin, was charged in Nachreiner's grisly torture and death. He was eventually convicted of her murder, thereby ending most people's concerns that a crazed serial killer was stalking that part of the state (the Nachreiner case and Brown's tale of terror is discussed later in this book).

The troubling Blackstone case has remained unsolved. Without an immediate arrest of a suspect in Hackl's case, the two murders lingered like raw, open wounds. But despite the passage of time, those grim summer days of 1987 remained fresh in the minds of all those involved and for anyone who knew the two women. While the gun used in Hackl's death has never been unearthed, the holster was found by Crystal Nolden while riding her horse near the death scene, about twelve months after the murder.[39]

A break in the Hackl case finally came in 1989. It took almost two years of sifting clues and interviewing suspects for authorities to reel in Terry Vollbrecht of rural Sauk City. The twenty-eight-year-old was arrested and charged in Hackl's death on February 13, 1989. He had been an initial suspect, but analyzing mounds of circumstantial evidence delayed his arrest, according to Attorney General Hanaway.[40] A pubic hair discovered in Hackl's Pontiac was similar to that taken from Vollbrecht, and became a major piece of evidence against him.[41]

Vollbrecht, who was well known to local authorities because of his record of burglary and cocaine selling, was questioned within two days of the discovery of Hackl's body. He denied killing her, although admitted he escorted the young woman from a tavern and confirmed that he had sex with her, using the red sleeping bag. He said that he met Hackl at the tavern and claimed they were "attracted to each other." They left to go to an after-hours party and later drove to a nearby marsh where they "made love." Afterward, according to Vollbrecht, Hackl drove him back to Sauk City where his car was parked and she left. They even talked about seeing each other again, he said. Vollbrecht said that he slept in his car the remainder of the night because he had lost the keys.[42]

Various witnesses indicated they were in locales where Vollbrecht claimed to be during the time of Hackl's death, but that they never saw him. Meanwhile, Vollbrecht roamed around the Sauk City area, telling acquaintances, "I didn't do it and if I did, I don't remember doing it."[43]

Vollbrecht, a self-employed auto mechanic, was brought into custody in July 1988, when authorities arrested him on a charge of selling cocaine and took a second hair sample. He was released on bail and there were reports that he might have planned on leaving Sauk City. He was rearrested February 6 on charges of felony possession of a handgun while hunting. That charge was pending on the day he was arrested in the Hackl case.[44]

The shackled suspect shook his head when Sauk County Circuit Judge James Everson related the first-degree murder and sexual assault charges. The judge set bail at $150,000 on the two charges and set a preliminary hearing for February 22. Ellen Berz, Vollbrecht's public defender, disagreed with the high bail, arguing that the man had remained in the area, even though he knew he was a suspect. "We feel that everything in the criminal complaint is false. The only speculation we have here is who is the real killer. I am not convinced the killer is any longer in Sauk County," she said. The court appointed Madison attorney Warren Kenney as Vollbrecht's lawyer. Kenney had also represented Vollbrecht in 1980 when the young man was convicted of burglary and given two-years probation.[45]

Vollbrecht's nine-day trial started on September 25 in Baraboo, the Sauk County seat. A jury of six men and two women deliberated only two hours before convicting him.[46]

In his closing statement, Prosecutor Matthew Frank, an assistant attorney general, said that Vollbrecht was "calm, cool, with ice water in his veins" during the killing. Frank maintained that Vollbrecht assaulted and then shot Hackl. The suspect then tried to make the crime scene appear as if it was "something other than a sexual assault and murder" by first attempting to hang the body in a kneeling position from a tree, using a tire chain and then clumping broken shrubs and wood around it to make it appear "as a satanic sacrifice," the prosecutor argued.[47]

On the other hand, Kenney, Vollbrecht's defense attorney, said that his client told the truth during his six hours on the witness stand. But "it was a truth they didn't and probably still don't want to believe," he said as the trial ended. Kenney asserted that the state's case was nothing more than "hype, smoke screen, window dressing, and red herrings" and he claimed that Frank's presentation "failed miserably" to prove that Vollbrecht had indeed killed the woman.[48]

Vollbrecht himself insisted that police lied and made up the evidence, railing against the Sauk County legal system. He called the authorities "incompetent and dishonest," and said that Prosecutor Frank had "disgraced the legal profession" and that the entire case was merely one "built on conjecture, assumptions, and opinions." In a loud voice, he added that he was "maliciously prosecuted and incarcerated," claiming again and again that the real killer was still at large.

Frank rebutted Vollbrecht's assertions, stating that the defendant delivered a "vintage performance on the witness stand" to hide the truth. He pointed out that Hackl's clothes had been torn off and that it was determined that no consensual sex had taken place. "Angela Hackl resisted a sexual assault from the defendant and it was the last mistake she ever made and she paid for it with her life," Frank argued.

After the verdict was delivered, Frank said he was quite pleased. As he left the courtroom, the prosecuting attorney hugged the weeping members of Hackl's family.[49]

Vollbrecht was sentenced to life in prison on Friday, December 1, 1989, and was immediately taken to Dodge County Correctional Institution in Waupun. While he is eligible for parole in 2007, Frank felt that the convicted man would not be released and would spend at least 25 years in prison.[50] As if a life sentence for murder were somehow insufficient, on the day of the sentencing Vollbrecht was also slapped with a paternity suit in Sauk County Circuit Court, and the Sauk County district attorney said he was going ahead with drug and gun possession charges.[51]

Hackl's father told reporters that he was pleased by the sentence. On the other hand, Vollbrecht's family still asserted his innocence. His brother, Richard, offered a $50,000 reward for any information leading to the reversal of the conviction, a prize still not handed out in the fifteen-plus years since the case was closed. The family even started a petition drive that collected 804 signatures, seeking to have Judge Virginia Wolfe dismiss the verdict. "We'll find the killer yet," asserted Vollbrecht's father, Herman.[52]

Yet as of 2007, Vollbrecht remained imprisoned in the general population unit of the Wisconsin Secure Program facility at Boscobel.

As the Angela Faye Hackl murder case was winding down, another tragedy unfolded three counties north of Sauk County, beneath the frowning crown of Rib Mountain in Marathon County. On Monday, October 4, 1989, the same day the suspect in Hackl's murder was convicted, Marathon County Dairy Princess Lori K. Esker was charged with strangling a high school friend.[53]

Esker was accused of killing twenty-one-year-old Lisa Cihaski, who was about to be engaged to Esker's sometime boyfriend. According to the complaint, Esker said she was pregnant by Bill Buss, the man Cihaski was set to marry.

Cihaski's body was found by her mother on September 21 in her car outside the Rib Mountain Holiday Inn where she was an assistant sales and catering manager. Esker, of Hatley, was a twenty-year-old agriculture journalism major at the University of Wisconsin–River Falls who worked at the Wausau Area Chamber of Commerce promoting farm products.[54]

Esker was considered a prime suspect after police questioned the twenty-eight-year-old Buss, who worked on his parents' farm. Buss said he had dated Cihaski over the course of six years and had occasionally gone out with Esker. The three attended Wittenberg–Birnamwood High School, where Esker belonged to the National Honor Society and was president of Future Farmers of America. However, Buss said he was planning to become engaged to Cihaski on her birthday, October 25. He recalled that both women had been in a shouting match at his farm that June.[55]

Esker told investigators that Cihaski died after the two struggled in the car, saying her first thoughts were, "Oh, my God, I killed her." She said that she hadn't intended to hurt her friend. Sheriff's Deputy Randall Hoenisch wrote up Esker's statement, asking that she demonstrate how the other woman was killed. He was surprised at her strength, noting that "she was not shy or hesitant how she did this." In fact, the deputy said, Esker became quite aggressive when applying pressure to his throat with her forearm, lifting him up off his chair and pushing him against a wall in the interview room. She quickly took his belt and, he indicated, she "had it wrapped around my neck and once again, applied a good amount of pressure."[56]

In June 1990, Esker was convicted of first-degree intentional homicide and sentenced to life imprisonment. She is serving her sentence at Taycheedah Correctional Institution in Fond du Lac.[57] A state appeals court upheld her murder conviction in 1992, unanimously rejecting her claims that some of her statements to authorities were forced and that the judge's instructions to the jury were confusing and misleading.[58] But Esker wasn't forgotten. In 1995, NBC aired *Beauty's Revenge*, a thriller inspired by her case.[59]

* * * *

One more horrific murder ended the 1980s in central Wisconsin. Sixty-year-old Dorothy Raczkowski was a hard-working single woman found dead on November 17, 1989, at her 240-acre farm in western Adams County. Early that morning, neighbor Stanley Buchanan discovered the corpse on the floor of her garage, her crushed head in a pool of blood. Authorities believed she was attacked and beaten when she returned from work at Ore-Ida Foods in Plover, where she worked the 3–11 p.m. shift, sifting potatoes after a long day caring for her Black Angus cattle and her flock of chickens.

Police said it did not appear that robbery was a motive because Raczkowski's purse containing money was found in her car and her home was not looted. As with the Barbara Blackstone case, the mystery remains unsolved.[60]

All is now mostly quiet in central Wisconsin. But somewhere out there lurk furtive characters who know what happened to a smiling schoolteacher, a hard-working dairy farmer, and other state residents whose lives were tragically snuffed out.

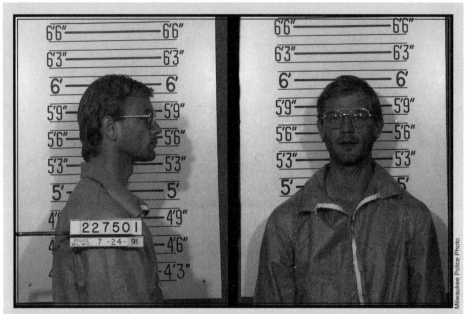

Jeffrey Dahmer's bizarre appetites were not sated by cheese and brats.

Chapter 7

Slaughter House on Twenty-fifth Street

Milwaukee, Wisconsin
Late 1980s
Death toll: 16 (plus 1 in Ohio)

Oh, you're from Milwaukee. Isn't that where they eat people?

—bartender, Limerick, Ireland[1]

Milwaukee, 11 p.m., Monday, July 22, 1991. The fitful night was hot and gummy with the threat of a thunderstorm in the air. The pungency of unwashed dumpsters seemed to ooze heavily over the skyline, joining the odors of the yeast plant, the chocolate factory, and the tanneries. The rankness compounded the Brew City's traditional summer assault on the olfactory nerves.[2]

With all that ground-level ozone, particulate matter, carbon monoxide, sulfur dioxide, and nitrogen dioxide floating around Milwaukee, no one complained much about the strange odors wafting along the dim hallway of an apartment building just west of Marquette University's campus. Tenants noted that one room had been giving off a peculiar smell for several months. Many complained, talking with the tenant who lived there or slipping notes under his door. The thirty-one-year-old resident always had an answer. It was usually "the fish tank" or "the garbage." Then there were the late night thumpings, bumpings, and sawing sounds emanating from the man's rental unit.

Got Murder?

For the building's residents, the foul smells and noise were merely additional components of an uncomfortable life in the inner city.[3]

Tidings of evil seemed everywhere that year, from the First Gulf War to mayhem in Wisconsin. A sixteen-year-old boy in Polk County was ordered to stand trial as an adult on July 12 for murdering, dismembering, and incinerating a Balsam Lake mother and three children. On July 22, boxer Mike Tyson was arrested and charged with raping Desiree Washington, a Miss Black America contestant. There was the usual mayhem elsewhere around the world.

A front page story in the July 22 *Milwaukee Journal* bugled the headline "Satanic Elements Found in Slaying." Joachim E. Dressler of the Town of Raymond, a crossroads village near Racine, was being tried for the killing and dismemberment of James Madden, a twenty-four-year-old Whitefish Bay man canvassing for an environmental group.

Milwaukee County Medical Examiner Jeffrey Jentzen said in court that the wounds found on Madden's assorted body parts, plus the fact that the young man had been decapitated and his heart, liver, and genitalia removed, might have been part of a religious ritual. Over the preceding months, several dogs had been similarly carved up in the Raymond area. But while Jentzen agreed with law enforcement officials that satanic rites could be blamed in Madden's murder, he emphasized that the gruesome killing was more likely that of homosexual overkill.[4]

So, with dog butchers and fork-tailed demons possibly afoot in the Dairy State, Milwaukee slept fitfully that uncomfortably warm July 22. Its residents—at least those unfortunates without air conditioning— tossed and turned. Pillowcases and sheets were sticky with sweat. Overworked fans hummed dispiritedly and windows were open, hoping to promote a semblance of life in the thick, still air.

Around 11:15 p.m., Tracy Edwards, a lanky thirty-two-year-old black man, burst out the front door of the Oxford Apartments, 924 North Twenty-fifth Street. The building, managed by African emigrant Sopa Princewell, was one of the few neatly kept buildings in the bête noire neighborhood near Marquette. A shambled mix of mostly low-income residents of numerous ethnicities lived in the faded neighborhood, one that also hosted halfway houses, dingy bars, and tiny Indian- or Pakistani-managed grocery stores. In addition to apartments for students and other transients, there were scattered single-family homes well past their architectural prime.[5]

Naked and staggering, Edwards ran down the 2600 block of West Kilbourn Avenue, then spotted a passing squad car driven by patrolmen Rolf Mueller and Robert Rauth. The German-born Mueller, a ten-year department veteran, and his partner Rauth, with thirteen years on the force, were about to wind down their 4 p.m.–midnight shift. Hot and worn out, the men flirted with leaving the scene. If they ignored Edward's apparent predicament because they didn't want to face a resulting paperwork pile, that in cop-speak would be known as *FIDO*, or "fuck it, drive on." After all, it wasn't unusual to see such odd scenes late at night while patrolling their rough-and-tumble Third Police District. Even people running naked down the sidewalk were not considered as out-of-place as they might have been in suburban South Milwaukee or Fox Point.

So, torn between heading back to the locker room or investigating, they chose to call the distraught soul over to their squad car—especially when they noticed a handcuff dangling from one of his wrists. But even this detail didn't suggest to the officers that the incident was going to be anything but another chapter of life on Mean Street Milwaukee.[6]

Breathlessly, the bedraggled Edwards told of a "weird dude" who had cuffed him and held him hostage for several hours after a chance meeting at the Grand Avenue Mall. He said his captor threatened to cut out his heart. The tired officers decided to confirm the story and followed the gasping Edwards back to the Oxford. The officers were wary, knowing that another building resident, twenty-six-year-old Dean M. Vaughn, had been found strangled in his third-floor room there on May 4. The two knocked on the door of apartment 213, certainly noticing the foul hallway odor.[7]

The door was opened by Jeffrey Dahmer, a former Ambrosia Chocolate Company night laborer, who lived in what initially seemed to be a neatly kept suite. Responding calmly to the policemen's questions, Dahmer permitted the two policemen to look inside his home. From the safety of the hallway, Edwards warned them of a knife that Dahmer had waved at him. Hearing this, Dahmer then attempted bluffing out of the situation. He indicated that he had recently lost his factory job and lost his temper after drinking too much. After speaking with the officers, Dahmer then went into his bedroom to get the key to the handcuffs.[8]

Mueller and Rauth saw numerous pornographic magazines and posters featuring well-oiled weightlifters and muscular body builders scattered around the apartment. A security camera was mounted on the living room wall; the bedroom could be locked from the outside, rather than the inside.[9]

Mueller looked inside an open dresser drawer and pulled back in surprise. Assailing his eyes were numerous Polaroid photos of skulls and body parts, plus the graphic portrayal of a skeleton hanging from a showerhead.[10]

Realizing that Edwards' tale had more to it than initially expected, Mueller yelled for Rauth to take Dahmer into custody. Faced with arrest, Dahmer struggled, attempting to fight off Rauth before being subdued. After the tussle, Edwards pointed out that Dahmer had also become agitated when he wanted to get a beer from the kitchen refrigerator. "Maybe he's got one of those heads in there," Edwards exclaimed, referring to the photos being held by Mueller.[11]

The policeman cautiously opened the fridge door but slammed it quickly shut, involuntarily yelling, "There's a goddamn head in here."[12]

The startled Mueller was so loud that he woke Dahmer's neighbors. At the uproar, curious men and women cautiously peeked out of their apartments or entered the hallway to learn the cause of the commotion. Later, in talking to the press, many admitted that was one of the worst mistakes they ever made.[13]

The grinning face leering back at Mueller was a calling card inviting him into the labyrinth of Jeffrey Dahmer's twisted mind. But the policeman's shocking discovery was also the beginning of the end for the shy loner, destined to be forever labeled as one of Wisconsin's most notorious murderers.

Slaughter House on Twenty-fifth Street

As in the previous days, the early edition of the July 23 *Milwaukee Sentinel*, the city's morning newspaper, contained details of the Joachim Dressler trial. Kathleen Dressler's testimony about her alcoholic husband and his pornography collection was front-page stuff. But that sordid tale was pushed aside in the late edition that hit the streets. An eye-grabbing headline trumpeted "Body Parts Found Inside Apartment," as reporter Tina Burnside described the initial scene in her terse eleven-paragraph story. "It was a mess," one officer was quoted as saying.[14]

By the time the afternoon *Milwaukee Journal* came out, that policeman's understatement had extended to explosive stories covering several full-page spreads. The layouts included photos of workers clad in bio-hazard suits removing a barrel that was thought to contain acid allegedly used to strip the flesh from victims' bones. The *Journal's* coverage was provided by Anne E. Schwartz, the first journalist into Dahmer's apartment. She had been alerted to the crime by a police informant, almost as the first body parts were discovered.[15]

The police eventually uncovered three more complete human heads. Hunks of human flesh were located in Dahmer's freezer. Two boiled and fleshless skulls had been painted gray and placed on a bedroom shelf; two more skulls rested in a computer box. Pairs of hands and a penis were in a stockpot, hidden at the back of a closet. Several testicles were preserved in formaldehyde and a bottle of chloroform, probably used to subdue the victims, was also found. As the clincher, the authorities found numerous graphic photographs of the victims, both before their deaths and after they had been murdered. By 4:30 a.m., the police had gutted the apartment, removing its contents for evidence. Even the infamous refrigerator, emptied of its gruesome cargo, went out a side door of the Oxford, as did Dahmer's lava light. This prompted public defender Ray Valdez, who was on the scene, to exclaim that he had the same type of lamp.[16]

Following Dahmer's arrest, the discussion of "homosexual overkill" again made the newspapers; the associations with Dressler's Racine County trial were too tempting to ignore.[17] Richard D. Knudten, Marquette University professor of sociology and criminology, said that these types of murders usually were more of a sexual nature than others. "The killings usually involve mutilation of the sex organs or torture involving the sex organs," he said. He added that the person who would commit such crimes "probably did not have the social development skills needed to deal with others."[18]

On the other hand, University of Wisconsin–Milwaukee Professor Anthony Fazio pointed out that violence wasn't limited to sadomasochistic sexual relations; many kinds of sexual situations also could become violent. "I'd put the emphasis on the hate. I'd put the emphasis on the rage. What I see is the pathological manifestation that happens to be associated with sex—negative feelings about sex."[19]

Despite the abundance of armchair psychiatry, Milwaukee County Medical Examiner Jeffery Jentzen indicated that there was no hard evidence of "homosexual overkill" with Dahmer. The use of the term enraged the gay and lesbian community.[20] "They [the media] just want to make the killing seem more horrific. It's just using the feelings about how people feel about homosexuals," asserted Christopher Fons, of ACT UP, a gay rights organization.

"The guy who did that is just a sicko. Whether he's gay or straight doesn't matter. He's sick," said a patron at Club 219, a city dance club frequented by gays. Several others questioned pointed out that serial killer Ted Bundy was an example of a heterosexual murderer. Others emphasized that Dahmer actually seemed to be acting out his fierce hatred toward homosexuals.[21] This view seemed to be borne out by Episcopal lay brother Jean-Paul Ranieri who regularly ministered to the gay street scene in the early 1990s. Ranieri met Dahmer twice at local bars, and indicated that as Dahmer became more intoxicated, he became more antihomosexual. According to Ranieri, the word spread to "stay away from this man."[22]

With such a juicy story, the international media stampeded to Milwaukee. Camera teams from Madison and Chicago joined the locals. CNN called the situation "The Milwaukee Massacre." CBS led its evening news with a Dahmer update. The *Philadelphia Daily News* and the *Cleveland Plain Dealer* were among newspapers sending reporters. Both the *Journal* and *Sentinel* newsrooms, as well as the police, were inundated with inquiries from other publications across the United States, as well as from New Zealand, Australia, and Great Britain. Reporters were reduced to interviewing reporters. Yet by the second day, it seemed that almost everyone within an ever-expanding radius of the Oxford was eager for their fifteen minutes of fame, recounting personal Dahmer tales.[23]

At least two filmmakers and several television producers quickly sought to get Dahmer's story. Charles Spicer, senior editor at St. Martin's Press, said he had several book proposals within a couple of days of Dahmer's arrest. Such a story would sell, according to Spicer, because Dahmer was educated and middle class, unlike the public stereotype of a serial killer or mass murderer. "Mass murders are hot right now," he added, referring to the then current popularity of *Silence of the Lambs*, featuring the cannibal Hannibal Lecter character.[24]

Over the next several days, Milwaukee residents learned with increasing horror what had been happening under their collective noses. On Wednesday, July 24, they read how Dahmer, the master predator, was capturing and secretly carving up his victims, thereby giving new meaning to Milwaukee's international reputation as a leader in the meat packing industry. Through his graphic photographs, Dahmer replayed his experiences. Always on the prowl, he preyed on young men, trolling for them at secluded bus stops, gay taverns, and on Milwaukee's lonely, late-night alleyways. Dahmer even visited Chicago's New Town neighborhood, a well-known homosexual hangout. Persuasive in setting the bait with promises of free drinks, porno videos, and cash for sex, Dahmer lured intended victims to his Caligula-esque den of horrors.[25]

"It was like I was confronting Satan himself," almost-victim Tracy Edwards told interviewers several days after he escaped Dahmer's clutches. Since moving from Mississippi, Edwards had been in Milwaukee only five weeks when he met Dahmer at the Grand Avenue Mall. Dahmer invited Edwards and another man to come to his apartment for drinks. In order to get Edwards alone, he gave the second man a false address as he went to get his girlfriend for the proposed "party." So the thirty-two-year-old Edwards wound up solo with Dahmer, who, according to the intended victim, "changed from Mr. Nice to Mr. It." While watching *The Exorcist*, Dahmer handcuffed Edwards and pulled out a knife; however, the captive was able to punch Dahmer and escape. Edwards said his mental alertness, his self-taught karate, and God "delivered" him from a grisly death. As he spoke with *Milwaukee Sentinel* reporters, Edwards broke down and cried.[26]

Eager to capitalize on his escape from Dahmer's apartment while still in handcuffs, Edwards sold his story to numerous media outlets. He also testified at Dahmer's trial in a confusing mix of commentary that often did not jibe with the initial police report. The blaze of publicity that followed him attracted the attention of police in his home state of Mississippi. Apparently, he had been indicted by a Tupelo grand jury in November 1990 for raping a fourteen-year-old girl. He jumped bail and fled to Milwaukee.

On August 8, 1991, the same day that the Reverend Jesse Jackson came to Milwaukee to lobby for racial unity, Edwards was charged in Milwaukee County Circuit Court and returned to Tupelo. In Mississippi, he pleaded guilty to the rape charge but disappeared again while awaiting sentencing. In 2006, Edwards was still considered a fugitive by Mississippi authorities.[27]

Even living on the run, however, Edwards can count himself a lucky man; Dahmer's other victims were not as fortunate. Once they were ensnared, Dahmer drugged and strangled his captives, slicing up their bodies with an electric carver and a hacksaw. The extent of the mutilation made identifying the victims a particular challenge. "We're just doing good old-fashioned forensic work right now," medical examiner Jentzen offered shortly after the discoveries. Fingerprints provided the most reliable clues; dental records, scars, and other distinguishing marks also helped.[28]

By July 27, the identities were confirmed for eleven murdered men whose body parts were found in the now-infamous apartment 213. Of those, eight were black, one was Asian, and one was white.[29] The expense of identifying so many victims forced Jentzen to ask the county budget director for additional funds to cover the costs.[30]

When Dahmer appeared for his initial hearing on Thursday,

July 25, it was as if a movie star had entered Circuit Judge Frank T. Crivello's courtroom. All heads turned as the killer was led in. At least eighty spectators and press packed the room and another seventy or more reporters were outside, along with a crowd of the public. One man remarked, "I wanted to see what the creep looked like." Yet Dahmer failed to provide the monsterlike appearance they expected. What was frightening, journalists wrote, was that Jeffrey L. Dahmer didn't "look" like a creep at all—more like a slightly disheveled guy-next-door.[31] He was "just" a rumpled young man who, incidentally, was being charged with four counts of first-degree intentional homicide and habitual criminality. More charges were soon to be issued.

As the story unfolded, it became obvious that Dahmer deliberately set out to find young men who led here-today-gone-tomorrow lifestyles, especially those with minor criminal records or drug or alcohol addictions. As such, their disappearances often failed to show up on the community's sensibility screen. Distraught families understandably felt that the authorities had not done enough to safeguard their loved ones.[32]

Police pointed out, however, that while several of the victims were innocents caught in Dahmer's web, others contributed to his criminal acts by making it easy for him to be their murderer. While not excusing Dahmer's crimes, they said that most of his victims were quite careless, placing themselves in danger by agreeing to accompany him to his apartment, whether for money, sex, or alcohol.[33]

Nevertheless, more than one relative complained to reporters that the police should have known earlier what Dahmer was doing and thus prevented him from expanding his web of death. Their anguish was palpable. A strong network of family and friends drew tightly around weeping mothers, fathers, siblings, and grandparents. Grief-stricken, they spoke tearfully with the media about their lost sons and brothers.[34]

In addition, leaders of the city's black community demonstrated their anger and dismay that such a large number of young African American men were killed. The figures would be folded into an ongoing statistical horror. As of July 15, 1991, there already had been eighty-eight homicides in Milwaukee; the city was on track to exceed the previous year's total of 165 victims, a majority of whom were black.[35]

The disturbing perception that Milwaukee's community of color was not getting the security it needed only increased when authorities revealed that Dahmer had murdered and dismembered Laotian teenager Konerak Sinthasomphone. The youngster's family had fled to the United States in 1980 to escape the Communist regime in their homeland. He was identified when police showed the family a photo of Konerak flexing his muscles that had been found in Dahmer's apartment.[36]

"People are venting their frustration," said Walter Farrell, professor of educational policy and community studies at the University of Wisconsin–Milwaukee. "They're very angry. It seems clear that he [Dahmer] was not targeting just males and homosexuals, but black males or males of color, with the Laotian boy," he added grimly.[37]

A rally on Tuesday, July 30, brought out dozens of marchers to protest the perceived lack of police support. Numerous city and county officials turned out to listen to the speeches in MacArthur Square behind the Police Administration Building. The next day, other demonstrators assembled along North Twenty-fifth Street, near the site of Dahmer's many killings. Carrying homemade signs, they supported the police chief but complained about the handling of neighborhood security.[38] On the other hand, police wives formed Operation Blue Ribbon, which distributed ribbons to show support for the police.

Neighbors cited police neglect of complaints by African Americans as one of the reasons they didn't complain earlier about the odd things occurring around Dahmer's apartment, particularly the stench. Police denied that the area was mostly written off by the authorities; four regular squads and three extras were on duty in the vicinity, police replied. Alderman Paul Henningsen also said that he had not received any complaints about the Oxford Apartments from any constituents who lived in his district.[39]

Yet the story of young Sinthasomphone was hard for police to explain away. The youth was walking to Mitchell Park to play soccer on May 26, 1991, when he disappeared, apparently picked up by Dahmer.

The fourteen-year-old managed to escape from Dahmer's clutches early in the hazy morning of May 27. Summoned to the scene by a woman who had been alerted by passersby, officers John Balcerzak, Joseph Gabrish, and Richard Porubcan found the dazed and bleeding teen wandering in the alley near the Oxford Apartments. But, despite seeing him in handcuffs, Balcerzak and Gabrish returned the boy to Dahmer's apartment. The killer coolly said the naked youth was his nineteen-year-old lover.[40]

After talking with Dahmer, the police felt the incident was "merely" a homosexual lovers' quarrel and did not pursue the matter. Defending their actions later, Balcerzak and Gabrish said that Sinthasomphone appeared to be older than his actual age and never seemed to be struggling or objecting to going with Dahmer. In fact, it was later shown that the boy was so drunk he could barely stand. Compounding the problem, Sinthasomphone had difficulty speaking English. So, back he went into Dahmer's death lair. After killing the boy, Dahmer kept his head as a trophy.

Although Balcerzak, Gabrish, and Porubcan were suspended and eventually fired for their negligence in the Dahmer affair, courts dismissed civil rights claims made by most of the victim's families.[41]

While the case polarized Milwaukee along racial lines, one question preoccupied the minds of people throughout the city: Who was this Jeffrey Lionel Dahmer?

* * * *

Dahmer was born May 21, 1960, in Milwaukee and was named after his father, Lionel, a chemist. When he was eight years old, young Dahmer moved with his family to Bath, Ohio, an upscale community near Akron. He played the clarinet at Revere High School and worked on the school newspaper. Dahmer's classmates recalled that he was quite shy, fascinated by dead animals, and was already a heavy drinker. Although he was considered a prankster, he wasn't a discipline problem in school. His parents, Lionel and Joyce, went through a heated divorce when Dahmer was eighteen, fighting nastily over custody of his twelve-year-old brother, David. The divorce was granted on July 24, 1978.[42]

Got Murder?

After breaking up with her husband, Joyce Dahmer reassumed her maiden name, Joyce A. Flint. She took David with her to Chippewa Falls, a northern Wisconsin city near where she had been born, and enrolled at the University of Wisconsin–Eau Claire. Jeffrey was left to live alone in Bath.[43]

Dahmer's father always lamented the fact that his older son was so secretive and never opened up to him. He would eventually write *A Father's Story*, a book describing his on-and-off relationship with his tortured elder son.[44] Dahmer's brother David changed his last name and now lives in anonymity.[45]

A month before his parents' divorce was finalized, Jeffrey Dahmer had already claimed his first victim: an eighteen-year-old hitchhiker named Steven Hicks. The young man was last seen on June 18, 1978, after leaving a rock concert in Chippewa Lake Park, Ohio, and was reported missing on June 24. Hicks had the misfortune to meet Dahmer, who invited him to his house. According to police interrogations in 1991, Dahmer confessed the two drank and smoked pot. Dahmer then blugeoned his guest from behind, because, he later told officers, he "didn't want him to leave." (Ironically, a barbell would one day be the instrument that brought Dahmer's life to an end). After knocking the young man unconscious, Dahmer had sex with Hicks and then killed him. After cutting up Hicks, Dahmer buried the remains near a pet cemetery he had established in the woods near his house while a youngster. Hick's partial remains were found when the family's Ohio property was searched in 1991.[46]

Dahmer enrolled in Ohio State University then dropped out, as his apparent alcohol abuse became so noticeable that he occasionally passed out on the street between classes. His father married his second wife, Shari Jordan, on December 24, 1978. Jordan never had much good to say about either of her two stepsons and kept the two at a distance.[47]

Following his failure at college life, Dahmer joined the army in 1978 and became a medic, although he had hoped to be a military policeman. Dahmer was stationed in Baumholder, in the former West Germany, from July 1979, until his discharge in March 1981. According to fellow soldiers, Dahmer regularly became drunk, especially on weekends when he zoned out in his bunk while listening to Black Sabbath rock albums. He also often disappeared on long leaves.[48] No one paid much attention to that behavior until Dahmer's arrest in Milwaukee more than a decade later. As a result, German police reopened their investigations in several missing persons cases, but nothing overseas was ever linked to the Milwaukeean.[49]

After being released early from military service for alcohol and drug abuse on March 28, 1981, Dahmer returned to the States and lived for a short time in Miami, where he worked in a sandwich shop. He then traveled back to his old haunts in Bath, Ohio, and moved in with his dad and stepmother. There, he secretly dug up Hick's bones, pulverizing them with a hammer, and then scattered the pieces around the forestland near his house. On October 7, Dahmer was charged with disorderly conduct and resisting arrest after being found with an open bottle of alcohol at a local motel. It was his first official brush with the law.[50]

Feeling that his son needed a change of scenery, Lionel Dahmer suggested that Jeffrey go to West Allis to visit his grandmother, whom he had been close to as a youngster. Dahmer decided to take up permanent residence in Wisconsin and got a job at the Milwaukee Blood Plasma Center, drawing blood from donors. But his move did not improve his behavior. Dahmer was charged and fined fifty dollars for being drunk and disorderly at the 1982 Wisconsin State Fair, where he exposed himself to the crowd.[51]

In January 1985, Dahmer got a job with the Ambrosia Chocolate Company as a night laborer, but he was regularly reprimanded for sleeping in the lunchroom and frequent tardiness.[52]

On September 8, 1986, Dahmer was arrested again for masturbating in front of two boys; he received a year's probation and was ordered to do therapy. In April 1988, an Illinois man complained to police that Dahmer had drugged him and stole his money and jewelry. Lacking hard evidence, authorities dropped the case.[53] It was during this time that Dahmer began frequenting Milwaukee's gay bar scene and became a regular visitor to the Club Baths, a gay hangout. He was told not to return after several clients said that Dahmer drugged them in the club's private rooms.[54]

In 1987, Dahmer's demons broke free. On September 15, 1987, he made what might have been his first Milwaukee kill: Steven W. Toumi, twenty-four, another gay tavern regular, originally from Ontonagon, Michigan. The two had drunken sex at the downtown Ambassador Hotel and then passed out. Dahmer later told police he didn't remember what had happened but that Toumi was dead and bleeding from the mouth when he woke up. Dahmer purchased a large suitcase at the nearby Grand Avenue Mall, stuffed it with the corpse, and took a cab to his grandmother's house, entering by a rear door. He then stripped off the flesh, deposited it in trash bags, and tossed the remains into the garbage. He was not charged with Toumi's death because the district attorney felt there was no clear evidence of attempt to kill. Since it already had other unequivocal counts against Dahmer, the D.A.'s office did not pursue this one.[55]

The next to die was fourteen-year-old James "Jamie" Doxtator, a Native American who stood more than six feet tall and often passed for an adult. He disappeared around January 16, 1988. Dahmer drugged the youth and killed him in his grandmother's house, cutting up the body with a sharp knife, smashing the bones, and then throwing the pieces into the trash.[56] Dahmer's fourth victim was Richard Guerrero, a twenty-five-year-old Mexican last seen by his family on March 24, 1988. He lured Guerrero to his home, killed him, and again chopped up the body.[57]

Finally, his grandmother had enough of Jeffrey's coming and going at all hours and asked Lionel Dahmer to encourage his son to find his own apartment. The young man moved out, finding a temporary place at 808 North Twenty-fourth Street, where he would live for about a month. His room was near the Oxford Apartments, where he soon began his rampage in earnest.

On September 26, 1988, Dahmer lured a thirteen-year-old Laotian into his apartment by offering him fifty dollars to pose for a photo. The child was drugged and molested but managed to get away. It was later revealed that the boy was an older brother of Konerak Sinthasomphone,

one of Dahmer's future victims. Dahmer was subsequently arrested and charged with second-degree sexual assault and enticement of a child for immoral purposes. Lionel Dahmer paid his son's $10,000 bail and hired noted Milwaukee defense attorney Gerald Boyle to represent Jeffrey.[58]

Assistant District Attorney Gail Shelton sounded discouraged while summarizing that case, heard before Milwaukee County Circuit Judge William D. Gardner. In her view, Shelton said, "It is absolutely crystal clear that the prognosis for treatment of Mr. Dahmer within the community is extremely bleak. . . . and is just plain not going to work."[59] On January 30, 1989, Dahmer pleaded guilty.

Shelton sought a six-year prison sentence for Dahmer but Judge Gardner felt that the accused would better benefit from psychiatric treatment if he was not incarcerated. On May 24, 1989, Dahmer was subsequently ordered to serve a one-year sentence in the Franklin House of Correction. The work-release program allowed him to keep his job at Ambrosia Chocolate. Standing before the judge, Dahmer blamed his troubles on alcohol abuse and claimed, "I can't stress enough that I desperately want to change my conduct for the rest of my life."[60]

In a letter he wrote to Gardner, December 10, 1989, Dahmer sought leniency. "Sir, I have always believed that a man should be willing to assume responsibility for the mistakes that he made in life. The world has enough misery in it without my adding more to it. Sir, I assure you that it will never happen again. This is why, Judge Gardner, I am requesting from you a sentence modification. So that I may be allowed to continue my life as a productive member of our society."[61]

During his time at the corrections facility, Dahmer was generally a model prisoner, serving his sentence quietly and not causing any trouble. Yet prison records indicate that he did have two violations. Once he returned six hours late and smelling of alcohol after a visit to his grandmother on Thanksgiving Day in 1989. He lost two days of "good time" for the infraction and was prohibited from going to work for two days. In another situation, Dahmer was cited for not going to work when his paycheck indicated that he had not worked a full work week. Dahmer blamed the gap on a snowstorm that closed the Ambrosia plant for a day, and the charge was dropped.[62]

Dahmer completed his time in March 1990. Later it was revealed that no probation officer ever visited Dahmer in his home; supervisors of Dahmer's caseworker waived the visitation requirement because the worker had an overly large file of cases to handle. However, it was noted that Dahmer met the other requirements of probation, such as making appointments with his caseworker and undergoing alcohol counseling and treatment.[63]

On October 4, 1990, Dahmer was recorded as voluntarily visiting the Milwaukee County Mental Health Complex in Wauwatosa. However, he apparently waited only fifteen minutes before leaving without getting any treatment or speaking with anyone. Around the same time, he told his probation officer that his life seemed to be deteriorating and he was thinking of suicide. As late as July 19, 1991, he told his agent that he was about to be fired from his job at Ambrosia, which would be a good reason to kill himself. The caseworker arranged for Dahmer to get psychological assistance, provided a list of free meal programs, and helped place him on a Salvation Army housing list pending his eviction from the Oxford for nonpayment of rent.[64]

Yet, while Dahmer was passing like a ghost through the rehabilitation bureaucracy, his merry-go-round of horror had already begun twirling. On March 25, 1989, Milwaukeean Anthony Sears, twenty-four, had disappeared from La Cage Aux Follies, a well-known gay bar in Milwaukee's Walker's Point area. Three years later, Sears became the first of Dahmer's eleven known victims from his apartment murders to be positively identified. During Dahmer's trial in 1992, Gerald Boyle, his defense attorney, related how his client kept Sears' head in his locker at Ambrosia Chocolate. Boyle was hoping this would help show Dahmer's insanity. Ambrosia Chocolate was frantic, concerned that some body parts might have been chucked into their vats. But apparently Dahmer was never inclined to so spice up the confections he prepared.[65]

The casualty list grew longer. Thirty-three-year-old Ricky Beeks, also known as Raymond Lamont Smith, was last seen on May 29, 1990.

Beeks was never in close contact with his family, and relatives thought he had been shot to death a year earlier on Milwaukee's East Side. They had no idea he was a Dahmer death statistic until alerted by police.

Ernest Miller, twenty-four, was last seen on September 2, 1990. He had come to Milwaukee from Chicago to escape that city's violence. "Never bothered nobody," said Vivian Miller, an aunt of the victim. Curtis Straughter, eighteen, disappeared March 7, 1991. He lived with his grandmother, but felt separated from his family because of his homosexuality. The high school dropout, who had just lost his job as a nursing assistant, wanted to go to modeling school. Pals later wondered how he hooked up with Dahmer, because Straughter was suspicious of white men.[66]

Errol Lindsey was only nineteen when he vanished on April 7, heading to the Grand Avenue Mall to have a key made. A rap music and weight-lifting fan, friends said he avoided bars and rarely drank. Madison's Tony Hughes, thirty-one, was deaf and unable to speak. But he supposedly had known Dahmer for at least two years. When hearing Dahmer's name in the media, his mother cried, "I knew deep inside my heart that he would be one of those bodies found." The last time his friends saw Hughes was May 24 at a gay dance club on Milwaukee's South Side.[67]

Dahmer met Matt Turner, a twenty-year-old also known as Donald Montrell, at a Chicago bus station on June 30, 1991. He offered to pay Turner to pose nude and watch videos. The man accompanied Dahmer back to Milwaukee by bus and the two then took a cab over to the Oxford. Turner was drugged, strangled, and dismembered. His body parts were placed in a fifty-seven-gallon barrel and his head made into a sickening display in the refrigerator.[68]

The Milwaukee Journal reported that around July 5, Dahmer met Jeremiah Weinberger, twenty-three, at a Chicago gay bar and also convinced him to return to Milwaukee to appear in photos. Weinberger stayed for two days and when he wanted to leave, Dahmer killed him. Weinberger's father, David, later related that his son was "hypnotized by a cobra. Unfortunately, he was bit."[69]

The next victim was twenty-three-year-old Oliver J. Lacy, a high school track star who grew up in Oak Park, Illinois. He had last been seen on July 12. Dahmer apparently ran into Lacy on North Twenty-seventh Street, between West State Street and West Kilbourn Avenue about July 15. After luring Lacy to his apartment, Dahmer drugged and strangled his visitor, then had sex with the dead body. In addition to other body parts, Dahmer kept the heart in the freezer, allegedly, as the charges stated, "to eat later."[70]

Dahmer continued his hunt. He met Joseph Bradehoft, twenty-five, on July 16 on West Wisconsin Avenue near Marquette University. Bradehoft had recently moved to Milwaukee to live with a brother while seeking a job. He was married with three children and was waiting for a bus when Dahmer offered him money to pose for photos. Just as with the others, Bradehoft was then drugged, strangled, and cut up. His head went into the freezer and his limbs and torso made their way into the death barrel.[71]

It was only a matter of days before Tracy Edwards' July 22 encounter with Dahmer resulted in the killer's arrest, ending an almost-invisible reign of terror that might otherwise have claimed dozens more lives.

The scale of Jeffrey Dahmer's crimes sent renewed calls for capital punishment echoing across Wisconsin. The state has not had the death penalty since 1853, the longest state ban of the death penalty in the nation. The last execution in Wisconsin had been in 1851, attended by scores of thrill seekers . . . and pickpockets.

Usually, the demands to reestablish capital punishment are made by grandstanding office holders seeking political gain by appearing "tough on crime." Opponents of capital punishment, including the Office of the State Public Defender, contend there is no evidence the death penalty lowers crime rates. "I think almost all experts would agree now that there isn't a deterrent effect on capital punishment on homicide," according to Dana Smetana of the Office of the State Public Defender. *Milwaukee Journal-Sentinel* columnist Eugene Kane chimed in, "The state hasn't exactly been overwhelmed with notorious murderers in the 153 years since Wisconsin repealed the death penalty. Sure, we had Jeffrey Dahmer, and Ed Gein before him, but nothing you could call an epidemic. Yet some apparently feel it's time for a death penalty to discourage such mayhem."[72]

Proponents, on the other hand, often claim that the families of murder victims require capital punishment for crimes to gain closure and relief. They often neglect to acknowledge that many relatives of victims feel that murder and the death penalty don't cancel out each other, but only increase violence in society.

Following Dahmer's arrest in 1991, a number of prominent Wisconsin politicians, including Republican Governor Tommy Thompson, jumped on the death-by-decree bandwagon. However, even Thompson admitted that capital punishment would not have much influence on the actions of the mentally ill. A number of other Republican legislators supporting such punishment also agreed that even threat of the death penalty wouldn't deter mass killings on the scale of Dahmer's crimes.[73]

At a hearing on September 10, 1991, defense attorney Boyle attempted to use the insanity defense, with Dahmer pleading not guilty by reason of mental disease or defect. A two-part trial was set. The first would determine if Dahmer had committed the killings and the second would establish whether or not he was insane. On September 24, prosecutors in Summit County, Ohio, charged Dahmer for the 1978 murder of Steven Hicks, after police there used a map drawn by Dahmer to find the victim's bone fragments at his boyhood home.[74]

If Dahmer was insane in connection with the murders he committed before 1989, he might have been able to seek release from a mental hospital six months after confinement. On the murders after 1989, he would have been up for release within a year.[75]

During a pretrial session opening on January 13, 1992, Dahmer entered the locked-down courtroom of Judge Laurence C. Gram Jr., wearing a jail-issued orange jumpsuit, brown socks, and blue tennis shoes. The room full of reporters stared at the accused killer. Judge Gram denied Boyle's requests for a change of venue and his suggestion that jurors be selected from outside the city. The judge responded that it would be difficult to find anyone in Wisconsin who probably hadn't heard something about the case. It took until January 29 to select the six white men, seven white women, and one black man to serve as jurors. The fact that there was only one African American on the panel enraged many relatives of the victims.[76]

In a surprise move at that hearing, Dahmer changed his plea to guilty, leaving the jury to determine whether he was insane or knew what he was doing while committing the murders. Under the state law, Boyle had to prove insanity, so he emphasized that only a madman could have done what Dahmer did.[77]

But prosecutors, led by District Attorney E. Michael McCann, maintained that Dahmer was a clever liar who knew what he was doing, planning each murder in gruesome detail.[78] Using Dahmer's own words against him, Milwaukee police detectives read from his 160-page confession. The sordid details related how he tried various seasonings to add to his victim's cooked flesh and once tried to drink a vial of blood but didn't care for the taste. Through it all, the jurors sat stone-faced and motionless.[79]

William Kunkle, a former Cook County prosecutor who helped convict John Wayne Gacy Jr., in the murders of thirty-three young men and boys between 1972 and 1978, met with McCann. The two had known each other professionally for years. The Chicago attorney, by then in private practice, had taught with McCann at the National College of District Attorneys in Houston. Kunkle provided McCann with transcripts of the Gacy trial, for legal research and help in preparing motions. Although the killer's defense team also tried to show Gacy was insane, the jury rejected the claim. In 1990, Gacy was convicted of twelve separate death sentences and twenty-one of life in prison without parole. He died by lethal injection on May 10, 1994.[80]

The fact that Jeffrey Dahmer was a serial killer didn't necessarily make him insane, legal experts said when asked about the case. They pointed out that the standards for an insanity defense were hard to meet; just because an act is abnormal doesn't make the perpetrator crazy.[81]

The case became a titanic struggle between expert witnesses, with each side bringing in psychiatrists and other specialists who argued convincingly about the perceived whys and wherefores of Dahmer's state of mind. Civilian witnesses included a man who cleaned

Dahmer's stained carpet, as well as his apartment manager, and friends of victims.

FBI agent John Douglas, who helped the bureau develop a system of profiling serial killers, sided with noted California forensic psychiatrist Dr. Park Dietz, who testified for the prosecution at $3,000 a day that Dahmer was not insane. Dietz indicated that Dahmer was a paraphilic—in the old days that would be a "pervert"—but not psychotic.[82]

"Whatever the decent men and women of Milwaukee might have intellectually felt about Jeffrey Dahmer's sanity or lack thereof, I don't believe they were willing to entrust his future (and their community's) to a mental institution about whose security and judgment in keeping him they couldn't be sure," Douglas later recalled. "If they put him in prison, his dangerousness would more likely be held in check."[83]

At the closing arguments of the trial, McCann held up color photos of each victim and theatrically urged the jury "Don't forget Richard Guerrero" and on along for each of the names and likenesses. Boyle, on the other hand, called his client "a runaway train on a track of madness."[84]

The jury went into deliberations on Valentine's Day 1992. After five hours, they returned to Gram's courtroom. Dahmer was found guilty and sane on all counts as the victims' families screamed and shouted with relief.[85] Dahmer's consecutive life terms totaled 957 years in prison. The trial was the most expensive ever conducted in Milwaukee County up to that time, with expenses reaching more than $120,000.

McCann said he learned two lessons from what he called the "terribly sad" Dahmer case. "Never part with your kids in anger over their lifestyle. There may be no recovery. They could walk out of the house and never return. Be sure you let your kids know that you love them no matter what. And secondly, as the nuns used to say, 'Watch out,' especially with the power of imagination," he said, adding that, as a kid, Dahmer first started thinking about murder and what it would be like to take a life.[86]

Dahmer was marched off to serve his time at the Columbia Correctional Institute in Portage. He kept a low profile, accepted

Got Murder?

Christianity, and was baptized on May 10 in the prison whirlpool. On that day, there was a solar eclipse, and Illinois serial killer John Wayne Gacy was put to death. Even locked up, however, Dahmer still wasn't safe. He was attacked by another prisoner who stabbed him in July 1994, but the attacker's plastic knife broke before any serious injury resulted.

Fate finally caught up with Jeffery Dahmer on November 28, 1994, in the person of Christopher Scarver, a fellow inmate serving life for a 1990 Milwaukee murder. Scarver killed Dahmer and another inmate, Jesse Anderson, beating them to death with a bench-press bar from the prison's weight room—the same kind of bludgeon Dahmer used to murder his first victim. The three were on work detail cleaning a gymnasium bathroom at the time. Scarver stated that he was the "son of God" and was commanded from on high to kill Dahmer and Anderson. A commission appointed by the governor investigated the two deaths to determine if they could have been examples of "prison justice," a setup by the guards or other prison officials. The staff subsequently was exonerated.[87]

Immediately after Dahmer's death, an autopsy was undertaken by state pathologist Dr. Robert Huntington III, at the University of Wisconsin Hospital in Madison. Thirteen witnesses jammed in to watch as Dahmer was sliced and diced, chains still on his feet.[88] Huntington kept the brain, but the rest of the Milwaukeean Massacre Man was forwarded to the county morgue, located in the basement of the Dane County Public Safety Building until Scarver's trial. Dahmer's remains were the first to be stored in the new building's shiny walk-in freezer. In May 1995, Scarver pleaded no contest to killing Dahmer and was sentenced to life in prison. In September 1995, Dahmer's body was cremated as he wished.[89]

In a bit of irony befitting a man who played with the bodies of his victims, Dahmer's preserved brain became the object of a custody battle. Dahmer's mother, Joyce Flint, wanted the brain to go to Dr. Jonathan Pincus, a Georgetown University researcher who wished to study it. But Lionel Dahmer wanted it destroyed.[90]

Columbia County Circuit Court Judge Daniel George was charged with figuring out what to do with the brain. In settling Dahmer's estate, the jurist had to decide if scientists could analyze Dahmer's brain or whether it should be destroyed in accordance with Dahmer's wishes. Neither Pincus nor Flint had specific ideas on what should be done with the brain if it wasn't destroyed, so the judge was never convinced that allowing any testing was worthwhile. In December 1995, he decided to have the brain disposed of after weighing the knowledge to possibly be gained from research against the anguish that victims' survivors would experience.[91]

Milwaukee County District Attorney E. Michael McCann always wished that Dahmer had remained alive so he could have talked with psychologists and psychiatrists about what drove him to kill. "I think he would have cooperated, just as he did in telling about his murders," said McCann.[92]

The aftermath of Dahmer's crimes continued to reverberate. In 1992, Judge George settled several multimillion-dollar wrongful death claims against Dahmer by his victims' survivors, dividing Dahmer's few assets among the claimants. Campus Circle, Marquette University's neighborhood development arm, purchased the Oxford in August 1992, intending to raze the building and stop the flood of sightseers to the site. The forty-nine-unit building was demolished in November 1992. The site remained vacant for years.[93]

In 1996, to block anyone from setting up a Dahmer museum or otherwise capitalizing on the deaths, several concerned Milwaukeeans raised $407,225 to buy the killer's collection of infamous tools, the refrigerator, and other furnishings. Several of the families had obtained a court order that gave them the items; they planned to auction the artifacts and use the proceeds as compensation for their pain and suffering. McCann said that the last thing anyone would have wanted was having some restaurant owner offering to serve a meal on a Dahmer plate as part of a promotion. Horrified at any such possibilities, Milwaukee realtor and investor Joseph J. Zilber led a group of civic leaders who put up the money for the odd lot of macabre items, which was then destroyed. The action was taken after an agreement was reached between Zilber's group and the victims' families. Under the arrangement, eleven families seeking restitution from Dahmer's estate received $32,500 before lawyers' fees.[94]

Many sex killers such as Dahmer end up emotionally exhausted, not able to differentiate between passion, sex, or illusion. Shortly before he died, Dahmer supposedly bemoaned his prison stay, saying "I couldn't find any meaning for my life when I was out there. I'm sure as hell not going to find it in here."[95] Many years after the Dahmer trial, his defense attorney Gerald Boyle said, "Dahmer was lonely, the loneliest person I ever met."[96]

In autumn of 2006, Reverend Roy Ratcliff, the pastor who baptized Dahmer in prison, released *Dark Journey Deep Grace: The Story Behind a Serial Killer's Journey to Faith*, a book relating that he felt Dahmer was sincere in his conversion and that he was forgiven by God. Not that Dahmer should be excused for his actions, but the minister thought the murderer was saved from eternal damnation. Ratcliff emphasized that his faith gave him strength to believe that no sin was so great that it couldn't be forgiven. Even Dahmer's list of horrors.[97]

Perhaps there could be something to that belief. After all, the prophet Joel cried out, "Everyone who calls on the name of the Lord will be saved." (Joel 2:32).

Kim Brown's cocaine binge ended in murder.

Chapter 8

Unlocked Doors

South-central Wisconsin
Summer of 1987
Death toll: 7

*She was face down. Her hands were tied
behind her back.*

—Robert White, Adams County sheriff's investigator[1]

To the casual eye, south-central Wisconsin is a mixed palette of pasture and cornfields fading into forlorn expanses of sandy flatland, scrub woods, and marsh. Clumps of pasqueflowers purple the early spring, sometimes before the last snow has melted. Along the ditches, wild roses blossom under the summer sun. Streams tickle the feet of limestone outcroppings, shaded by limb-to-limb pine, oak, and maple. Autumn frosts the landscape before the snow again drifts across the county highways. And the people are generally pleasant, caring, and good-natured; they still say hello to visitors on the streets of towns and villages that are truly Lake Woebegonesque.

Yet terror lurked in darkened corners of Wisconsin's heartland during the hot, dry summer of 1987. A horrible series of tragedies was slowly unfolding. Whispers of "serial killer" entered the gossip chain, a breath-stopping phrase for those who lived and worked here. With the June murder of Angela Faye Hackle of Lone Rock, and the mysterious disappearance of Barbara Blackstone of Lyndon Station shortly afterward, central Wisconsin residents were jittery. Was a madman actually on the loose?

On July 24, 1987, police reported a break-in and arson at a house in Oxford, a village of 508 in Marquette County. The home owners, Corey and Linda Gage, were away at the time, but the family dog had been stabbed and its body tossed into a bedroom. A braided rug was also draped across the kitchen stove with the burners turned on high. Liquor had been poured around the room, apparently to feed the blaze.[2] Several slugs were later found shot into a sofa. It was believed that the bullets were fired at the family cat.[3] A pile of Mrs. Gage's underwear was heaped on the floor.[4] Stolen were a Smith & Wesson .357-caliber Magnum revolver, a black holster, and a black balisong, commonly known as a "butterfly," an easily concealed folding pocketknife favored by martial artists and urban gang members.[5]

On July 28, barely a week after the Gage break-in and following the cases of the two missing women, twenty-nine-year-old Linda Nachreiner disappeared from her secluded home in Dell Prairie, a village of 1,415 residents six miles from the burglary site. Her husband, Brian, was a construction worker on a job in Illinois at the time; she worked part time at the Tofson Insurance Company in Wisconsin Dells. Their modern, comfortable house was twenty miles from Barbara Blackstone's residence. Nachreiner's mother, Gertrude Leege, had last talked to her on the telephone that morning around 10:30 a.m., but there was no response at the house when Leege dropped by there a few hours later. She found her two granddaughters, Casey and Ashley, alone in a crib. A basket of wet laundry seemed to have just been removed from the washing machine. Leege immediately contacted police.[6]

More than 150 determined searchers combed the vicinity for days, using a helicopter, horses, and bloodhounds. Nachreiner's body was found about 1 p.m., August 5, with her hands tied behind her back, nude from the waist down; her head was wrapped in her blue jeans. A pink sock was on her right foot, the mate of one that had been found in her bedroom. Nachreiner's corpse was only three miles from where she vanished, dumped along a remote one-lane pathway, known to locals as Beer Can Alley because of its regular use by underage drinkers.

The victim had been raped before being killed by a single bullet fired into her head. Careful investigators found tire tracks matching others outside Nachreiner's home. The state crime lab eventually recovered a slug apparently fired by the .357 Magnum stolen from the Gages' home on July 24.[7]

With the mysterious killings of Hackl and Nachreiner, and Blackstone's puzzling disappearance, previously unlocked doors were again being bolted across central Wisconsin. Neighbors were wary of neighbors. Outsiders were viewed with caution, even in a community long used to vacationing tourists flooding to the nearby Wisconsin Dells and to area campgrounds.

Tips poured into police departments throughout Marquette, Richland, Adams, Sauk, Columbia, and Juneau counties. Sergeant Manny Bolz of the Sauk County Sheriff's Department said that reports of suspicious-looking persons had soared since Hackl's murder. "I think people are scared right to their souls," added Juneau County Sheriff Gervase Thompson. Gun shops reported brisk sales of small pistols, mainly sold to women. Classes in self-defense were fully booked. However, the million-plus visitor engine at the Wisconsin Dells continued pumping. "I think people are busy with their vacations and barely read the papers," offered Tom Diehl, president of the Wisconsin Dells Visitors and Convention Bureau, though he agreed that the ever-growing complexity of the situation was tragic and worrisome.[8]

Unexpected help came in the form of Curtis Sliwa and his Guardian Angels, a volunteer crime prevention organization that started in 1979 in New York. A Madison chapter was organized by state coordinator Willie Brooks in the early summer of 1986, patrolling that city's south side after a spate of area murders. The sight of the Angels' van, marked by signs reading "Stop the Dells Serial Killer," stopped tourists in their tracks. For a time in early August, their vehicle was parked on the city's Oak Street municipal lot across from the police station. Sliwa said that he received some forty requests for house guardians, young men and women who had come from Milwaukee, Minneapolis, and Chicago. Many were people of color, an anomaly in that predominately white swath of the state. Among the sitters was Maureen Villiers, a

Got Murder?

fifteen-year-old black woman trained in martial arts who stayed with a grateful single woman and her children in a rural Oxford home about five miles from where Nachreiner's body was found.[9]

Sheriff's departments met within days to discuss potential links between the discovery of the bodies of Hackl and Nachreiner and the still-missing Blackstone. Blackstone's father, Herbert Fisher, requested that the governor's office seek National Guard assistance to help in the search for his daughter, a personable, outgoing teacher who seemed to have simply melted away. After the 400 acres around the Blackstone home was combed, the search area was expanded to a five-mile radius. Hot, humid weather, accompanied by irritating mosquitoes and ongoing drizzle made the task difficult.[10]

As the Blackstone inquiry proceeded, five agents from the state's Division of Criminal Investigation, along with Robert White and Kenneth Probyn, Adams County sheriff's deputies, remained on the Nachreiner investigation.[11] This was evolving into a textbook murder case, according to Adams County District Attorney Mark Thibodeau.[12]

* * * *

It wasn't Thibodeau's first murder investigation. Six months after he was appointed to his position in March 1978, the twenty-one-year-old divorced daughter of Sheriff Edwin Williams, Janna Williams Henningsen, apparently strangled and bludgeoned romantic rival Nancy Potts. The deadly instrument of choice: a heavy frying pan.

That situation had more twists and turns than some of the county's Rustic Roads. Henningsen, the mother of twin daughters, had been living with Rick Reichoff, brother of Kenny Ray Reichoff, a pulp cutter who had been convicted of the shooting deaths of his boss and another man in 1974. At the time, Kenny Ray was serving two consecutive life terms in the Wisconsin State Reformatory in Green Bay.

The lawman's daughter had testified at Kenny Ray's trial. She and Kenny Ray conducted a torrid correspondence even during the year she was living with his brother. But another woman, nurse Nancy Potts, had also been Kenny Ray's romantic pen pal—hers was just one of several long distance love affairs the locked-up lothario apparently had enjoyed.

Potts and Kenny Ray subsequently dated seriously after a new trial in 1977 exonerated him and he was released. Throughout all this, it was well known in the Adams–Friendship area that Henningsen and Potts did not get along for many reasons, most of which concerned their passionately convoluted love entanglements.

On April 10, 1978, Henningsen slashed Potts' bike tires and seat, a case that also came up before Thibodeau. In a court hearing, the woman was fined $130 for criminal damage to property. But the women's rivalry intensified as the summer wore on.

Six months later, on October 10, Henningsen asked Potts to come to her home in the Parkland Mobile Village trailer park after her shift at Adams County Memorial Hospital. Co-workers later testified that Potts agreed, thinking Henningsen wished to apologize for the bike incident and end the feud raging between them.

That was a Tuesday. On that coming Saturday, Potts and Kenny Ray Reichoff were to be married.

Once lured to Henningsen's trailer, Potts was attacked, strangled with a scarf, and beaten to death. Henningsen was aided by her thirteen-year-old baby-sitter, Mary Collins, who had just shown up to care for Henningsen's daughters. Refusing to beat Potts, the terrified girl still held one end of the scarf as Henningsen pounded her love competitor to death. Henningsen and Collins then stuffed the nurse's battered body into the trunk of her car, which had been a prewedding gift from her fiancé, Kenny Ray.[13]

Thibodeau worked around the clock on the case, aided by a wide range of investigators, a team that included both locals and those from the State of Wisconsin Department of Justice's Division of Criminal Investigation. Without a staff, the young DA admitted he was in desperate need of assistance, and Assistant Attorney General J. Douglas Haag was assigned to ride to the aid of Adams County. "As a result of this legal tag teaming, we successfully prosecuted Henningsen who was convicted, after approximately 10 days of jury trial," Thibodeau indicated.[14]

Got Murder?

* * * *

The Henningsen case had given Thibodeau experience in handling the kind of high-profile homicide case he now faced again nearly a decade later, especially the pressure of conducting a complicated investigation with scant resources while under the constant scrutiny of the news media. On September 2, 1987, Thibodeau was relaxing at Moundview Golf Course after another grueling day of work when he received a phone message he had been eagerly awaiting. Investigator White called and excitedly said he found "the" car.[15]

Investigators had assembled a list of thirty-three individuals in the area around Adams and Marquette counties whose names were reported as "potentials" in the case, even if they were not officially considered linked to the Nachreiner murder. Meeting every morning at their command center in the Wisconsin Dells, the investigators doggedly ran down the names, scratching each off as alibis were confirmed, car tires checked, and DNA samples taken.[16]

By chance, the thirty-third name on the roster was that of Kim S. Brown, a truck driver from Oxford who lived near the burglarized Gage house. The man's name had been given to Investigator White by Lowell Benedict, a Montello landscaper who shared White's enthusiasm for trapping. Benedict phoned White at 9:30 a.m., July 29, to advise him to take a close look at Brown, also an avid outdoorsman. Benedict told White that he had seen the trucker behaving "oddly" in the woods. In a follow-up call to the detective on August 5, Benedict called Brown a "weird bastard" and told White that he felt the Oxford man was capable of committing a murder because Brown had cut up a dog and used it to bait his traps. "When I heard about a dog being stabbed at the Gage place, I knew it was him," Benedict said.[17]

White and Ernest "Ernie" Smith, a special agent with the state's Division of Criminal Investigation, went to the Columbia County trucking company where Brown worked. Confronting the tall, chunky trucker, the investigators asked to speak with him in the firm's parking lot. While waiting for Brown to join them, White strolled over to Brown's vehicle, a 1975 Pontiac. He immediately realized he had a match with the treads found at the Nachreiner house and the murder scene.[18]

Brown at first refused to allow police to comb through his car, but relented when he learned that a search warrant was to be issued. Smith later testified that he found a gun, two used cartridges, and a knife that contained blue jeans material, human body hair, and animal hair.[19] A look into the vehicle's glove compartment uncovered a second knife, with animal hair and blood on the blade that were later matched to those from the dead dog. Brown was taken into custody on charges of possessing stolen goods, the items taken from the Gage house.[20]

Brown initially claimed that the stolen weapons belonged to an acquaintance. His story soon changed. The accused man indicated that he had found the revolver and the butterfly knife along Highway 82 the day Nachreiner's body was discovered. Samples were then taken of Brown's blood and saliva, which matched those found on a bed comforter inside the Nachreiner home.[21] A search of Brown's trailer home turned up a .357-caliber Magnum with slugs that were described by authorities as "similar" to those dug out of the Gages' sofa.[22]

The investigation picked up speed throughout the night, as Thibodeau prepared search warrants at the Columbia County district attorney's office. He notified his old ally Haag, who was preparing another murder prosecution in a rural northern county, that "we had our man."[23]

On Thursday, September 3, Brown was charged in Columbia County Circuit Court for possessing the gun. He posted the $1,000 cash bail bond and was handed over to Adams County authorities. They immediately arrested him in connection with Nachreiner's murder. The state and local authorities had worked forty-four straight hours tying up details of the case before bringing seven felony charges against the suspect.[24]

Among the evidence was the possibility that the reclusive Brown might have been acquainted with Linda Nachreiner's husband. The two worked at the Warren W. Coon Trucking and Excavating Company, although at different times; both men occasionally had drinks in the same bar, the Fur, Fin and Feathers along Highway B. The tavern was a half mile south of Nachreiner's house in Dell Prairie. Yet bar owner

Got Murder?

Rob Bauer told the media that he couldn't remember if the two men ever spoke or even seemed to know each other.[25] After the charges against Brown were filed, Brian Nachreiner told reporters that he once met the man but didn't know him very well. According to Bauer, Linda Nachreiner rarely dropped by the tavern, except once in a while to order a pizza.[26]

Brown was never involved in a fight or seen flirting with other women, Bauer said. "Kim was Kim—just a quiet individual," he said.

A native of Adams County, Brown grew up with two sisters, graduated from Wisconsin Dells High School in 1969, and held a long line of jobs throughout the area. At various times, he was a logger, drove cross-country for a freight hauler, and was a heavy-machine operator. Brown worked two years for Coon Trucking, but lost his job in 1984 because he had several accidents that put him in a high-risk insurance category.[27]

For a time while a truck driver, he lived with his parents, Joann and Daniel Brown, respected members of the community who were friendly but who not known to socialize much.[28] He regularly parked his vehicle outside their Eighth Avenue home, only a few miles west of Highway B where the Nachreiners eventually built their house.[29]

After he married in 1984, Brown moved to within a half mile of the Gage place. He lived in a trailer with his wife, Cindy, and two-year-old son, Daniel, at Coon's Deep Lake mobile home park on Fish Lane about six-and-a-half miles southwest of the Nachreiners.[30] The family had a puppy that neighbors said Brown sometimes kicked across the yard when its barking seemed to annoy him. Others, however, said he appeared to be a good family man, often flying kites with his toddler. Yet Brown rarely talked with his neighbors. When he did, the conversation usually centered around hunting and fishing.[31]

At the time of his arrest, Brown was driving trucks for the Davis Construction Company of Mauston. "You don't know how to think about it. He was a run-of-the-mill truck driver. He never missed a day of work," according to company owner Joseph Davis. Warren Coon, who had earlier employed Brown, also said that Brown seemed like an ordinary guy. "He was burly and husky, yet he seemed to be very meek and mild," he said of the six-foot-plus suspect.[32]

Brown's time clock records at work demonstrated that he claimed to be ill on July 24 and was not at his job. Brown said he was at home and had seen the fire at the nearby Gage house. Brown also left work only two hours after checking in on July 28. His wife told police that she believed her husband had worked a full shift on both days.[33]

Held in the Adams County Jail on $500,000 bond, Brown was represented by state public defender Tom Flugaur of Stevens Point and carefully interrogated. The bespectacled trucker was told that tires on his car closely resembled police casts taken around the Nachreiner home. Yet Brown continued to assert that he remained at home throughout the day on July 24, adding that he went with his wife shopping four days later. When asked about his whereabouts when Nachreiner disappeared, Brown told Detective Robert White that rain had shortened his work day and that he and his wife drove to Madison for shopping about noon. However, when special agent Richard Berghammer of the state's Division of Criminal Investigation questioned Cindy Brown, she indicated that the couple had not gone to Madison until that evening.[34]

On Friday, September 4, 1987, Brown was charged with first-degree murder, first- and second-degree sexual assault, kidnapping, burglary, armed burglary, and arson. A second first-degree sexual assault charge was added later. The suspect appeared that afternoon and heard Adams County Circuit Court Judge Raymond Gieringer declare the charges against him "tragic." The judge set a preliminary hearing for September 16, as Cindy Brown broke down and cried in the courtroom. No further charges were filed, because authorities did not see any links to the murders of Hackl and Blackstone.[35]

When charged, Brown hung his head, answering "yes" in a barely audible voice as the counts were read. The packed courtroom was heavily guarded, with families of both the victim and suspect present. Only Nachreiner's husband, Brian, was not in the room. Cindy, Brown's wife, began weeping when Thibodeau uttered the dismaying word, "murder."[36]

"Mr. Brown's demeanor can best be described as, 'Oh shit, they got me,'" Thibodeau recalled. "Mr. Brown said very little and showed no emotion. When his fingerprint was identified on the liquor bottle from the Gage arson, Mr. Brown knew he had met his Waterloo."[37]

Assistant Attorney General Haag told reporters that Brown's actions were an "escapade of brutality the likes of which have seldom been seen in Wisconsin . . . rape, torture, and murder, not to mention arson and burglary." Due to the complexity of the crime and multiple jurisdictions, the state was helping prosecute the case.[38]

Although Attorney General Donald J. Hathaway refused to indicate whether Brown was involved in the deaths of Hackl and Blackstone, he did say that the state's Justice Department and Sauk and Juneau county officers were cooperating in the investigations of the two other women's deaths. Despite the fact that the area's frightful murder spree screeched to a halt when Brown was taken into custody, by September 11, authorities had formally discarded the idea that Brown was a serial killer.[39]

According to the complaint filed on October 19, 1987, with the clerk of circuit court in Friendship, the Adams County seat, Brown allegedly broke into Nachreiner's home on July 28 and sexually assaulted her in an upstairs bedroom before driving off with her and eventually murdering the woman.[40]

The maximum penalties Brown faced included life imprisonment, five additional twenty-year stretches, and up to $20,000 in fines. Appearing in open court, Brown pleaded not guilty to each count.[41]

Seeking the best representation they could find in the state, Brown's parents hired Milwaukee attorney Gerald Boyle, a noted Milwaukee County assistant district attorney who had turned defense counsel. Boyle was noted for his no-nonsense approach to the law as a prosecutor and represented a number of suspects in headline-attracting trials after he switched to the other side of the table. (He'd later defend Jeffrey Dahmer.) "When I was called, I had to take the case. You don't pick and choose," he said. "Every case needs to be dealt with. More often than not, there is some shred of decency left in these individuals, even when they've done the most indecent thing."[42]

A preliminary hearing originally set for September 15 was delayed so Boyle could get up to speed on the case.[43]

The session was rescheduled for Wednesday, September 30. The day unfolded dramatically as Brown sat quietly before Judge Gieringer. Prosecutor Haag described Linda Nachreiner's death as similar to those depicted in books on torture and bondage found in Brown's home. Defense attorney Boyle countered that the books were not relevant to the case. "What books a person has in their home is immaterial and inconclusive," he argued, saying that there was no evidence that Brown owned the books or even read them.[44]

The next day, Brown was ordered to stand trial for Nachreiner's murder as both prosecution and defense debated their positions. As Haag said, the circumstantial evidence in the case "is so overwhelming and points the finger so directly at Mr. Brown." Boyle admitted that the crimes as described were committed, but claimed that the state failed to show that it was Brown who perpetrated them.[45]

In an interesting twist, Judge Gieringer withdrew from the case on October 20, citing a potential conflict because his own family was acquainted with the Nachreiners. After all, it was a small, close-knit community. Wood County Circuit Judge Edward Zappen was named to replace Gieringer.[46]

Over that winter, the two sides prepared their cases, with Boyle promising to challenge every bit of evidence the prosecution had. He was as good as his word: On February 11, Brown testified that he was not informed of his rights when he made statements to authorities about Nachreiner's murder and asked that the court withhold as evidence the pistol seized from his car. Judge Zappen rejected Brown's assertion, saying that the man had given his permission to search the auto and that his statements were offered voluntarily. Brown spoke slowly, sometimes not responding for up to thirty seconds to questions asked him by prosecutor Haag.[47]

Citing problems finding an impartial jury in Nachreiner's home county, Boyle told the courtroom, "In the best interests of Mr. Brown, the jury should be as far removed from Adams County as possible, some county where the jury has not been contaminated by the effects of the news media." The state agreed on Thursday, November 12, to move

Got Murder?

Brown's murder trial to Wisconsin Rapids and pick jurors from yet another county. Judge Zappen set a hearing on motions filed by Boyle for February 16, 1988, emphasizing that he would then set a definite trial date. Prosecutor Haag also agreed to the shift, primarily because Wood County provided better security for the jury and housing for Brown. Defendant Brown also gave his assent during the one-hour hearing.[48]

However, Haag disagreed with Boyle's assessment of media coverage. "The state has not felt that news media coverage of these proceedings has been anything but proper and appropriate but knows from past experience that it can be difficult to select a jury in this county in high-profile cases such as this."[49]

Testifying on Wednesday, February 10, 1988, Brown still maintained his innocence and complained that he was not informed of his constitutional rights prior to his arrest. Boyle pointed out that Brown was held for nine hours at the Columbia County sheriff's office before being formally arrested. He was never informed that he could leave or contact a lawyer, the defense said. But Judge Zappen again rejected the claim, and set a trial date of May 16.[50]

Not long after that hearing, Brown and Boyle sat down for a heart-to-heart talk. The lawyer had just filed another motion to gain Brown's release, and he laid out all the potential results to Brown if he were to be convicted. "I finally told him the state would put in a case so strong that he would be found guilty," Boyle recalled.[51] The man sat quietly for a few minutes, then turned to Boyle and admitted his guilt. "That was so incredible," Boyle recalled. "The only time I really know someone is guilty when going into a case is when they tell me. I work hard to have them tell me in their own time. Then I see what I can do. I won't go to trial for the sake of a trial," he pointed out.[52]

"I had to take care of his poor family then. They were convinced that he was innocent. The wailing, the tears. The shrieks were incredible," a somber Boyle remembered. "It was a human tragedy for all concerned. I was very sympathetic toward the Nachreiner family. And Brown's mom and dad, such nice people. Mrs. Brown reminded me of [actress] Angela Lansbury."[53]

On Friday, May 13, Boyle met with Judge Zappen, Adams County District Attorney Thibodeau, and Special Prosecutor Haag in the judge's chambers. Boyle said Brown would admit his guilt, just as the trial was scheduled to start that following Monday in Wisconsin Rapids. Opening testimony had been expected to begin on Tuesday, after the jury visited the wooded site where Nachreiner's body had been found. Later, Judge Zappen told the media that Brown was pleading guilty to save the expense of jury selection and a trial. "I've also been advised that his change in circumstances has not come as a result of any plea bargain," he pointed out.[54]

At the same time, reporters learned that the state identified Brown's fingerprint on a liquor bottle that he was believed to have held in the Gage burglary shortly before Nachreiner's murder. Haag did not discuss such evidence, citing that he was bound by judicial ethics "not to comment on the pending guilty plea." Yet he did confirm that all evidence not previously made public would be disclosed; "That will be a testament to the thorough investigation that was conducted in this case."[55]

Reflecting on the case, Thibodeau credited Adams County Investigator Ken Probyn as responsible for linking the Gage break-in and arson with the Nachreiner murder. "Local knowledge and determination impressed the most seasoned investigators. The proof is in the pleas," he said.[56]

On Tuesday, May 17, 1988, Brown formally changed his plea to guilty and Zappen ordered a pre-sentence investigation to be completed within two months. The study by the Department of Correction Division of Probation and Parole was meant to help the judge determine the sentence. The investigators studied Brown's background and talked with both with his family and that of the Nachreiners, as well as acquaintances, to make recommendations as to where to best place him. The pre-sentence report was completed on September 27, 1988, and copies were delivered to Boyle for the defense, District Attorney Thibodeau as prosecutor, and the judge.[57]

The evidence in the Brown murder case was considered so overwhelming that even Boyle admitted that his defendant "would have been found guilty of all those charges whether he admitted it or not." Among the evidence was a pair of Brown's gloves found at the murder scene. Authorities also introduced a strip of paper used to carry cocaine, which they called a "coke fold"; it was apparently made from a sportsmen's magazine that Brown and two acquaintances used for packaging the drug.[58]

The crowded courtroom gasped when it heard the results of toxology reports showing that Nachreiner had ingested a bit of cocaine before her death—there was never any previous evidence of her drug use. Prosecutor Haag also told of witnesses seeing a husky, bearded man in the vicinity of the murder driving a car that matched a description of Brown's. At the time of his arrest, Brown sported a beard and had long, scraggly hair. Keys found in Brown's car also fit a broken padlock found at the murder site.[59]

At his trial on May 17, back in Friendship at the Adams County Courthouse, Brown described his crime. He said he left Nachreiner tied to a tree while he went away for several hours on a drinking and cocaine spree. Brown said he returned and shot her in the head.[60]

"I am deeply sorry for the victims and what I did; I deserve, your honor, whatever sentence you give me," Brown told the court. His voice was so muted that everyone there needed to strain to hear him. But when asked by Judge Zappen why he pleaded guilty to "such serious crimes," Brown responded loudly, "I am guilty. I done it. I just want to put everything to rest."[61]

Defense attorney Boyle said that Brown's admission "showed that he had killed Linda Nachreiner and committed all the other acts he was charged with." Boyle indicated that his client did not provide any motive for the slaying, but he pointed out that Brown was using cocaine at the time of the murder and for several months previously. "There is a real trail of cocaine abuse here," Boyle added.[62]

The attorney said that he was not able to create a defense because of Brown's guilty plea, "but I had to explore all the possibilities." He even had Brown examined by several psychiatrists in Madison and Milwaukee but they indicated there was no possible defense that Brown "suffered from mental disease or defect."[63]

Brown was formally processed May 17, 1988, at the Dodge Correctional Institution in Waupun.

Almost immediately after Brown was sent away, several people came forward to claim a $25,000 reward put up by ten Wisconsin Dells area business leaders for information leading to the arrest and conviction of Nachreiner's murderer. Among them was trapper Lowell Benedict, the first person to pass along Brown's name to authorities. Benedict pointed out that he had come forward even before any reward was offered. Despite his request to receive the entire amount, however, the fund donors studied those who provided other leads "Right now, there is one person claiming the reward, but there may be as many as seven who had a part in solving this thing," said P. Warren Anderson, of the Bank of Wisconsin Dells.[64]

It wasn't until that September that the money was finally divided among the claimants, with Benedict receiving $12,500. Dennis and Marion Coon earned $6,250. Coon was Brown's former employer and Mrs. Coon had told authorities that Brown had once made sexual advances toward her. Donna Manley also picked up the same amount. She approached police after Brown's arrest, confirming that his car was near the dirt road leading to Nachreiner's body.[65]

At a sentencing hearing on November 2, 1988, the Nachreiner family cried as Thibodeau held up a color print of Linda and Brian Nachreiner and their children, ages two and three. A letter to the court was read, saying, "Linda left a part of herself behind with many loved ones and friends. We all share memories of Linda and are proud of the person she was. She also left a part of herself in Casey and Ashley . . . they now know Mommy is with Jesus, but they don't understand why. . . . Someday, this whole terrible story will have to be told to the girls—hopefully we can tell them Kim Brown will be in prison for all of his natural life." Brown was sentenced to life; Judge Zappen added another 120 years.[66]

The convicted man's wife, Cindy, later told a reporter, "I'm glad they caught him. I'm glad he's getting punished. I wish they would give him the death penalty for what he did to that woman." She said she was tired of making excuses for Brown, but that while he sometimes "acted strange," she had no idea that he had killed Nachreiner until his arrest.[67]

Brown was moved to the 110-acre Columbia Correctional Institution on August 8, 1988. Situated near Portage in Columbia County, the institution's high fences are barely forty miles south of the Nachreiner murder scene in Dell Prairie.[68]

Boyle filed an appeal dated December 15, 1988, but the initial judgment was affirmed and returned on May 23, 1989. A twelve-page response filed by Marilyn Graves, clerk of the state Court of Appeals, read: "We find nothing in the record to support an argument that Brown's statements were procured by coercive means or were the product of improper police pressure . . . Brown was 35-years-old at the time and of average intelligence. He was cooperative and the interrogation was of relatively short duration. The police ceased the interrogation immediately upon Brown's request for an attorney. We conclude that Brown's statements were voluntarily made." An ensuing petition to the Wisconsin Supreme Court was denied.[69]

The years crept past. Brown was confined to his cell for three days because of one minor conduct report dated September 13, 1993, that indicated he "altered contraband." The infraction involved his having four rubber bands, a box altered for storing cassette tapes, and two boxes of cereal.[70]

Brown was later assigned to helper/carpenter maintenance duties at the prison by Columbia's Program Review Committee. He was confined at Columbia on November 28, 1994, the day Wisconsin's most notorious serial killer, Jeffrey Dahmer, was beaten to death by inmate Christopher Scarver with a twenty-inch-long metal bar from the prison weight room.[71]

Due to overcrowding in the Wisconsin prison system, Nachreiner's killer was transferred from Columbia to a county jail facility on September 24, 1999, and from there to the 1,505-inmate Whiteville Correctional Facility in Tennessee on October 11, 1999.[72]

When space opened up in Wisconsin, Brown was shifted to the Redgranite Correctional Institution in Waushara County on February 21, 2003. His good behavior early on indicated that he no longer warranted high-risk status in a top-security facility.

"Brown has been a model prisoner, which means he can be held in a more relaxed setting such as Redgranite," said Steve Beck, assistant warden at Redgranite. But Beck affirmed that "he remains a risk to society," and reiterated, "He's doing his time."[73]

In 2006, Brown's far-from-fancy "home" was cell G77-North, which he shared with a roommate serving a forty-five-year sentence for third-degree sexual assault, domestic abuse, intimidating a witness, and violation of a restraining order. Brown's daily regime is simple. He gets up around 7 a.m., dresses in green prison garb, makes his bed, and cleans the functional six-by-ten-foot cell. The gray-painted room is simply furnished with two chairs, two desks, a mirror, and bunk beds. Brown sleeps in the lower bunk. Prisoners are allowed to have a few posters and photos on the wall, plus rugs. Toilets are located down a hall. The lone window overlooks the outside recreational area.

The inmate generally has a day free of chores because, as of 2006, he had yet to be assigned a permanent job within the prison. To fill in his time, Brown walks freely around the day room and plays cards or checkers. He rarely visits the library but an outdoor yard is available for exercise. Brown, still a loner, does not engage in any hobbies or attend church services or counseling sessions. Lights out is required at 11 p.m., with a jailer calling out a ten-minute warning prior to lockdown. On weekends, inmates can remain up until 12:30 a.m., if they wish. Brown has occasional visitors, although prison authorities decline to identify them.[74]

Nachreiner's murderer is eligible for his first parole hearing on September 17, 2031, when he is eighty. For now, however, convicted killer Kim S. Brown has no choice but to wait and stare out his only window on a relieved world.

LaCrosse police chief Ed Kondracki speaks to anguished townspeople to answer
the disturbing question: Was a serial killer in their midst?

Chapter 9

Deep, Deadly Waters

La Crosse, Wisconsin
1997–Today
Death toll: 8 and rising

None of it makes any sense.

—Scott Effenheim, University of Wisconsin–La Crosse student[1]

Drinking and drowning. The roll call of dead young men seems never-ending. Mothers weep. Fathers rage. Lawsuits are filed. Denials fly. Memorials are placed by rolling waters. Promises are made.

Yet after the tears and prayers, life goes on. Memories fade.

Until the next time.

Between 2000 and 2005, death by drowning claimed a number of college-age students: Brian Shafer, Ohio State University; Scot Radel, St. Cloud State University; Chris Jenkins, University of Minnesota; Justin Haydek, West Virginia University; Josh Guimond, St. John's University; Albert Campbell, Clarkson University; Patrick Kycia, Minnesota State University–Moorehead; Joshua Snell, Hastings, Minnesota; Patrick M. Welsh, York College of Pennsylvania; Arvin Sharma, University of Maryland; and Christopher S. Thiem, Vincennes University, among others.[2]

In Wisconsin, Eau Claire resident Craig Burrows, twenty-three, had disappeared on September 29, 2002. A week later, he was discovered

Got Murder?

dead in the city's fifteen-foot-deep Half Moon Lake, once a holding pond for logs on their way to its sawmills. The small body of water, with its rugged western shoreline, is located in the 130-acre Carson Park at the corner of Lake and Farwell streets and close to the heart of the city and its bars. Scenic hiking trails wend their way around Half Moon.[3]

Little more than a year later, University of Wisconsin–Eau Claire student Michael Noll disappeared after leaving a bar on the frosty night of November 6, 2002. On March 25, 2003, the twenty-two-year-old's body was discovered wedged under the ice of, yet again, Half Moon Lake. He was one of four midwestern, college-age men who drowned under similar circumstances that same November. The three others were in Minnesota. Police could not find any link between the deaths.[4]

Yet there was actually one uniter throughout these cases: alcohol.

More than 13,000 people drowned in the United States between 1999 and 2002, according to data from the Centers for Disease Control and Prevention.[5] Drowning is a frightening, horribly lonely way to die. A person drowns in several gruesome stages, beginning with trying to hold his or her breath until no longer possible. This urgent resolve to live soon breaks, a reflex followed by involuntary gasping. This spasm leads to loss of consciousness. After that point is reached, the victim sucks in water for several minutes until respiration ceases. Loss of consciousness happens within three minutes of being underwater. Soon, irreversible cerebral hypoxia occurs, a drop in the oxygen supply to the brain, although there is still plenty of blood flow.[6] Permanent brain damage results after four to six minutes.[7] Usually, death occurs within ten minutes. During this time, large volumes of water pass through the body and enter the circulatory system.[8]

Under certain circumstances, drowning does not follow the normal pattern.

In 10% of such deaths, laryngeal spasms can form after exposure to small amounts of water. This causes production of a thick mucus that blocks the airway, causing what is called a "dry drowning." The mucus plug prevents water from entering the lungs yet the victim still suffocates. Dry drowning victims are often intoxicated.[9] Death, some forensics experts believe, comes faster this way.

For almost a decade in La Crosse, the cluster of authorities huddled around the body of a drowning victim has been an all-too familiar scene along the Mississippi River's sloughs and city parkland. The picturesque frontage abuts La Crosse's bustling, historic commercial district.

La Crosse's downtown covers six blocks of buildings ranging from two-story 1860s brick structures to turn-of-the-twentieth-century architecture. Many renovated buildings sport what are purported to be some of the best bars in the state. A number of these establishments are popular with University of Wisconsin–La Crosse student partiers. They are also within three blocks of the largest, most powerful river in the country.[10]

The Mississippi River has a sheer drop-off of more than eighteen feet immediately off the La Crosse municipal shoreline. The current past the city's sprawling Riverside Park averages 20,000 cubic feet per second, ranging from a low of about 15,000 cubic feet per second in the summer's low water to a high of 90,000 cubic feet per second at the height of spring runoff. At flood stage, as much as 150,000 cubic feet of water per second can surge past the city.[11]

The drowning scenarios are similar: La Crosse County sheriff's deputies and La Crosse police officers, along with tracking dogs from Milwaukee, scour the shoreline. Some officers ride horses along the riverbank while others putter about in small watercraft, poking beneath the river's surface. Divers probe under downed logs and other obstacles churned over by the roiling waters. Friends of the victim pace the shoreline, weeping and hugging each other. Someone throws a rose on the muddy waters, watching the bloom as it is carried swiftly downstream.

Another missing college kid. Another headline. More hand-wringing. More tears at memorial services.

Serial killer on the loose? Or urban legend?

Luke Homan, twenty-one, a former star basketball player at Brookfield Central High School in suburban Milwaukee, was last seen

Got Murder?

at 2:15 a.m., Saturday, September 30, 2006. Oktoberfest, the city's annual celebration of La Crosse's German heritage, was in full swing, and Homan spent the early part of the evening visiting bars. The young athlete was eager for a morning golf game with high school friends from the Milwaukee area who'd come to La Crosse to help him celebrate the festival. Shortly before he disappeared, Homan hit a popular club called the Vibe before departing alone to head to another tavern. It was the last time anyone saw him alive.[12]

When Homan didn't show up for the golf outing, his friends were worried. They knew how much he was looking forward to playing. When roommates found his cell phone under his empty bed, they knew something was wrong and reported his absence to police. Over the weekend, his concerned pals circulated posters to help authorities in the search.[13]

Homan's body was found Monday, October 2, by the La Crosse Area Underwater Rescue and Recovery Unit in about ten feet of water near the south end of the Riverside Park levee. His remains were transported to the Regina Medical Center in Hastings, Minnesota, for an autopsy by forensic pathologist Lindsey Thomas.[14]

The six-foot-three-inch shooting guard played varsity ball for his high school, going to state two of the three years he played for Brookfield. A finance major, Homan initially attended the University of Wisconsin–Milwaukee and was a walk-on player for the Panthers for two seasons. He had transferred to UW–La Crosse in the fall of 2005, playing in each of the Eagles' twenty-eight games, which helped the school obtain its first twenty-victory season in more than twenty years.[15]

Homan's dad, Jerry, was on the Marquette University squad that advanced to the NCAA finals in 1974 under fabled coach Al McGuire. The elder Homan and his wife, Patti, were understandably devastated by the death of their son, as was the entire UW–La Crosse campus and the wider community. Once again, the city asked itself what could have happened to cause the tragic accident.[16]

La Crosse Mayor Mark Johnsrud pointed out Homan's death was evidence that his community and the school had yet to deal completely with dangerous drinking patterns that cause young people to wander off alone. Johnsrud urged that "people need to look out for one another to make sure that these things don't happen in the future."[17]

An autopsy showed that Homan died of drowning and did not find any signs of trauma to indicate that a struggle or other force had caused his death. But the same questions arose with Homan's death that have followed each of the decades-long string of dead young men in La Crosse.[18]

Homan was the eighth young man since 1997 to disappear along the shores of the Mississippi River—and the twenty-third since 1974. Five of those most recent deaths were caused by alcohol use and led La Crosse to create an Alcohol Task Force to study ways to warn young people about the dangers of overdrinking. The city beefed up police patrols and increased fines for bartenders drinking on the job, a factor that might have contributed to overpouring refreshing beverages for their patrons.

Yet, in the Homan case, overdrinking seemed too easy an answer. The tragedy resulted in more than one thousand e-mails to the *La Crosse Tribune*. They were a mixture of complaints about police, praise for Homan as a friend, and condolences to the family. Many wondered why there seemed to be no drowning deaths of young women or city residents. Others rapped La Crosse as being a "booze town" or used more colorful language to describe the city's drinking atmosphere. A number had suggestions to help prevent similar incidents, such as placing cameras along the riverbank or organizing special security patrols.[19]

* * * *

A 2004 presentation made by the La Crosse County Medical Examiner's office offered facts and similarities in seven cases of college-age males who drowned in the La Crosse area between 1997 and 2004.

The report indicated that the La Crosse drownings were, tragically, not all that unusual. Nationwide, males accounted for 92% of drowning victims ages fifteen to nineteen, and alcohol use was a major factor in both adult and adolescent drownings. La Crosse's location in the cold, remote western region of the state played its part, as well. Incidents of drowning occur three times more in rural areas; and when water temperatures dip below 42ºF—a frequent occurrence in local waters— life expectancy is less than five minutes.

There were also commonalities with several drownings near other midwestern college campuses over those years:

The victims were Caucasian males between the ages of eighteen and twenty-seven.

- They lived in Minnesota, Wisconsin, Michigan, Indiana, or Chicago, which was the extended area surrounding Lake Michigan. These areas had high populations of colleges students living near large bodies of water.
- All but one were students or had recently graduated.
- Most were high achieving.
- Most were in good physical condition or were athletes.
- They were last seen out drinking with friends or at a party.
- Each was under the influence of alcohol.
- They became separated from friends.
- All disappeared between the bar-time hours of 10 p.m. and 4 a.m.
- All disappeared between the school months of September and April.

After discussing each La Crosse case, the examiner's office said, "After completion and review of all these tragic cases, it is the opinion of the La Crosse County Medical Examiner that these deaths are due to several factors, with those being the following:

- Alcohol use by all the victims; out of these five victims, only two were of legal drinking age. They all had at least two times the legal limit, with one being four times the limit.
- Depression in at least two cases.
- Poor or unsafe design of the levee, allowing unsafe access to the river.
- Lack of enforcement of existing ordinances."

The report cast doubt on the possibility that a serial killer was responsible for the deaths. For one thing, it noted, there were no physical injuries or trauma to the bodies, and the cause of death for each was attributed to drowning. Autopsies showed that the victims were alive prior to entering the water. There was no evidence of robbery, sexual assault, or other motive. Homicide by drowning is relatively rare: it occurs in less than 5% of murders. Then, too, there were no reported attacks on individuals who escaped to report the incident. As the Jeffery Dahmer case had demonstrated, even the most prolific serial killer does not have a 100% success rate.

The solution, according to the medical examiner's office, was for young people to take responsibility for their own safety by avoiding excessive alcohol consumption and staying in familiar surroundings among friends. It also suggested that the city build fences to keep people from falling into treacherous waters, install monitoring cameras in the park, and do a better job of enforcing liquor laws and park closing hours.[20]

Despite the 2004 report's reassuring findings, Homan's death two years later resurrected an undercurrent of fear and frustration, a feeling that something more insidious than merely overindulgence caused the strange string of La Crosse drownings.

Contributing to the apprehension was the terrifying regularity of the tragedies. A mere two-and-a-half years prior to Homan's drowning, Jared Dion, of the Waukesha County Town of Merton, was pulled from the Mississippi off La Crosse's Riverside Park on April 15, 2004. The muscular young man was a popular wrestler who had just turned twenty-one. It was known that he took one of the university's Safe Ride program buses from the university's sprawling campus into downtown La Crosse on April 9 and then disappeared. Apparently, Dion became inebriated and sometime early the next morning wandered off from friends waiting for the so-called drunk bus, the final ride returning to the school. Police officers indicated that the disoriented young man must have stumbled across the park before tumbling into the Mississippi River and drowning. The student had a blood-alcohol level of 0.289—more than three-and-a-half times what Wisconsin DUI law considers intoxicated. La Crosse County Medical Examiner John

Got Murder?

Steers said that Dion's body was in cold water for only five days, which prevented it from decomposing significantly.[21]

An autopsy on Monday, June 7, 2004, confirmed that a body spotted the previous Saturday floating in the Mississippi was that of a missing La Crosse resident who had vanished the previous December. The initial autopsy on the body of thirty-seven-year-old Gordon J. Stumlin "revealed that there was no trauma or injury to the body and no evidence of a crime." The examiner's report also indicated that Stumlin's body might have been in the water since his disappearance. Boaters saw the bloated corpse near Pettibone Resort. Stumlin's billfold and identification were found on the body, but authorities had a difficult time identifying the dead man because of the advanced state of decomposition.[22]

After his disappearance in 2003, it was thought Stumlin might have left La Crosse to live with out-of-town friends without notifying his mother, Norma Jean Thompson of Onalaska, or his two brothers, John Stumlin of La Crosse and Daniel Stumlin of Madison. La Crosse police and Wisconsin's Division of Criminal Investigation sought help from the public to determine how Stumlin might have died, but there were no leads. He was buried in a graveside ceremony in the secluded Lewis Valley Lutheran Church Cemetery.[23]

* * * *

Some cases in the string of deaths were unambiguous. In July 1997, brothers James and Richard Hlavaty were chased from the downtown corner of Third and Pearl streets by a gang of youths after a fight. The Hlavatys jumped into the river to escape and the group threw rocks at them while the two tried to swim away. While James escaped the Mississippi, his brother was less fortunate. The medical examiner said that nineteen-year-old Richard Hlavaty drowned as a result of the incident. The autopsy showed that the rocks caused numerous cuts and contusions, but the injuries were not severe enough to cause Hlavaty's death. Witnesses, including James Hlavaty, were unable to identify the attackers. If the suspects had been identified, they would have faced such charges as reckless homicide or manslaughter. An autopsy showed that Richard Hlavaty's blood alcohol content was 0.271 at the time of death.[24]

Other deaths were more puzzling. Charles Blatz, twenty-eight, of Kiel, a University of Wisconsin–Platteville student, disappeared early in the morning of September 28, 1997. Blatz had come to La Crosse for Oktoberfest and was last spotted alive heading to a downtown bar. Five days later, on October 3, an alert fisherman found the man floating face down in the river near the Seventh Street landing. His blood alcohol content was 0.31. The death was considered accidental. While there was no pre-death trauma, police said the body was mangled after it was struck by a barge. The water temperature was 66°F.[25]

In 1999, two years after her son's drowning, Henrietta Blatz sent posters to twelve La Crosse taverns at the start of another Oktoberfest. She urged, "Chuck is dead. Next could be you. Don't go anywhere alone." Mrs. Blatz indicated that she was simply trying to warn students to be careful and hoped to prevent another tragedy.[26]

Such warnings were much too late for Anthony D. "Tony" Skifton, nineteen, of 820 Caledonia Street, La Crosse, who wandered off from a house party carrying a case of beer on October 5, 1997. It was barely a month since Blatz had drowned. Last seen by a beer truck driver near Houska Park, Skifton appeared intoxicated. He disappeared and was not found until October 10, in Swift Creek near the Hood Street Bridge. Authorities theorized that Skifton, who could not swim, probably fell off a dock there. Foul play was not suspected because no injuries were noted on his body. Therefore, the medical examiner ruled the death an accident. However, "acute alcohol intoxication" was called a contributing factor in Skifton's death, especially given his blood alcohol content of 0.23.[27]

Nathan "Ko-cheese" Kapfer, twenty, a Viterbo College sophomore from Glendive, Montana, disappeared February 18, 1998, and was reported missing on February 22. A fisherman found the student's floating body on April 4. The water temperature was 37°F. The young man was last seen walking by himself.[28] Kapfer's wallet, his drinking citations, and baseball cap were neatly stacked near *The Big Indian*, the statue sometimes nicknamed "Hiawatha." Erected at the north end of

Got Murder?

Riverside Park, the statue commemorates the hometown legend that there will never be a natural disaster where the Mississippi, Black, and La Crosse rivers join.[29]

At the time of his death, Kapfer had already received four underage drinking citations. The medical examiner's report was simple: "Findings: Pulmonary Congestion. Watery gastric contents. Mastoid petrous ridge hemorrhage. No injuries of Trauma noted. Toxicology: Alcohol .22. Cause of death: Drowning. Manner: Undetermined."[30]

A year after their son's death, Doris and Mark Kapfer wrote in the *La Crosse Tribune*: "It was not our wish to have this story spotlighted again, but rather to bring into focus that the problems and perceptions that led to his death still exist. A major problem is the lack of awareness of the underage drinking problem. People either do not perceive it as a problem or think it will never effect [sic] them. They may not realize the dangers involved in such risk-taking behavior." The Kapfers pleaded with students and their friends, parents, and the broader community to be more aware of what could happen . . . what *did* happen to their underage son. "The ultimate goal should be prevention," they said.[31]

Still, the list of dead stubbornly and insidiously continued to grow. Jeffrey F. Geesey, twenty, a University of Wisconsin–La Crosse student, was last seen alive talking with two young women at Club Millennium in downtown La Crosse in the early hours of April 11, 1999. Police officers said the young man was also partying with two friends who were so drunk that they could not remember which bars they had visited on their rounds. They found no indication that trauma or foul play was involved in Geesey's death, the cause of which was listed as undetermined but probable drowning. Geesey had a history of attempted suicides, with scars on his left arm as a reminder of a previous try. His decomposing body was pulled from the river on May 24, 1999. The water temperature was 49°F. His toxicology reading was 0.42.[32]

"This summer I buried my son," wrote Laurie Geesey to the *La Crosse Tribune* after Jeffrey's death. She urged stricter watch over student identification and made other suggestions to curtail underage drinking. Mrs. Geesey concluded, "Jeffrey's future is over, but there are lots of other Jeffreys in Wisconsin who can be saved. Let's do something to make sure they have a future."[33]

A forensic pathologist with the Minnesota Regional Coroner's Office in Hastings, Minnesota, Dr. Lindsey Thomas, who conducted autopsies in the Skifton, Kapfer, and Geesey cases, reiterated that there were no links between the three tragedies except for the volatile mix of alcohol and the river's harsh waters.[34]

* * * *

Despite the pleading of anxious officials and a legion of grieving parents, that lethal cocktail of booze and frigid water kept claiming lives. Patrick Runingen, twenty-three, drowned in the Black River on March 1, 2001. On Thursday, March 8, authorities pulled the body of the young West Salem man from the river where it was spotted near the French Island beach. Witnesses said he appeared intoxicated as he left the Nut Bush Bar alongside the slow-moving Black, which feeds into the more powerful Mississippi. The medical examiner's office bluntly indicated that physical evidence showed "that subject had fallen through the ice. Autopsy was done. Cause of death drowning/no signs of altercation or trauma. Manner of death: accident."[35]

In case after case, the evidence was unambiguous: drowning deaths preceded by intoxication, with no other sign of injury or struggle. But put any set of points close enough to each other, and people will begin to see patterns; and for many La Crosse residents, the pattern of so many young men dying, one after the other, raised the invisible specter of a serial killer. After all, it had not been so long before that a string of missing young men in Milwaukee had been completely dismissed by authorities—until an almost accidental encounter led them to the horror chamber of Jeffery Dahmer. Could police be certain that a similar fiend wasn't stalking the streets of La Crosse?

Questions persisted. Why were women not dying in the same numbers as the men? "Maybe it's because women are taught from a young age to stay together. There just isn't the panic when a guy wanders off. We're tough and macho and can watch out for ourselves, especially when we've been drinking," wrote *La Crosse Tribune* columnist Matt James. Why La Crosse? James discussed the beauty of the city, its parks, and water. "But the downside of all that beauty is a powerful river that doesn't know any better. It's not a sparkling little lake that you tumble into, crawl out and have a good laugh. There is a reason it happens more here than anywhere else. We have the perfect setup for a tragedy," he concluded.[36]

Even as the drowning cases mounted, the city and police positions remained constant. Captain James Schleifer, chief of the La Crosse Police Department's detective bureau, regularly pointed out that there were no signs of trauma, identification was found on the victims, and there were no indications of robbery. These factors suggested that at least Blatz, Skifton, Kapfer, and Geesey were not victims of homicide. La Crosse officials have often said that if a serial killer was involved, the murderer was amazingly successful every time he struck; over these years in which the various deaths were recorded, authorities had not received reports of any unsuccessful murder attempts, such as someone being pushed into the water.[37]

This police position did not sit well with some of La Crosse's residents, particularly those within the student community. At a citywide meeting in 2004, Chief Edward Kondracki reiterated that investigators did not have any evidence of crimes being committed in the deaths. He believed concerns should be placed elsewhere. "I personally see these young men as victims of an alcohol culture that targets them and encourages binge drinking," he said. For this, he was roundly heckled. Some even accused the police of pushing drunken students into the river. The overflow crowd of 1,500 in the Central High School auditorium finally quieted shamefacedly when police Lieutenant Dan Marcou chastised the audience for theorizing about murders. His nephew, Anthony Skifton, drowned in the river after leaving a party drunk in October 1997. "This community has a drinking problem," said the tearful Marcou. "It will never fix itself because it denies and denies. When is the community going to pull its head out of the sand and fix this?"[38]

Despite police denials, detectives from New York City gave the serial killer theory some credibility when they visited Wisconsin in 2005. The detectives were investigating a series of drownings in

Brooklyn and were looking into any correlation. If there was a serial killer involved, they speculated that he might have moved between communities. But no links were discovered between the East Coast tragedy and the Midwest drownings.[39]

By 2006, most of the recommendations of a 2004 drowning task force has been acted on. After a delay due to liability concerns, the city finally approved gates at the entrances to the Riverside Park levee. The La Crosse Common Council made it harder to register beer kegs and increased police patrols of drinking parties. Hot lines were established to gather information about the drownings, and efforts to educate young people about the dangers of drinking and wandering off alone were redoubled.[40]

And yet, barely two weeks after Luke Homan's death and burial, at 1:16 a.m., Sunday, October 15, 2006, a drunken twenty-two-year-old University of Wisconsin–La Crosse student was picked up by police. Discovered lying in the grass at the south end of Riverside Park, he was found talking on his cell phone sprawled outside the Logistics Health building, a short distance from the river. The man was taken to Gundersen Lutheran Medical Center for detoxification with a 0.19 blood-alcohol level. The student told police officers he was heading home but he was stumbling, slurring his speech, and was not wearing warm clothing. Although he lived east of the park, the student informed police he lived to the north.[41]

To date, no evidence has surfaced suggesting that a deranged killer stalks young men in the back alleys of La Crosse. And yet, in 2004, La Crosse police issued 1,095 citations for underage drinking by those aged eighteen to twenty. In 2005, police issued 1,350 citations. By September 2006, authorities had issued 799 citations. So it seems that a very real killer is on the loose, unchecked.

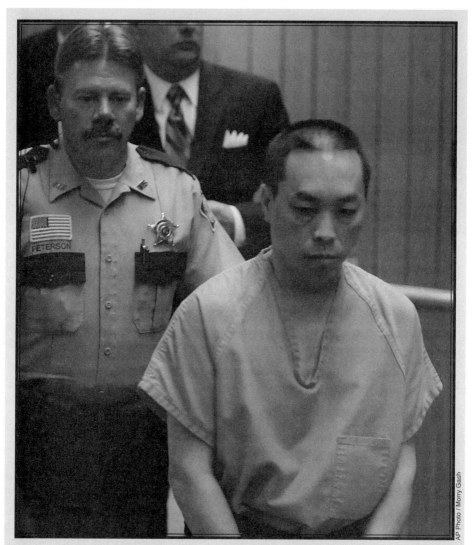

Deer hunting gone terribly wrong: Chai Soua Vang on his way to prison.

Chapter 10

Death Stalks the Blue Hills

Northwestern Wisconsin Woods
November 21, 2004
Death toll: 6
Wounded: 2

There've been a lot of surprises, but I've never imagined such a horrible thing as this.

—Pete Weatherhead, Birchwood police chief[1]

Wisconsinites are passionate about their *Odocoileus virginianus*, the scientific name for the state's abundant white-tailed deer. Deer season in Wisconsin draws out the best and, sometimes, the worst within the hunter world as the availability of prime hunting land decreases and more space is posted with No Trespassing or No Hunting warnings. Yet hunting remains popular, with more than half a million licenses issued by the Wisconsin Department of Natural Resources issued every year.[2]

This delicate balance between private property rights and hunters' enthusiasm became the basis for a deadly confrontation in 2004. Underlying racial issues clouded the situation and perhaps contributed to the horror.

Opening day that year, Saturday, November 20, was damp, with mist hanging low on the hills and threatening, overcast skies blanketing most of the state. It was hard to track deer because of the lack of snow; the drizzle that dampened the forest floor made it hard to hear deer

Got Murder?

moving through the woods. Conditions grew better by the afternoon, and Sunday dawned even brighter.[3]

Hunting license sales hit 644,233, only 585 short of the 2003 total of 644,818. But a rise in hunting accidents had Wisconsin's wardens concerned as the nine-day gun-deer season was about to start. Already in 2004, hunters seemed to be shooting themselves and each other at a much higher rate than in 2003. By November 19, twenty-nine had been wounded in the small-game and archery seasons compared with seventeen at the same time the previous year. None of the accidents, however, were fatal, even the one in which an Antigo man was shot in the neck by an arrow as he was sitting in his car. All the same, officials waited anxiously to see what the onslaught of men with shotguns would bring.[4]

The answer, terrible as it was, would come by noon of the season's second day. Five hunters were slain and three were wounded in a shooting rampage in the Sawyer County town of Meteor, about 120 miles northeast of the Twin Cities. One of the wounded died the next day. Chai Soua Vang, thirty-six, a Hmong truck driver and former soldier from St. Paul, Minnesota, was arrested just before dark, about five hours after the killings. Jeremy Peery, a twenty-eight-year-old DNR game warden, captured Vang around 4 p.m. on De Jung Road, a trail south of Deer Lake about a mile from the massacre. Vang was picked up just across the Sawyer County border in Rusk County in what are called the Blue Hills. He was carrying a SKS semiautomatic assault rifle. The weapon's twenty-round chamber was empty. After his arrest, Vang was held in the Sawyer County Jail in Hayward on cash bail of $2.5 million.[5]

Vang's rampage apparently started after a hunting party saw him in their tree stand, a platform that elevates hunters above the ground and out of the deer's line of sight. Two of the aggrieved hunters were the property owners, and did not recognize Vang; a confrontation resulted and weapons were fired. One of the wounded called for help on a walkie-talkie, and when his hunting partners arrived they also were shot. The victims were gunned down as they fled from their pursuer, their bodies later found scattered across a hundred-yard swath of ground.[6]

Those killed on the scene were Robert Crotteau, forty-two; his son, Joey Crotteau, twenty; Al Laski, forty-three; Mark Roidt, twenty-eight; and Jessica Willers, twenty-seven. The wounded included Dennis (Denny) Drew, fifty-five; his brother-in-law Lauren Hesebeck, forty-eight; and Terry Willers, forty-seven, Jessica Willers' father. Drew would die of extensive wounds to his abdomen after a three-hour surgery the next day. The victims were in a party of about fourteen friends and relatives who gathered each year to hunt on land owned by Crotteau and the elder Willers.[7]

One of the hunters was able to write Vang's hunting tag number, 685505, in the dust on an all-terrain vehicle parked at the scene. The tag, matching the number on Vang's back when he was taken into custody, made it easy to identify him. The injured tried calling for aid on their cell phones, but reception was bad in the heavily wooded, rolling countryside.

Two of the hunting party made it into the woods without being attacked. Brandon Willers was able to get his father, Terry, into his pickup and drove him to Rice Lake's Lakeview Medical Center. Later, another member of the hunting party ferried the wounded Drew and Hesebeck to Ed's Pit Stop, a deer-kill registration site in Birchwood, where they were met by medical personnel and taken to area hospitals. Hesebeck was sent to the Rice Lake hospital and the critically wounded Drew died November 22, after being airlifted to St. Joseph's Hospital in Marshfield.[8]

Police, led by Birchwood Chief Peter Weatherhead and armed with military-style rifles, walked into the forest, alert for an ambush. Deputies from three counties and state wardens quickly cordoned off the area and used dogs and helicopters to try to find the shooter. Authorities cruised logging trails and narrow, bumpy back roads where the massacre occurred, using loudspeakers to warn other hunters to flee.[9]

The flood of lawmen and game officials were able to arrest Vang when he eventually emerged from the forested area. Vang had apparently strayed from public land to the private property where the shootings took place. Without a compass, the Minnesotan had become lost and was aided by Walter Cieslak and Darrell Glass, two other hunters not involved in the incident. On his ATV, Cieslak gave Vang a ride toward to his cabin in northern Rusk County, only a few miles from the shooting scene in southwestern Sawyer County. Vang was then arrested by the authorities who had been searching for him.[10]

According to police reports, Vang had climbed up the tree stand and was discovered by Terry Willers who radioed Crotteau at their hunting shack a quarter mile away. Willers then approached Vang and asked him to leave. According to the surviving hunters, Vang crawled down from the stand and walked a short distance before taking off the scope of the semiautomatic rifle he carried and opening fire. Willers was the first hit but was able to radio to others that the party was being fired upon. As more hunters came closer, Vang kept firing and hit several more than once, even as they dove for cover. Three of the victims were shot from fifty yards or more, according to doctors.[11]

Back at the cabin, the unarmed Laski and Jessica Willers climbed onto an ATV and rode out to the scene. Vang, an avid hunter who was dressed in the requisite blaze orange, shot and killed both as they approached, then ran into the woods.

The entire group of killed and wounded hunters was from in and around the close-knit community of Rice Lake, a town of 8,300 adjacent to a 939-acre lake of the same name. The murders delivered a stunning blow to residents' sense of security and neighborliness.[12]

Vang, on the other hand, lived in East St. Paul in a diverse working class neighborhood where he also raised chickens, a favorite hobby of many Hmong immigrants. After siding with American forces during the Vietnam War, Hmong refugees were forced out of their homes in the Laotian highlands; many eventually came to the United States. The Twin Cities have the nation's largest urban Hmong population, with sixty thousand living in Minnesota.[13]

Vang arrived in the United States from Laos in 1980. At the time of the shootings, he was a married army veteran with six children, spoke English, and was an American citizen. During his six years in the California National Guard, Vang earned an Army Service Ribbon as a sharpshooter with the M-16 rifle, according to Army Human Resources Command records. A medical clerk, Vang was released from the military in 1997, living for a time in California before coming to Minnesota. Described by some neighbors as standoffish, community organizers who worked with the Hmong said that alleged aloofness was a common trait among such immigrants. Vang was considered a respected spiritual leader, often leading traditional Hmong ceremonies at funerals and feasts.[14]

All the same, St. Paul police had been called to his home five times since June 2003, although none of the calls was for a violent incident. Two were for domestic disturbances, two for theft complaints, and one was for a warrant that did not involve Vang, who was not arrested in any of the instances. However, Minneapolis police said they did arrest Vang on Christmas Eve 2001, when he threatened to kill his wife with a gun. No charge was brought because the woman would not file a complaint and did not cooperate with the officers.[15]

Not unlike other sportsmen, Hmong immigrants have a strong tradition of hunting, love of the land, and camaraderie. Vang had held Minnesota Department of Natural Resources hunting and fishing licenses since 2001. In Minnesota, he was cited for a fishing violation in 2001 after taking ninety-three crappies over the limit. Vang had passed all required weapons safety courses and also had a valid Wisconsin firearms license for 2004. Although Hmong hunters had hunting rules and regulations explained to them in their own language, rural landowners in both Minnesota and Wisconsin had complained that some of the former refugees were not familiar with the concept of private property and hunted wherever they wanted. In 2004, there were fourteen thousand licensed hunters of Hmong heritage in Wisconsin. The only DNR staff person assigned to act as a liaison with the community at the time was Kou Xiong, who worked only half time organizing meetings and workshops to explain Wisconsin's regulations. At the same time, Minnesota had five staffers working with only seven thousand Hmong hunters.[16]

Vang was charged with a trespassing offense while hunting with Ber Xiong in Wisconsin's Green Lake County in 2002, apparently after straying from private land where he had a permit to hunt to restricted property owned by Badger Mining. The two men and Xiong's twelve-year-old son, Dang, left peacefully when requested to do so by a Badger employee. Vang and Xiong were given $244 fines, although there is no record of Vang's payment.[17]

Vang's account of what occurred in the woods during the bloody Sunday in November 2004 understandably diverged from the unprovoked attack described by witnesses. Vang told police interviewers that he feared for his life after the hunters threatened him and used racial epithets, such as "gook" and "chink." He claimed he needed to return fire because of the shots aimed at him and at one time said one of the hunters actually shot his friends. Vang said he reversed his coat from orange to camouflage and had to reload his weapon. He did admit that he crept up on one of the unarmed victims and shot him in the back as the man fled. Yet mental health experts interviewed at the time said Vang's actions that day did not seem to indicate that he was afraid.[18]

At 10:15 a.m., Monday, investigators including an FBI agent read Vang his rights and made sure he understood them; Vang said he wanted to talk with a lawyer. The interview ended, but about fifteen minutes afterward, according to court records, Vang said he still wanted to talk and did so in detail after signing a statement and again being read his rights.[19]

Vang claimed he saw Terry Willers point his rifle at him. Subsequently, the Minnesota man dropped into a crouch position as Willers allegedly fired, the bullet striking the ground thirty to forty feet behind him. Vang said he then fired two rounds at Willers, the second hitting him in the neck and causing the Wisconsinite to fall to the ground. As the other men in the party ran away, Vang kept shooting, seeing Denny Drew and Mark Roidt collapse. Lauren Hesebeck tried to hide behind an ATV, but Vang walked around it and shot him in the shoulder. Vang admitted he chased Robert Crotteau and his son, Joey, shot the unarmed boy in the back, heard him groaning, and then walked away. Vang also said he shot another hunter, believed to be the elder Crotteau.[20]

Death Stalks the Blue Hills

Responding to the call for help, Carter Crotteau, eighteen, drove toward the shootings on an ATV and picked up Brandon Willers, twenty-three. They were able to take the wounded Terry Willers from the scene without being fired on. Then, Vang said, Al Laski and Jessica Willers roared up on another ATV and he began running. When the small vehicle passed him, Vang said the driver removed a gun from his shoulder while holding onto the handle bar, but that he was able to fire three or four times at the pair, hitting them. Vang went back to where the others were downed, firing another round at Hesebeck, who told police that he fired back. Vang took off, deciding he would not shoot anyone else, and tossed his ammunition into a marsh. When he heard planes overhead, he decided he should surrender. Shortly afterward, Vang met the other hunters who helped him out of the woods.[21]

At a Monday afternoon press conference, Sawyer County Sheriff James Meier said Vang was "extremely calm," adding, "I find it frightening." Governor Jim Doyle also attended the media event and visited with the victims and their families. He said the incident was "a terrible tragedy to such a great family tradition. . . . On behalf of all the citizens of Wisconsin, I express my deepest condolences." The governor went on to say, "Our prayers and thoughts go out to the community."[22]

As Circuit Judge Norman L. Yackel signed a court order indicating there was probable cause to try the St. Paul man for the murders, some two dozen Hmong leaders, meeting at the Lao Family Community Center west of the Minnesota State Capitol, voiced concerns about racial tension in the Minnesota and Wisconsin woods. They were alarmed by Vang's testimony that he was set off by racial slurs and that the others shot at him first. They also indicated that the shootings were "in no way" representative of the wider Hmong community. Not everyone accepted the disavowal; one member of an Eau Claire area rod and gun club went so far as to warn Hmong hunters at a public forum to stay out of the woods.[23]

Over the next few days, the shooting victims were buried. The people of Rice Lake made an impressive demonstration of their unity and support for the families of the slain, as hundreds turned out for memorial services.[24]

On Monday, November 29, Vang was charged with first-degree intentional homicide and use of a dangerous weapon. Prosecutors in the state attorney general's office also charged Vang with two counts of attempted first-degree homicide for shooting and wounding Lauren Hesebeck and Terry Willers. The official complaint was at odds with Vang's account of the events. The complaint said that only Terry Willers was armed during Vang's initial rampage, and that Hesebeck eventually used Willers' gun to fire at Vang, chasing him away and ending the attack. At least twenty shots were fired in the confrontation. Although Vang said that Laski and Jessica Willers had a rifle when they passed him on their ATV, no weapon was found near their bodies.[25]

A shackled Vang made his first court appearance Tuesday, November 30, to answer the charges against him. Flanked by his Milwaukee attorneys, Steven Kohn and Jonathan Smith, Vang appeared before Judge Yackel in the secure basement of the county sheriff's department as a precaution in case someone might have wanted to take revenge. More than a dozen journalists attended the ten-minute session. A closed-circuit television had been set up in a courtroom across the street to accommodate the public, but no one took advantage of the screening.[26]

Vang's attorneys waived his right to a preliminary hearing and entered pleas of not guilty on Wednesday, December 29. A third count of first-degree attempted homicide was added to the charges in the state's original complaint, indicating that Vang tried to kill Lauren Hesebeck twice. However, Vang's lawyers later objected, saying he could not be charged twice for the same crime. Following the pleas, a trial date of September 12, 2005, was set and the defense was given until March 1 to file motions in the case. A plea of not guilty by reason of insanity was considered by Vang's legal representative and the accused killer began undergoing examination by two psychologists.[27]

Vang's defense team filed motions declaring that excessive pretrial publicity and racial prejudice deprived Vang of his right to a fair trial in Sawyer County. His lawyers pointed to fliers circulating in the community and on online blogs about the case that called Vang names and slammed the defense teams as "Jews."[28] The state prosecutors countered by arguing that the legitimate media coverage was informational, not inflammatory, and that the defense failed to prove any prejudice against Vang. Attorney General Peg Lautenschlager argued that Vang's attorneys and the court could weed out any prospective jurors with preconceived ideas of the accused's guilt or innocence, and that the trial should stay in Sawyer County. [29] In June, Sawyer County Judge Yackel ruled that the trial would be held in his jurisdiction, but the jury would be selected from Dane County, about three hundred miles south of where the shootings occurred.[30]

Ruling out an insanity defense or plea bargain, Vang claimed he shot the victims in self-defense, according to court papers released Friday, August 26. "This is not a case that can be resolved through plea negotiations," said defense attorney Kohn. "There is so much disagreement on the facts that there's no real middle ground, and the charges as now alleged are not something you plead guilty to; they carry mandatory life terms."[31]

The jury selection was accomplished quickly; the process took only two hours, although Judge Yackel had set aside two days for it. Ten women and four men were chosen to hear the case. Helping speed the selection, about four hundred people in Dane County received questionnaires that filtered out those who could not be sequestered, were biased, or already had determined Vang's guilt or innocence.[32]

Vang's trial began Saturday, September 10. As he entered the courtroom, he nodded to his family and supporters. Attorney General Lautenschlager, taking the lead prosecutor's role, requested that jurors use "common sense" to convict Vang. The defense asked the jurors to wait until all the evidence was presented before reaching a conclusion. Both sides then gave detailed and conflicting accounts of what transpired that November afternoon the previous year. Many of the victims' friends and relatives in the courtroom cried as a videotape taken shortly after the murders showed the five victims sprawled in the woods.[33]

Survivor Terry Willers was the first to take the witness stand on the second day of the trial. Testifying with a stoic demeanor, he denied that any racial slurs were used in the confrontation. Willers said that he yelled, "Don't you shoot at me, you son of a bitch," when Vang pointed his weapon at him. He said Vang then fired several times, hitting him. Another testimony that day focused on what happened after the shootings, with Willers' son, Brandon, and Denny Drew's brother, David, describing how they heard radio calls asking for assistance. Brandon Willers, who had transported his father out of the woods in the truck, recalled that his father kept saying, "It was stupid, it was stupid."[34]

In his testimony on September 13, Lauren Hesbeck, the second survivor, agreed that Vang initially was walking away from the hunting party but then turned and fired. He also indicated that when landowner Robert Crotteau first challenged Vang, he swore roundly at the interloper, threatening to beat him and report him to authorities. But he denied that Crotteau used racial slurs.[35]

When Vang had his chance to testify over the course of three hours on Thursday, September 15, he said that he feared for his life and started shooting only after another hunter's shot narrowly missed him. He demonstrated ducking around trees and traversing the rugged ground while he chased after the fleeing hunters. "I was afraid. I was confused. I wished it wasn't happening," Vang testified, adding that the problems began when he became lost. He said that he apologized to Willers when he crawled down out of the tree stand but Crotteau called him a "chink" and a "gook" and threatened him. When he completed his testimony, Vang held his hands together and knelt in front of ten or so of his family who had gathered in the courtroom. They spoke briefly in Hmong before the accused was led away.[36]

In her closing arguments Friday, Attorney General Lautenschlager said that Vang had responded from anger, not fear, as he stalked his victims. "His response was grossly disproportionate to whatever remarks were made," Lautenschlager added later. She also indicated that the incident was a disagreement gone bad between two hunting parties, not a confrontation between different races.[37]

The jury took three hours to convict Vang, rejecting his self-defense claims. It found him guilty of six counts of first-degree intentional homicide and three counts of attempted homicide. Families on both sides cried as the verdict was announced. The hunters' families felt their dead relatives were vindicated, but Vang's family told reporters he was unfairly convicted and that the jury didn't take into consideration that he faced a hostile situation.

On November 8, Judge Yackel sentenced Vang to six consecutive life terms without parole, calling him a "ticking time bomb" and that the man demonstrated a "pattern of antisocial conduct."[38] After first being incarcerated at the Dodge Correctional Institution in Waupun, Vang was transferred to Iowa State Penitentiary in Fort Madison for precautionary safety concerns in April 2006.[39]

Memories of the dead hunters remained fresh. More than $400,000 was contributed to a survivors and victims fund at Dairy State Bank in Rice Lake, earmarked for funeral services, hospital bills, attorney fees, and college tuition for the children of the deceased.[40] Hunters Memorial Park in Rice Lake—an acre of land with a basketball court, picnic areas, green space, and a pavilion with a kitchen—was dedicated in August 2006, Area contractors donated much of the labor and materials for the park. Individuals and hunting groups paid $100 each to inscribe messages on fifteen hundred bricks that make a walkway from the parking lot to the pavilion; rock star, outdoor fan, and hunting advocate Ted Nugent bought three.[41]

Even after the tragedy, hunters continued their traditional quest in the woods that year, and some commented that continuing the hunt was what the dead would have wanted them to do.[42]

Today, the wind ruffles through the forests carpeting the picturesque Blue Hills, beautiful in their northern Wisconsin ruggedness. On the far side of the world, in the Southeast Asian highlands where Vang was born, another breeze dances. But it's calm within the walls of that Iowa penitentiary, a place where a man with time on his hands can only remember how life once was.

But the outside world remains a deadly place. A chance encounter between squirrel hunters during the unseasonably warm winter of 2007 resulted in the death of another Hmong refugee, Cha Vang, thirty, a Green Bay factory worker. Vang was reported missing by friends on

Got Murder?

January 5; his partially concealed body was found by a search dog the next day. He allegedly was stabbed and killed by twenty-eight-year-old James A. Nichols of Peshtigo. Nichols had gunshot wounds in both hands but nevertheless was arrested on homicide charges after going to a hospital for treatment of his injuries. Both men were in the Peshtigo Harbor Wildlife Area when the tragic incident—perhaps due to an argument over hunting territory—occurred.[43]

Terry Ratzmann parked his pickup in the lot of the Sheraton Hotel in Brookfield, walked inside, and gunned down seven members of his church.

Chapter 11

Church of the Living Horror

Brookfield, Wisconsin
March 12, 2005
Death toll: 7 victims, plus 1 slayer suicide
Wounded: 4

He planned to shoot us all.

—Chandra Frazier[1]

March 2005, has earned the dubious title of "The Month of Death." On March 9, Bart Ross, a disfigured cancer patient who unsuccessfully sued his doctors for malpractice, shot and killed himself on a side street in West Allis. Police were seeking Ross for the double murders on February 28 of the mother and husband of United States District Court Judge Joan Humphrey Lefkow. The two were shot mobster-style in the judge's North Chicago home. Ross had appeared before the judge in his case against the physicians, a suit that Lefkow dismissed. After his suicide, authorities found a detailed confession in Ross' van describing the murders. Authorities said that the killings were the first in the United States in which family members were slain in revenge for a judges ruling.[2]

On March 11, in Atlanta, Georgia, rape suspect Brian Nichols, thirty-three, overpowered a guard and killed a judge, a court reporter, and a deputy sheriff in a shooting spree that began in the Fulton County Courthouse. He later turned himself in to police after an intensive

Got Murder?

manhunt.[3] But Georgia was a long way from Milwaukee and nobody was really giving much thought to the unfortunate Ross by the time March 12 rolled around. Despite the chill, it was a festive morning for the 50 or 60 congregants of the Living Church of God. Dressed in their best, the racially mixed group of assorted ages were holding services in the Wisconsin Room of the Sheraton Milwaukee Brookfield Hotel that Saturday, just south of busy Interstate 94 along a strip of other hotels and fast-food outlets.

The Wisconsin assemblage was one of two hundred like-minded congregations of about sixty-three hundred adherents in forty countries who observed Saturday as the true Christian Sabbath. Members considered themselves the spiritual heirs of the original Jerusalem Church of the New Testament.[4]

The nondenominational Living Church of God was founded in the 1990s after a split from the Worldwide Church of God amid contentions over docrine and governance. From that split came the Global Church of God, which in turn became divided, with one of the larger groups becoming the Living Church of God. In 2003, this church moved its headquarters to Charlotte, North Carolina, from San Diego and began broadcasts of a program called *Tomorrow's World* heard in cities such as Wausau, Wisconsin, and similar mid-tier markets.[5]

Randy Gregory, pastor of the Milwaukee branch of the Living Church of God, was a denomination veteran, traveling with his wife and children throughout the Midwest to serve in several cities. Considered friendly but reserved, Gregory and his family lived in a comfortable two-story home on a quiet cul-de-sac in Gurnee, Illinois. They had moved there from Texas in 2000 because it was the midway point between Milwaukee and Chicago, where Gregory also had a congregation. The couple's youngest son, James, was a junior at Warren Township High School. Their oldest, Jonathan, had recently concluded studies at the University of Wisconsin–Parkside.[6]

For at least four years, members of the Living Church of God drove to Brookfield from around northern Illinois and southeastern Wisconsin to pray and socialize in rented space at the hotel. This particularly bright, snowy spring weekend, they were to hold a talent show with a ventriloquist and a potluck dinner after services. Everyone was in high spirits. The prayer session had been moved back from its usual 10 a.m. starting time to 12:30 p.m. to accommodate the afternoon activities.[7]

None of the believers had any inkling that within minutes, seven of them would be murdered. They would be killed by one of their own, Terry Ratzmann, a forty-four-year-old bachelor who then took his own life. Four of their friends would be seriously wounded.

The ensuing massacre remains one of the worst mass murders in Wisconsin history. The carnage was the second deadly hotel shooting in the Milwaukee area in less than a year. On November 5, 2004, two guests had been murdered in another shooting rampage at an Oak Creek hotel.

It was a busy morning at the Sheraton. The lobby was packed with young hockey players eager to head to a tournament. Other youngsters frolicked in the hotel pool. A Catholic group was also holding a conference at the Sheraton that weekend. They were attending Mass in one of the hotel meeting rooms, to be followed by lunch.

The morning was also hectic at the Waukesha County Communications Center. False alarms. Fire reports. An auto crash. Suicide threats. Dispatchers shook their heads, wondering about the day's next catastrophe.[8]

The Living Church of God worshippers started their prayer services around 12:30 p.m. Wearing dark glasses, Terry Ratzmann actually arrived early, parking his silver Toyota pickup in his usual spot. He then left briefly, returning to his home for a half hour. His mother, Shirley, was still in bed when Ratzmann first left the house and she greeted him when he came home. When he arrived back at the Sheraton, Ratzmann carried a briefcase but remained outside the room where the service had started. Ratzmann had missed the previous week's prayers for some reason.[9]

Arriving some eight minutes after the service started, Chandra Frazier took a seat in the third row from the back, next to Gerald Miller. Frazier was in front of Pastor Randy Gregory, his wife, Marjean, and their son, James, all of whom were in the back row of the crowded room. They arrived around 12:28 p.m. and had said hello to Ratzmann as he walked out the first time. Frazier began leafing through her Bible and reviewing some notes she had made about some of the passages. Her sixty-one-year-old mother, Ella, and Ella's husband, Earnest, fifty-nine, found a place to sit in the third row and settled in to pray. The older woman had passed Ratzmann in the hallway outside, but he hadn't sat next to her as he often did. She and Ratzmann liked to chat about gardening and their trips to Australia.[10]

Harold Diekmeier, a native of Cudahy, was a union carpenter who had moved to Delafield in 1994. He loved stock cars and strolling with his German shepherd, Dina. Diekmeier sat in a back row, intent on a short homily delivered by his son, Glenn, about Jonah in the belly of the whaled by his son, Glenn . Father and son often worked together on building projects around the Milwaukee area. [11]

Twenty minutes or so into the service, Ratzmann, wearing blue jeans and a brown jacket, entered the room and stood at the rear, directly behind the Gregorys where the pastor was studying his sermon. Church member Fred Critari glanced up at Ratzmann and then looked down at his prayer book. He was in charge of the public address system, so he, his wife, Gloria, and their granddaughter, Lindsay, were sitting in their usual places at the rear. [12]

Ratzmann's fellow worshipers had no idea that the man had in his briefcase a 9 mm Beretta he had purchased a few days earlier. After his first brief visit to the hotel that morning, Ratzmann had gone back to his house in nearby New Berlin and apparently exchanged his Bible for the pistol.[13]

About 12:51 p.m., Ratzmann glanced around the room and pulled the pistol from his briefcase. A volley of twenty-two gunshots echoed through the room. Witnesses later said the sound was like rapidly popping balloons. Jacodi Morris, thirteen, thought at first that an electrical circuit blew. Anne Varichak assumed it was some children's prank. But from his vantage point at the front of the congregation, Glenn Diekmeier could see Ratzmann with his weapon, and he ducked behind the podium. His father, however, stood up at the sound of the gunfire—and was immediately killed.[14] Ratzmann walked toward the right side of the room, firing as he strolled deliberately along the rows of chairs. After hitting the pastor in the back, he shot Marjean and James Gregory and Bart Oliver, a fifteen-year-old sitting in front of the pastor's family. Oliver's cousin, Robert Geiger, yelled out, "Not Bart!" But it was too late. The teen crumbled to the floor, dead.[15]

In the chaos, worshippers scrambled for cover, overturning chairs and tossing aside songbooks. People piled on each other to protect their loved ones. As the shooter reloaded, congregant David Mohr pleaded with Ratzmann to stop and consider what he was doing.[16] Ignoring Mohr, the gunman fired three more times and turned the gun on himself, blasting a hole in his right temple, splattering a wide swath of brains and gore. He fell to the floor near a table.

Following that single minute of murderous rage, there was an oppressive silence. The once peaceful room was heavy with the stench of death. Within seconds, that brief, stunning calm was overcome by desperate wailing for aid and pleas for God's mercy.[17]

After the shooting, Mrs. Gregory was barely alive, painfully crying for help and water. A bullet had entered her shoulder and had come through her chest. Gerald Miller, who was also shot, had thrown himself over a woman sitting next to him. Staggering to his feet, he cried out, "It's real," and stumbled over to the aisle where he collapsed. A pool of sticky, warm blood slowly puddled around his body. [18]

Using a cell phone, one breathless caller was the first to reach dispatcher Kerri Weindorfer at the county emergency communications center. The man's voice gasped out that at least six people had been shot. "Oh, crap," Weindorfer thought. Four additional 911 messages came in in less than a minute. Several callers were hysterical, so distraught they could not even explain where the shootings had occurred. More calls then flooded the police lines, interspersed with more typical mundane phone messages, as the ten dispatchers cringed. They could hear screaming in the background.[19]

Within three minutes after the initial call was received, Officer Frank Riederer and three other Brookfield police officers burst into the death room, M-16 semiautomatic rifles ready to fire. Another dozen Waukesha County police and fire departments assembled at the scene to assist as needed.[20]

An estimated seventy-five witnesses, many snugly wrapped in blankets, were divided among one of the hotel's guest suites and three meeting rooms to write out statements. Tearful survivors asked what would happen to the victims' bodies, where the wounded were being treated, and how to help the children cope with what they had witnessed.[21]

Waukesha County District Attorney Paul Bucher was shocked when viewing the crime scene. Later, shaking his head, he would say," Heartbreaking. Overwhelming. Human carnage."[22]

The authorities began counting the dead, listing them dispassionately as relatives wailed: Randy L. Gregory, fifty, Gurnee; James Gregory, seventeen, Gurnee; Harold Diekmeier, seventy-four, Delafield; Richard W. Reeves, fifty-eight, Cudahy; Bart Oliver, fifteen, Waukesha; Gloria Critari, fifty-five, Cudahy; and Gerald Miller, forty-four, Erin. The wounded included: Marjean Gregory, fifty-two, Gurnee; Angel Varichak, nineteen, Hellenville; Matthew Kaulbach, twenty-one, Pewaukee; and Lindsay Maughmer, ten, Cudahy.

Four of the victims died at the hotel: James Gregory, Diekmeier, Critari, and Oliver. Those dying at Froedtert Memorial Lutheran Hospital were Pastor Gregory, Reeves, and Miller. Twenty-five physicians, nurses, and technicians attended the six wounded and dying victims who arrived within minutes of each other. Young Maughmer was cared for at Children's Hospital of Wisconsin in Wauwatosa and later released.[23]

The crime scene took on a surrealistic air. At one end of the building, draped bodies of the dead were cordoned off by police. Curious passersby overflowed the parking lot, seeking a glimpse of the action. A few people left flowers near a side entrance where emergency vehicles and television camera trucks were arrayed. Within an hour, registered hotel guests were allowed to come and go at will. At the far end of the facility, new arrivals were already checking in, oblivious to the investigation going on down the hall.[24]

Four days of vigils and funerals followed the massacre, allowing the healing to begin. The slaying brought the congregation even closer together, as they put the killings into God's hands. Few seemed ready to question the why and wherefore of the slayings.[25]

But the faith of at least one person was shaken by the deaths. Claiming that the church shooting proved that God didn't exist, a woman motorist rammed her auto into Waukesha's St. Joseph's Catholic Church at 11 p.m. the night of the massacre. The distraught woman totaled her car but did not damage the side of the church. She was subsequently taken to the Waukesha County Mental Health Center.[26]

Eight hundred pages of grimly detailed documents pertaining to the case were released in September 2005, including extensive interviews with surviving congregation members. Investigators could not identify a motive, but police and District Attorney Bucher indicated that the lonely, depressed Ratzmann apparently had targeted Pastor Gregory and his family. No single reason was determined.[27]

Ratzmann, forty-four, was a bachelor who lived with his mother and sister in a small, comfortable, seventy-five-year-old home on New Berlin's north side. Joining the church just a few years before his 2005 rampage, Ratzmann was a devoted church member and once turned down an invitation to a wedding because it conflicted with the group's Saturday services. Yet he had a dark undercurrent to his nature, often snapping back at friends or being uncommunicative even with people he knew. Called "smart" by his friends, Ratzmann lacked social skills yet was still uncomfortable about being single. His church did not permit members to date nonmembers, so a singles organization it sponsored was subsequently the only pool from which he could find a potential wife.[28]

Folks who lived in Ratzmann's neighborhood thought he was generally pleasant, called "a normal Joe" who built his own greenhouse and a garage. Neighbor Patricia Herrmann, seventy-two, said Ratzmann often brought fresh tomatoes and zucchini to her door in summer. She and the Ratzmanns both lived on the same block since the 1970s. "There's never been any problems over there at all, they've never had any police over there or anything like that," Herrmann said. "They're just a nice quiet family. I was never aware that he could do anything like that."[29]

Got Murder?

Ratzmann's contractor job as a computer engineer at GE Healthcare was about to terminate on March 25. Authorities indicated that didn't seem to be root cause of his depression, yet the man had walked out of a February 26 sermon about how misfortune befalls those who have made bad choices. In taped remarks aired that day, church leader Roderick C. Meredith also discussed what he called a coming "spiritual war" that was to change the world.

Terry Ratzmann always asserted to friends that he never shot a thing in his life. In fact, one acquaintance said that "the guy caught bunny rabbits in a humane trap and drove twenty miles to release them, because he didn't want to kill them." He had a fish tank in which he raised trout, and enjoyed camping, albeit alone, and listening to the coyotes howling.[30]

Martyrdom in Milwaukee, a book released in the summer of 2006, questioned whether or not Satan had a role in the Brookfield church slayings. Congregant Thomas Geiger, who wrote the work, said that he was temporarily barred from services because of writing that his longtime friend, Ratzmann, was a "hapless victim," one possibly under the devil's influence. In the book, Geiger's twelve-year-old son, Robert, also graphically related how he responded to the slaying of his cousin, Bart Oliver.

Other church members felt that Geiger's thesis was an over-simplification, that Ratzmann had free will and made a terribly wrong decision on how to vent his frustrations. Geiger, in response, indicated he was not attempting to absolve Ratzmann from responsibility for the shootings, but he found it "difficult to ascribe all of that to him humanly." He said he wanted the book to promote healing.[31] But as the controversy over Geiger's writings demonstrates, Terry Ratzmann's pistol shots continue to ring through the congregation.

Notes

Introduction: Cesspool of the Human Soul

1. AC/DC, "Night Prowler," *Highway to Hell,* 1979, http://www.songfacts.com/detail.php?id=11792.

2. Walters, Steven, "Abused children, buried body found." *Milwaukee Journal Sentinel*, June 15, 2007; Held, Tom and Tom Kertscher, "4 charged in murderous torture spree." *Milwaukee Journal Sentinel*, June 20, 2007; Kertscher, Tom, "Fantasy blamed in Portage violence." *Milwaukee Journal Sentinel*, June 23, 2007.

3. Interview, Frank Meyers, retired director, Division of Criminal Investigation, Wisconsin Department of Justice, December 22, 2006.

4. Interview, Dale Mueller, retired director of the polygraph exam unit, FBI Milwaukee Field Office, December 22, 2006.

5. Wisconsin Crime Rates, 1960–2005, http://www.disastercenter.com/crime/wicrime.htm.

6. Wisconsin Office of Justice Assistance, January 1, 2007.

7. Ibid.

8. Federal Bureau of Investigation, http://www.fbi.gov/ucr/prelim06/t4ok_wi.htm; Wisconsin Office of Justice Assistance, January 1, 2007.

9. Diedrich, John, "Homicides in City Drop 16% in 2006," *Milwaukee Journal Sentinel*, January 1, 2006.

10. "Defining Serial Murder," http://en.wikipedia.org/wiki/Serial_killer; Rummler, Gary, and Mark Ward, "How Could Anyone Do That," *Milwaukee Journal*, July 24, 1991; "Rewriting 'Psycho,' UW Prof Works to Demystify a Loaded Term," On Wisconsin (Winter 2006); correspondence, Joseph Newman, MD, Department of Psychology, University of Wisconsin–Madison, January 5, 2007.

11. Eric Hickey, Department of Criminology, California State University in Fresno, http://www.csufresno.edu/criminology/faculty/hickey.htm.

12. Rolli interview.

13. "Types of Serial Killers," http://www.karisable.com/crserial1.htm.

14. "Investigative Programs Critical Incident Response Group," Federal Bureau of Investigation, http://www.fbi.gov/hq/isd/cirg/ncavc.htm; "Types of Serial Killers."

15. "Joseph Paul Franklin," http://www.geocities.com/verbal_plainfield/a-h/franklin.html; "Joseph Paul Franklin," http://en.wikipedia.org/wiki/Joseph_Paul_Franklin; "Joseph Paul Franklin," http://www.francesfarmersrevenge.com/stuff/serialkillers/franklin.html; "Joseph Paul Franklin," http://www.geocities.com/verbal_plainfield/a-h/franklin.html.

16. Ibid.

17. Evans, Joyce, "Writing Off Killings Is Too Simple," *Milwaukee Journal Sentinel*, November 29, 1997; McBride, Jessica, "North Side Victim Died of Strangulation," *Milwaukee Journal Sentinel*, February 19, 1998.

18. Mueller interview.

19. McBride, Jessica, "Killer Remains Key Suspect in 3 Other Deaths," *Milwaukee Journal Sentinel*, August 23, 1998.

20. Philipin, John, "Science, Intuition, and Hope: The Art of Personality Profiling," http://www.karisable.com/crserial2.htm.

21. Derleth, August. *Wisconsin Murders*. Sauk City, Wis.: Mycroft & Moran Publishers. 1968. vii.

22. Ibid.

23. Ibid., viii.

Got Murder?

24. Skiba, Katherine, M., "Files Show 882 Wisconsinites Are 'Missing Persons,'" *Milwaukee Journal*, July 24, 1991.35. Ibid.

25. Interview, Milwaukee County District Attorney E. Michael McCann, September 25, 2006.

26. Skiba, "Files Show 882 Wisconsinites Are 'Missing Persons,'"; interview, E. Michael McCann, retired Milwaukee County district attorney, September 25, 2006.

27. Meyers interview; Mueller interview.

28. Milwaukee Police Department, June 22, 2007

29. Derleth, *Wisconsin Murders*, vii.

30. Pattison, Tom, "Sociology Class Explores Fascination with Serial Murder Cases," News and Publications, University of Wisconsin–Whitewater, July 19, 2004; http://www.uww.edu/npa/news_releases/story.php?id=541.

31. "Multiple Murder in Popular Culture," http://www.mayhem.net/Crime/serial2.html.

32. Martens, Cynthia, "Psycho Killer Possibly on the Loose," *Badger Herald*, November 12, 2003.

33. "Multiple Murder in Popular Culture."

34. "Ed Gein's Car," http://www.artistdirect.com/nad/music/artist/card/0,,426497,00.html.

35. "Gein and the Graverobbers," http://www.geinandthegraverobbers.com.

36. "Marilyn Manson," http://en.wikipedia.org/wiki/Marilyn_Manson.

37. Church Of Misery, "Room 213," http://www.seeklyrics.com/lyrics/Church-Of-Misery/Room-213.html.

38. "Geiners," http://www.serialkillers.nl/ed-gein/geiners.htm.

39. "Digest of Jokes on Serial Killer Jeffrey Dahmer," http://www.netfunny.com/rhf/jokes/91q3/killer.html.

40. "Stilton Cheese," http://www.stiltoncheese.com; "Sweet Dreams Are Made of Cheese," British Cheese Board, September 25, 2005, http://www.cheeseboard.co.uk/news.cfm?page_id=240.

41. Ibid.

42. "All about Wonderful Wisconsin," http://www.wfop.org/wisinfo/aboutwis.html.

43. Larson, Ron, "List of Unsolved Murders," *Wisconsin State Journal*, May 27, 2006.

44. McCann interview.

Chapter 1: The Hatchet Man of Taliesin

1. *Wisconsin State Journal*, August 17, 1914.

2. Wright, Frank Lloyd, "An Autobiography," http://www.pbs.org/flw/buildings/taliesin/taliesin_wright04.html.

3. Ibid.

4. Wright, "An Autobiography."

5. "Frank Lloyd Wright,"; Secrest, Meryle, *Frank Lloyd Wright* (New York: Alfred A. Knopf, 1992), 212.

6. Burns, Ken, "The Master Builder," *Vanity Fair*, 459 (November 1998): 302–18; http://www.gpaulbishop.com/GPB%20History/GPB%20Archive/Section%20-%201/F.L.%20Wright/article_-1.htm.; Secrest, Meryle, *Frank Lloyd Wright* (New York: Alfred A. Knopf, 1992), 212.

7. Burns, "The Master Builder."

8. "Cheney Turns from Body of Former Wife," *Milwaukee Sentinel*, August 17, 1914; Secrest, *Frank Lloyd Wright*, 217.

Notes

9. Drennan, William R., and Ron McRea, *Death in a Prairie House* (Madison, WI: Terrace Press/University of Wisconsin Press, 2007), 92.

10. "Insane Negro Kills Five in Frank Lloyd Wright's 'Love Bungalow,'" *Wisconsin State Journal*, August 16, 1914; "Frank Lloyd Wright,"; Farr, Finis, *Frank Lloyd Wright* (New York: Charles Scribner's Sons, 1961), 137.

11. "Tragedy End of Soulmate Cottage Life," *Milwaukee Sentinel*, August 16, 1914.

12. "Murderer of Seven: Sets Fire to Country Home of Frank Lloyd Wright Near Spring Green," *Weekly Home News*, August 20, 1914; http://www.pbs.org/flw/buildings/taliesin/taliesin_wright02.html; Secrest, *Frank Lloyd Wright*, 217.

13. *Weekly Home News*, "Murderer of Seven: Sets Fire to Country Home of Frank Lloyd Wright Near Spring Green" ; http://www.pbs.org/flw/buildings/taliesin/taliesin_wright02.html; Friedland, Roger, and Harold Zellman, *The Fellowship* (New York: Regan/Harper Collins, 2006), 37–39; Drennan and McRea, *Death in a Prairie House*, 98–101.

14. *Milwaukee Sentinel,* "Tragedy End of Soulmate Cottage Life"; "Negro Axman Gives Self Up," *Milwaukee Journal*, August 16, 1914; *Weekly Home News*, "Murderer of Seven: Country Home of Frank Lloyd Wright Near Spring Green,"; http://www.pbs.org/flw/buildings/taliesin/taliesin_wright02.html.

15. *Milwaukee Journal,* "Negro Axman Gives Self Up"; *Milwaukee Sentinel*, "Cheney Turns from Body of Former Wife" ; "Bury Victims of Black Chef," *Milwaukee Journal*, August 17, 1914; Secrest, *Frank Lloyd Wright*, 217.

16. "Three Are Killed: Two Hurt by Man with Ax on Sauk County Farm," *Wisconsin State Journal*, August 15, 1914; *Milwaukee Journal*, "Negro Axman Gives Self Up"; "Carlton Better and Will Live to Face Trial for Seven Murders," *Wisconsin State Journal*, August 21, 1914; Secrest, *Frank Lloyd Wright*, 217.

17. ed., "Tragedy End of Soulmate Cottage Life," *The Milwaukee Sentinel*, August 16, 1914; ed., "Negro Axman Gives Self Up," *Milwaukee Journal*, August 16, 1914; Drennan, William R., *Death in a Prairie House*. Madison, Wisconsin,: Terrace Press/University of Wisconsin. 2007. 108.

18. Secrest, *Frank Lloyd Wright,* 6, 139–140.

19. ed, "Horror Created by Julian Carlton," http://www.caribvoice.org/Features/carlton.html; Secrest, Meryl, *Frank Lloyd Wright*. New York: Alfred A. Knopf. 1992. 220. ed., "Tragedy End of Soulmate Cottage Life," *The Milwaukee Sentinel*, August 16, 1914; ed., "Negro Axman Gives Self Up," *The Milwaukee Journal*, August 16, 1914; ed., title unknown, *Dodgeville Chronicle*, August 21, 1914.

20. "Mystery of the Murders at Taliesin," BBC News, January 14, 2001; Secrest, *Frank Lloyd Wright,* 222; *Milwaukee Sentinel*, "Tragedy End of Soulmate Cottage Life."

21. *Milwaukee Sentinel*, "Cheney Turns from Body of Former Wife"; "'Mamah of Hills' Buried at Night; Service of Silence by Wright for Whom She Defied Convention," *Wisconsin State Journal*, August 17, 1914; Wright, *An Autobiography*, 209–210; Farr, *Frank Lloyd Wright,* 139–140; Secrest, *Frank Lloyd Wright,* 222.

22. *Milwaukee Sentinel*, "Cheney Turns from Body of Former Wife."

23. *Milwaukee Sentinel*, "Cheney Turns from Body of Former Wife"; "Victims of 'Love Cottage' Has Reached Seven," *Milwaukee Sentinel*, August 19, 1914.

24. *Milwaukee Sentinel*, "Cheney Turns from Body of Former Wife"; *Milwaukee Sentinel*, "Victims of 'Love Cottage' Has Reached Seven"; *Wisconsin State Journal*, "Carlton Better and Will Live to Face Trial for Seven Murders."

25. *Milwaukee Journal*, "Negro Axman Gives Self Up"; Drennan and McRea, *Death in a Prairie House,* 102.

Got Murder?

26. *Milwaukee Sentinel*, "Victims of 'Love Cottage' Has Reached Seven"; "Negro Slayer May Be Eighth Tragedy Victim," *Wisconsin State Journal*, August 19, 1914.

27. *Milwaukee Sentinel* "Tragedy End of Soulmate Cottage Life,"; *Milwaukee Journal*, "Negro Axman Gives Self Up"; *Milwaukee Sentinel*, "Cheney Turns from Body of Former Wife"; "To Build Mansion on Bungalow Ruin," *Milwaukee Sentinel*, August 18, 1914; Secrest, *Frank Lloyd Wright*, 217, 220; Drennan and McRea, *Death in a Prairie House*, 149–150, 152–153.

28. Wright, Frank Lloyd, "Frank Lloyd Wright Issues a Statement to His Neighbors," *Wisconsin State Journal*, August 21, 1914; Wright, Frank Lloyd, "To My Neighbors," http://www.pbs.org/flw/buildings/taliesin/taliesin_wright02.html.

29. *Milwaukee Sentinel*, "To Build Mansion on Bungalow Ruin."

30. "Shining Brow," http://www.daronhagen.com/brow; ed, "Shining Brow," http://www.complete-review.com/reviews/muldoonp/shiningb.htm.

31. "American Dreams Festival, 2002," http://www.immigrantstheat.org/PLAYSdislocation2005.htm; "2004 O'Neill Playwrights and Musical Theater Conference," http://www.oneilltheatercenter.org/news/072304.htm.

Chapter 2: Deadly Big Bang

1. Milwaukee County Coroner's Inquest on the body of Charles C. Seehawer, et al., December 18, 1917: 4-5.

2. Declaration of Intention, No. 4784, Vol. 10, Milwaukee County: 484.

3. Spreng, Bishop S. P., *Evangelical Missionary World* (March 1930).

4. Ibid.

5. Declaration of Intention, No. 4784, 484.

6. Block, Herman A., "Wisconsin Conference Historical Data," Evangelical Association, The Evangelical Church, The Evangelical United Brethren Church, 1840–1969, 1971, Wisconsin Conference, Sun Prairie, Wisconsin: 45.

7. Bartelt, Arthur H. *Missionary Messenger* (July 1920).

8. Carini, Mario A., "Milwaukee's Italians: The Early Years," Italian Community Center, Milwaukee, 1984: 13; Andreozzi, John Anthony, "Contadini and Pescatori in Milwaukee; Assimilation and Voluntary Associations," (master's thesis, University of Wisconsin–Milwaukee, 1974), 34, 37.

9. Wisconsin Supreme Court, Peter Bianchi et al. v. State, 169 Wis. 75., October Term, 1918, No. 10 and January Term, 1919, March 7–April 2, 1919: 78-79.

10. Ibid.

11. Ibid., 80–81.

12. Milwaukee County Coroner's Inquest on the body of Antonio Fronasier [sic], September 14, 1917.

13. Wisconsin Supreme Court, Peter Bianchi et al. v. State, 169 Wis. 75., October Term, 1918, No. 10 and January Term, 1919, March 7–April 2, 1919: 80.

14. Ibid., 81.

15. Inquest on the body of Antonio Fronasier [sic], 34–35.

16. Bianchi et al. v. State, 81–82.

17. Inquest on the body of Antonio Fronasier [sic], 44.

18. Bianchi et al. v. State, 84.

19. Inquest on the body of Antonio Fronasier [sic], 55.

20. Bianchi et al. v. State, 84.

21. Ibid., 67.

22. "Round Them Up," *Milwaukee Sentinel*, September 11, 1917.

23. Inquest on the body of Charles C. Seehawer, et al., 11.

24. Ibid., 4–5.

25. "10 Killed by Bomb in Police Station," *New York Times*, November 25, 1917.

26. "Scene of Explosion Charnel House," *Milwaukee Journal*, November 25, 1917; "Body of Deckert Is Blown to Bits," *Milwaukee Sentinel*, November 25, 1917; ed, "The Wedding Ring Blown from the Finger," *Milwaukee Sentinel*, November 25, 1917; "Detective's Watch Blown From Pocket," *Milwaukee Sentinel*, November 25, 1917.

27. "Twelve Detained in Bomb Case," *Milwaukee Journal*, November 27, 1917.

28. Bianchi et al. v. State, 94.

29. "Arrest Italian Leaving Court," *Milwaukee Sentinel*, December 15, 1917; "Arrest Three More Italians," *Milwaukee Sentinel*, December 20, 1917.

30. *Milwaukee Leader*, date unknown, 1917: 2.

31. Inquest on the body of Charles C. Seehawer, et al.

32. Stone, Irving, *Clarence Darrow for the Defense* (Garden City: Doubleday, Doran & Company, 1941), 361.

33. Ibid., 361–362.

34. Bianchi et al. v. State, 97.

35. *Milwaukee Sentinel*, April 21, 1919, 3.

36. Gurda, John, "Terrorism Chilled Milwaukee in 1917," *Milwaukee Journal Sentinel*, November 4, 2001.

37. Stone, Irving, *Clarence Darrow for the Defense*. Garden City: Doubleday, Doran & Company. 1941. 361-362.

Chapter 3: Homegrown Body Snatcher

1. Bloch, Robert, *Psycho* (Mattituck, NY: Rivercity Press, 1959), 117.

2. Taylor, Troy, *Wisconsin's "Psycho," The Deviant Life & Times of Ed Gein,* http://www.prairieghosts.com/ed_gein.html.

3. Schechter, Harold, *Deviant: The Shocking True Story of Ed Gein* (New York: Pocket Books, 1989), 10–15.

4. Ibid.

5. Ibid.

6. Ibid., 18.

7. Schechter, *Deviant: The Shocking True Story of Ed Gein*, 28–30; "Gein, Edward," http://samvak.tripod.com/factoidg.html.

8. Taylor, *Wisconsin's "Psycho," The Deviant Life & Times of Ed Gein*.

9. Ibid.

10. Schechter, *Deviant: The Shocking True Story of Ed Gein*, 31.

11. Ibid., 31–32.

12. Taylor, *Wisconsin's "Psycho," The Deviant Life & Times of Ed Gein*.

13. Schechter, *Deviant: The Shocking True Story of Ed Gein*, 36.

14. Schechter, *Deviant: The Shocking True Story of Ed Gein*, 42; "Gein, Edward."

15. Schechter, *Deviant: The Shocking True Story of Ed Gein*, 44.

16. Schechter, *Deviant: The Shocking True Story of Ed Gein*, 53–59; "Ed Gein: Bluebeard or Ghoul?" *Milwaukee Sentinel*, November 21, 1957.

17. Schechter, *Deviant: The Shocking True Story of Ed Gein*, 60–61.

18. Schechter, *Deviant: The Shocking True Story of Ed Gein*, 61–64; Wells, Robert W., "Youth Recalls that He Saw Two Heads," *Milwaukee Journal*, November 20, 1957.

19. Schechter, *Deviant: The Shocking True Story of Ed Gein*, 71–73; "Missing from Store, Widow Found Dead," *Milwaukee Journal*, November 17, 1957.

20. Schechter, *Deviant: The Shocking True Story of Ed Gein*, 74–77; Holmes, Paul, "Hint Killer Is Cannibal!" *Chicago Tribune*, November 19, 1957.

21. Schechter, *Deviant: The Shocking True Story of Ed Gein*, 78–79; Holmes, "Hint Killer Is Cannibal!"

22. Schechter, *Deviant: The Shocking True Story of Ed Gein*, 78–79; Leonard, Richard H., "Plainfield Farmer Admits Grisly Act," *Milwaukee Journal*, November 18, 1957.

23. Schechter, *Deviant: The Shocking True Story of Ed Gein*, 81.

24. Ibid., 81–82.

25. Ibid., 82–83.

26. Ibid., 83.

27. Ibid., 84–86.

28. "Rundown Farm House Was Murder Factory," *Milwaukee Journal*, November 8, 1957.

29. Schechter, *Deviant: The Shocking True Story of Ed Gein*, 87–89; "Gein, Edward,"; Holmes, Paul, "15 Horror Victims Found," *Chicago Tribune*, November 20, 1957.

30. Schechter, *Deviant: The Shocking True Story of Ed Gein*, 89–90, 92; "Gein, Edward,"; Holmes, "15 Horror Victims Found."

31. "Woman Store Owner Dead; Suspect Held," *Milwaukee Sentinel*, November 17, 1957.

32. Holmes, "15 Horror Victims Found."

33. Schechter, *Deviant: The Shocking True Story of Ed Gein*, 93–94.

34. Holmes, "Hint Killer Is Cannibal!"

35. "Gein, Edward."

36. Schechter, *Deviant: The Shocking True Story of Ed Gein*, 106–110; Holmes, "Hint Killer Is Cannibal "; Bliss, George, "Tell Gein's Crime Motive," *Chicago Daily Tribune*, November 21, 1957; "Gein Says That He Was in Daze Whenever Robbed from Graves," *Milwaukee Journal*, November 19, 1957.

37. Schechter, *Deviant: The Shocking True Story of Ed Gein*, 110; Bliss, "Tell Gein's Crime Motive."

38. *Milwaukee Sentinel*, "Woman Store Owner Dead; Suspect Held."

39. *Milwaukee Sentinel*, "Murder 'Factory' on Farm!"

40. Interview, Richard Leonard, June 21, 2006.

41. Schechter, *Deviant: The Shocking True Story of Ed Gein*, 110–116.

42. Ibid., 117–120.

43. "Plainfield Butcher's Story! Ghoul Stole 10 Female Corpses, 'Moon-Mad' Gein Robbed Graves, Mutilated Bodies," *Milwaukee Sentinel*, November 18, 1957; Wells, Robert W., "Incredibly Dirty House Was Home of Slayer," *Milwaukee Journal*, November 19, 1957.

Notes

44. Holmes, "15 Horror Victims Found"; "Gein Realizes Medical Need, Lawyer Says," *Milwaukee Sentinel*, November 21, 1957.

45. Schechter, *Deviant: The Shocking True Story of Ed Gein*, 117–120, 147.

46. Ibid., 127–133.

47. "Shy Gein Feared Women, Pal Says," *Milwaukee Sentinel*, November 21, 1957.

48. Schechter, *Deviant: The Shocking True Story of Ed Gein*, 157–158.

49. Schechter, *Deviant: The Shocking True Story of Ed Gein*, 158–159; Wells, Robert W., "Publicity's Spotlight Enjoyed by Wautoma," *Milwaukee Journal*, November 22, 1957.

50. "Rules No Bar to Interview," *Milwaukee Sentinel*, November 22, 1957.

51. Schechter, *Deviant: The Shocking True Story of Ed Gein*, 136, 167.

52. Ibid., 136.

53. Schechter, *Deviant: The Shocking True Story of Ed Gein*, 169–170; "Gein Admits 2nd Slaying," *Milwaukee Sentinel*, November 21, 1957.

54. "Sexton Denies Graves Were Violated," *Milwaukee Sentinel*, November 22, 1957.

55. Schechter, *Deviant: The Shocking True Story of Ed Gein*, 137–140; *Milwaukee Sentinel,* "Gein Admits 2nd Slaying,"; Bliss, "Tell Gein's Crime Motive."

56. "Keating Quiz Results Inconclusive," *Milwaukee Sentinel*, November 21, 1957.

57. "Gein Acted Alone, Lie Tests Indicate," *Milwaukee Journal*, November 29, 1957; "Doctors Study 2 Gein Interviews," *Milwaukee Sentinel*, November 30, 1957.

58. Schechter, *Deviant: The Shocking True Story of Ed Gein*, 141.

59. "Bare Boyhood Obsession of 'Butcher' Gein," *Chicago Tribune*, November 19, 1957; "Obsessive Love for His Mother Drove Gein to Slay," *Milwaukee Journal*, November 21, 1957; "Mother Complex Led Gein to Kill," *Milwaukee Sentinel*, November 22, 1957.

60. Schechter, *Deviant: The Shocking True Story of Ed Gein*, 149–155.

61. *Milwaukee Sentinel*, "Doctors to Study 2 Gein Interviews."

62. "Friends Crowd Church at Worden Rites," *Milwaukee Sentinel*, November 21, 1957.

63. Ibid.

64. "Editor-Friend Pays Tribute to Slain Widow," *Milwaukee Sentinel*, November 21, 1957.

65. "Weeping Gein Prays in Cell with Minister," *Milwaukee Sentinel*, November 22, 1957; "Robbed Graves Ordered Opened," *Milwaukee Sentinel*, November 23, 1957.

66. "Kin of Grave 'Victims' to Be Contacted," *Milwaukee Sentinel,* November 22, 1957.

67. Schechter, *Deviant: The Shocking True Story of Ed Gein*, 165–167; Holmes, Paul, "Decide to Open Graves in Gein Case," *Chicago Daily Tribune*, November 23, 1957.

68. "Gein's Fate Hinges on Sanity Issue," *Milwaukee Sentinel*, November 22, 1957; Holmes, "Decide to Open Graves in Gein Case."

69. "'Butcher' Sent to Waupun," *Milwaukee Sentinel*, November 23, 1957; *Milwaukee Journal*, November 24, 1957; Powers, Thomas, "Hogan Slaying Reenacted by 'Butcher' Gein," *Chicago Daily Tribune*, November 24, 1957.

70. Schechter, *Deviant: The Shocking True Story of Ed Gein*, 205.

71. Holmes, "Decide to Open Graves in Gein Case"; "Sift Evidence for Bones of Gein Victim," *Milwaukee Sentinel*, November 25, 1957.

72. Schechter, *Deviant: The Shocking True Story of Ed Gein*, 185–192; Holmes, "Decide to Open Graves in Gein Case."

73. Schechter, *Deviant: The Shocking True Story of Ed Gein*, 193–194; "'Gein Graves' Empty,"

Milwaukee Sentinel, November 26, 1957; "Find Another Set of Bones on Gein Farm," *Chicago Daily Tribune,* December 1, 1957.

74. "Wisconsin Joins Prosecution in Gein Murder Case," *Chicago Daily Tribune*, December 12, 1957.

75. "Gein Admits Robbing 2 More Graves," *Milwaukee Sentinel*, November 28, 1957.

76. Schechter, *Deviant: The Shocking True Story of Ed Gein*, 200–219.

77. "Gein 'Incompetent,'" *Milwaukee Journal*, December 23, 1957; "Gein to Get Sanity Hearing; Rule He Can't Stand Trial," *Chicago Daily Tribune*, December 24, 1957; "Gein Is Not Fit to Stand Trial, Hospital Report Says," *Milwaukee Journal*, December 24, 1957.

78. Schechter, *Deviant: The Shocking True Story of Ed Gein*, 224–226; "Ed Gein Case Story of Year: State AP Poll," *Milwaukee Journal*, December 28, 1957.

79. Schechter, *Deviant: The Shocking True Story of Ed Gein*, 227–231; "Killer-Ghoul Ruled Insane; Escapes Trial," *Chicago Daily Tribune*, January 7, 1957.

80. Schechter, *Deviant: The Shocking True Story of Ed Gein*, 235–240.

81. Taylor, *Wisconsin's "Psycho," The Deviant Life & Times of Ed Gein.*

82. "Fire Destroys Gein Home; Arson Possibility Checked," *Milwaukee Journal*, March 20, 1958; "Fire Won't Halt Gein Farm 'Open House,'" *Milwaukee Sentinel*, March 32, 1958.

83. "Crowd Visits Gein's Farm; Auction Next Sunday," *Milwaukee Journal*, March 24, 1958; Dadisman, Quincy, "Tour Proves Strong Lure," *Milwaukee Sentinel*, March 24, 1958.

84. Schechter, *Deviant: The Shocking True Story of Ed Gein*, 244–248; "All That Gein Owned Auctioned; $5,000 Proceeds Held in Trust," *Milwaukee Journal*, March 31, 1958; "Gein's Farm Brings $3,925 at Auction," *Milwaukee Sentinel*, March 31, 1958.

85. "O'Connell, Bishop William Patrick," http://www.catholic-hierarchy.org/bishop/boconwp.html.

86. Sheriff Art Schley, Waushara County Courthouse, death notice.

87. Shaver, John, "Gein Goes on Trial in 1957 Slaying Case," *Milwaukee Journal*, November 7, 1968; Schley death notice.

88. Shaver, John G., "Links to 2nd Slaying Rejected at Gein Trial," *Milwaukee Journal*, November 13, 1968; interview, Robert Sutton, attorney, June 21, 2006.

89. Shaver, John G., "Ed Gein Guilty of Murder," *Milwaukee Journal*, November 14, 1968; Aschoff, Lee, "Lawyers Recount Bizarre Gein Case," *Milwaukee Journal*, July 27, 1984; Sutton interview.

90. Schechter, *Deviant: The Shocking True Story of Ed Gein*, 256–269.

91. "Notorious Murderer Ed Gein Dies at 77," *Milwaukee Journal*, July 26, 1984.

92. Dobish, Alex, "Plainfield Shows Anger, Patience in Gein Memories," *Milwaukee Journal*, July 27, 1984.

93. Aschoff, "Lawyers Recount Bizarre Gein Case."

94. Ibid.

95. Douglas, John, and Mark Okshaker, *Mind Hunter* (New York: Scribner, 1995), 96.

96. Jones, Meg, "Crime Doesn't Pay, But Will It Sell?" *Milwaukee Journal Sentinel*, April 7, 2006; Imrie, Robert, "Ed Gein's Farmland Is for Sale," *Wisconsin State Journal*, April 9, 2006; "Owner of Gein's Land Receives 1 Low Bid," *Chicago Sun-Times*, April 11, 2006.

97. "Ed Gein, MySpace," http://profile.myspace.com/index.cfm?fuseaction=user.viewprofile&friendid=2447488.

Chapter 4: Murders Most Foul

Notes

1. "Coed, 18, Slain on Campus at UW," *Milwaukee Journal*, May 27, 1968.

2. "Gen. Mitchell Field Closed by Dense Fog," *Milwaukee Sentinel*, May 27, 1968.

3. "Students to Control Patrols," *Milwaukee Journal*, May 30, 1968.

4. *Milwaukee Journal,* "Coed, 18, Slain on Campus at UW."

5. Dieckmann, June, "No Suspects, Motive Seen in UW Slaying," *Wisconsin State Journal*, May 28, 1968.

6. "She Liked UW Immensely," *Milwaukee Journal*, May 27, 1968; "A Happy Life Ends for Well-Liked Girl," *Wisconsin State Journal*, May 28, 1968; Schuetz, Lisa, "UW Woman Met Violent Death," *The Wisconsin State Journal*, May 26, 2006.

7. Dieckmann, "No Suspects, Motive Seen in UW Slaying."

8. *Milwaukee Journal,* "Coed, 18, Slain on Campus at UW"; Dieckmann, "No Suspects, Motive Seen in UW Slaying"; "No Motive Found in Coed Killing," *Milwaukee Sentinel*, May 28, 1968; Dobish, Alex F., "Worried Coeds Remain Indoors," *Milwaukee Journal*, May 28, 1968; Kreisman, Irvin, "Christine's Murder: Still No Clues a Year Later," *Capital Times*, May 26, 1969; Pittman, Sharon D., "Two Murders: Still Puzzles," *Capital Times*, August 25, 1983.

9. Dobish, Alex, "UW Crime No Cause for Panic, Madison, Campus Police Say," *Milwaukee Journal*, June 2, 1968.

10. "Coed Stabbed to Death at UW-Madison," *Milwaukee Sentinel*, May 27, 1968; Joslyn, Robert, "UW Co-ed Found Slain on Campus," *Wisconsin State Journal*, May 27, 1968.

11. Schuetz, "UW Woman Met Violent Death."

12. Dobish, "Worried Coeds Remain Indoors."

13. *Milwaukee Journal*, "She Liked UW Immensely."

14. *Milwaukee Sentinel*, "No Motive Found in Coed Killing"; Dobish, "Worried Coeds Remain Indoors."

15. Dadisman, Quincy, "Shock, Fear New Visitors to UW Madison Campus," *Milwaukee Sentinel*, May 28, 1968.

16. Joslyn, "UW Co-ed Found Slain on Campus."

17. Dobish, "Worried Coeds Remain Indoors."

18. "Were There Witnesses? The Murder at the University," *Wisconsin State Journal*, May 29, 1968.

19. Zweifel, Dave, "Psychiatrist Reports: Sees Wide Range in Type of Killer," *Capital Times*, May 31, 1968; "UW Victim Picked 'At Random,'" *Milwaukee Journal*, June 1, 1968.

20. Dobish, Alex, "Officers Called Lax Toward UW Crime," *Milwaukee Journal*, May 30, 1968; Zimmerman, Ken, "Crimes Unreported at UW," *Milwaukee Sentinel*, May 30, 1968.

21. Dobish, "UW Crime No Cause for Panic, Madison, Campus Police Say."

22. Ibid.

23. *Milwaukee Journal*, "Students to Control Patrols."

24. "Sen. Warren Tries to Milk Votes from Rothschild Tragedy," *Capital Times*, May 30, 1968.

25. Zimmerman, Ken, "100 Questioned in Coed Killing," *Milwaukee Sentinel*, May 31, 1968.

26. "Doctor Wanted for Questioning in Co-ed Murder," *Wisconsin State Journal*, September 18, 1968; "Detectives End Quiz of Doctor in Co-ed Murder," *Wisconsin State Journal*, September 21, 1968.

27. Dobish, Alex, "Police at UW Study Handkerchief, Pants," *Milwaukee Journal*, May 29, 1968; "No Suspect in UW Slaying, Police Say," *Milwaukee Journal*, May 31, 1968; "UW Victim Picked 'At Random," *Milwaukee Journal*, June 1, 1968.

Got Murder?

28. "Reward Sought to Aid Police in UW Slaying," *Milwaukee Journal*, June 4, 1968.

29. "Reward Upped in Co-ed Case," *Wisconsin State Journal*, June 15, 1968.

30. "Safety Council Asked for UW," *Milwaukee Journal*, June 11, 1968.

31. "Weapon Search Delayed at UW," *Milwaukee Journal*, June 12, 1968; Kreisman, Irvin, "What Makes a Killer? Who Really Knows?," *Capital Times*, June 12, 1968.

32. Dobish, Alex, "Police Study 'Confession' in Coed's Slaying," *Milwaukee Journal*, June 5, 1968.

33. Behrendt, David, "UW to Add $100,00 for Policing Campuses," *Milwaukee Journal*, June 13, 1968.

34. Kreisman, "Christine's Murder: Still No Clues a Year Later."

35. Schuetz, "UW Woman Met Violent Death."

36. Dieckmann, June, "Co-ed Possibly a Random Victim," *Wisconsin State Journal*, June 1, 1968.

37. "Murder Suspect Investigated for Rothschild Killing," *Wisconsin State Journal*, December 24, 1975.

38. Dieckmann, June, "Murder of Christine Rothschild Still Unsolved After Four Years," *Wisconsin State Journal*, May 28, 1972; Lovejoy, Steven, "New Link Is Eyed to Coed's Slaying," *Wisconsin State Journal*, September 16, 1972.

39. Schuetz, "UW Woman Met Violent Death."

40. Ibid.

41. "Sterling Hall Bombing," http://en.wikipedia.org/wiki/Sterling_Hall_bombing; "Sterling Hall Bombing," http://www.madison.com/library/LEE/sterlinghall.html.

42. Interview. Dane County Coroner John Stanley, September 12, 2006; ed., "Adopted Killers,": http://www.geocities.com/Wellesley/9950/adoption_serialkillers.html

43. Allegretti, Dan, and David Blaska, "Donna: Bright, Bubbly, Unafraid," *Capital Times*, July 2, 1982; Pitman, "Two Murders: Still Puzzles."

44. Pitman, "Two Murders: Still Puzzles"; Browne, Jeff, "UW Coed Stabbed to Death," *Milwaukee Journal*, July 2, 1982; Browne, Jeff, "No Motive Found in Campus Slaying," *Milwaukee Journal*, July 3, 1982; "Winding Down," http://www.crimelibrary.com/serial_killers/unsolved/madison_wi/3.html.

45. Browne, "UW Coed Stabbed to Death"; Pitman, Sharon D., and Mike Miller, "UW Student Murdered on Campus," *Capital Times*, July 2, 1982; Browne, "No Motive Found in Campus Slaying."

46. Miller, Mike, "Cops Appeal for Information in Slaying," *Capital Times*, July 6, 1982; "Police Seek Possible Witness for Questioning About Slaying," *Milwaukee Journal*, July 8, 1982; Pitman, Sharon D., "Stained Jeans Found Near Murder Site," *Capital Times*, July 9, 1982; Miller, Mike, "Lab Results Coming on Jeans Found Near UW Murder Site," *Capital Times*, July 12, 1982; Pitman, Sharon D., "Analysis of Blue Jeans in Mraz Murder Expected by Weekend," *Capital Times*, July 14, 1982; Pitman, Sharon D., "Jeans Not Tied to Murder, Officials Say," *Capital Times*, July 1982 (undated).

47. Browne, Jeff, "Many UW Students Fear Campus Area," *Milwaukee Journal*, July 4, 1982.

48. Ibid.

49. Browne, "Many UW Students Fear Campus Area"; Pitman, Sharon D., "In Wake of Mraz Murder, Students Feel Unsafe on Madison Streets," *Capital Times*, July 8, 1982.

50. Miller, Mike, "Body of Slain UW Student Is Exhumed," *Capital Times*, November 2, 1982.

51. "Reward in Mraz Murder Case Is Doubled," *Capital Times*, November 5, 1983.

52. Interview, Dale G. Burke, assistant chief, University of Wisconsin–Madison police department, October 13, 2006.

53. Ibid.

54. Kemmeter, Gene, "Unresolved Raasch Case Revived," *Portage County Gazette*, June 5, 2002.

55. "Winding Down."

56. Kemmeter, "Unresolved Raasch Case Revived."

57. Ibid.

58. Ibid.

59. Pitman, Sharon D., "Mass Murderer Coolly Describes Area Deaths," *Capital Times*, June 16, 1984; Lohr, David, "A Killer Emerges," *Court TV's Crime Library*, http://www.crimelibrary.com/serial_killersunsolved/madison_wi.1.html; Wachowski, Elizabeth, "Unsolved Murders Haunt Campus," *Daily Cardinal,* October 30, 2003.

60. Lohr, "A Killer Emerges"; Wachowski, "Unsolved Murders Haunt Campus."

61. Clark, Anita, "Woman's Body Found in Dunn Is Identified," *Capital Times*, April 21, 1981; Lohr, "A Killer Emerges"; Wachowski, "Unsolved Murders Haunt Campus."

62. "Body Found in Arboretum," *Capital Times*, April 18, 1980.

63. "Area Detectives to Interview Lucas," *Capital Times*, March 1, 1984; "Lucas Gets 60-year Sentence for Slaying of Texas Woman," *Capital Times*, January 25, 1985; "Police Urged to Reopen Lucas Serial Killer Cases," *Capital Times*, November 30, 1985.

64. "Pair Linked to 81 Murders, But Area Cases Remain Open," *Capital Times*, January 21, 1984; *Capital Times*, "Lucas Gets 60-year Sentence for Slaying of Texas Woman"; *Capital Times,* "Police Urged to Reopen Lucas Serial Killer Cases."

65. Pitman, "Mass Murderer Coolly Describes Area Deaths"; "Sheriff Sure Lucas Killed Two State Women," *Capital Times*, October 4, 1985.

66. "Two State Deaths Tied to Mass Killer," *Capital Times*, August 4, 1984.

67. *Capital Times*, "Area Detectives to Interview Lucas"; "Texas Inmate Tells Milwaukee Detective About a Murder Here," *Capital Times*, May 9, 1984; Lucas, O'Toole [sic] Linked to Another State Slaying," *Capital Times*, March 9, 1985.

68. "Lucas Murder Confessions a 'Grand Fraud,'" *Los Angeles Times News Service*, May 8, 1986.

69. University of Wisconsin–Madison Police, Campus Safety Report, 2005; University of Wisconsin–Madison Police, http://www.uwpd.wisc.edu.

Chapter 5: Death By Viciousness

1. Romenesko, James, "Retired Teacher Stabbed to Death," *Milwaukee Journal*, July 20, 1979.

2. Ibid.

3. "Woman, 78, Is Stabbed to Death," *Milwaukee Journal*, August 11, 1979.

4. "Murder Suspected in Death of Woman, 78," *Milwaukee Journal*, November 10, 1979.

5. Fauber, John, and Mary Zahn, "21-Year-Old Man to be Charged in 6 Slayings, Attempted Murder," *Milwaukee Sentinel*, May 31, 1980.

6. "Slaying Victim's Note Leads Police to Suspect," *Milwaukee Sentinel*, March 4, 1980.

7. "Woman, 28, Beaten on North Side," *Milwaukee Journal*, April 16, 1980.

8. "North Side Woman Found Beaten to Death in Home," *Milwaukee Sentinel*, April 26, 1980.

9. Fauber, John, "Ex-teacher Found Slain," *Milwaukee Sentinel*, July 20, 1979; Romenesko, "Retired Teacher Stabbed to Death."

10. Fauber, "Ex-teacher Found Slain."

11. Romenesko, "Retired Teacher Stabbed to Death."

12. "Woman, 78, Found Stabbed, " *Milwaukee Sentinel*, August 11, 1979; "Woman, 78, Is Stabbed to Death," *Milwaukee Journal*, August 11, 1979; "Survivor Identifies Suspect Linked to Six Slayings," *Milwaukee Sentinel*, June 11, 1980.

13. *Milwaukee Journal*, "Woman, 78, Is Stabbed to Death."

14. "Murder Suspected in Death of Woman, 78," *Milwaukee Journal*, November 10, 1979.

15. Janz, Bill, "Brutal Memories in Neighborhood," *Milwaukee Sentinel*, May 30, 1980; *Milwaukee Sentinel*, "Survivor Identifies Suspect Linked to Six Slayings."

16. "Slaying Victim's Note Leads Police to Suspect," *Milwaukee Sentinel*, March 4, 1980; "Victim's Note Leads Police to Suspect," *Milwaukee Journal*, March 4, 1980.

17. *Milwaukee Sentinel*, "Slaying Victim's Note Leads Police to Suspect"; *Milwaukee Journal*, "Victim's Note Leads Police to Suspect."

18. *Milwaukee Journal*, "Woman, 28, Beaten on North Side."

19. Janz, William, "The Only One Who Got Away Wonders Why It Happened," *Milwaukee Sentinel*, May 31, 1980.

20. Ibid.

21. "North Side Woman Found Beaten to Death in Home," *Milwaukee Sentinel*, April 26, 1980; "2 Were Seen at Slaying Site," *Milwaukee Journal*, April 26, 1980.

22. "Police Hold Suspect in 6 Slayings in the City," *Milwaukee Journal*, May 29, 1980; Fauber, John, and Mary Zahn, "21-Year-Old Man to Be Charged in 6 Slayings, Attempted Murder," *Milwaukee Journal,* May 31, 1980; "Charges Filed in 6 Slayings," *Milwaukee Journal*, June 3, 1980.

23. Fauber and Zahn, "21-Year-Old Man to Be Charged in 6 Slayings, Attempted Murder."

24. Ibid.

25. "Viciousness Betrayed Murder Suspect," *Milwaukee Journal*, June 1, 1980; "Necklaces Tied to Slaying Victim, Suspect," *Milwaukee Sentinel*, June 12, 1980; Stingl, Jim, "Killings Stir Memories of 1979–80 Murder Spree," *Milwaukee Journal Sentinel*, December 7, 1997.

26. Fauber and Zahn, "21-Year-Old Man to Be Charged in 6 Slayings, Attempted Murder"; "Charges Filed in 6 Slayings," *Milwaukee Journal*, June 3, 1980; Zahn, Mary, "Suspect Offers Grim Details of How Six Met Their Deaths," *Milwaukee Sentinel*, June 3, 1980.

27. Zahn, "Suspect Offers Grim Details of How Six Met Their Deaths."

28. "Trial Ordered for Suspect in 6 Slayings," *Milwaukee Sentinel*, June 14, 1980.

29. Interview, Barry Slagle, Milwaukee court commissioner, December 27, 2006.

30. Rothe, Karen, and John Fauber, "Suspect in 6 Murders Had Violent Childhood," *Milwaukee Sentinel*, May 30, 1980; Fauber and Zahn, "21-Year-Old Man to Be Charged in 6 Slayings, Attempted Murder."

31. Rothe and Fauber, "Suspect in 6 Murders Had Violent Childhood."

32. *Milwaukee Journal*, "Viciousness Betrayed Murder Suspect."

33. Slagle interview.

Chapter 6: Carnage in the Heartland

1. Fults, Kevin J., criminal complaint, filed Feb. 13, 1989, Sauk County Circuit Court.

2. Moe, Doug, "The Haunting of Adams County," *Madison Magazine*, February, 1983.

3. "2 Suspects sought in Deaths of 3," *The Milwaukee Journal*, October 5, 1975.

4. "Dream Ended in Nightmare of Death," *Milwaukee Journal*, October 6, 1975.

5. "2 Arrested in Triple Slaying," *Milwaukee Journal*, November 23, 1975.

Notes

6. *Milwaukee Journal,* "Dream Ended in Nightmare of Death."

7. Moe, "The Haunting of Adams County."

8. Derleth, August. *Wisconsin Murders.* Sauk City, Wis.: Mycroft & Moran Publishers. 1968. p. ix.

9. Interview, Doug Moe, *Capital Times*, April 4, 2006.

10. Ibid.

11. Moe, "The Haunting of Adams County."

12. Bergqiust, Lee, "Oxford Man Charged in Nachreiner Slaying," Milwaukee Sentinel, September 5, 1987; McCann, Dennis, "Arrest Quiets Fear, Even If It's Only 1 in 3 Slayings," *Milwaukee Journal*, September 6, 1987.

13. Moe, "The Haunting of Adams County."

14. Interview, Doug Moe, *Capital Times*, April 4, 2006.

15. Wisconsin State Climatology Office, www.aos.wisc.edu/~sco

16. http://www.sdc.com/swingers/Lone-Rock-swingers-Wisconsin.aspx

17. Lone Rock, Wisconsin, in http://www.tustison.com/hometown/history.shtml

18. *Baraboo Daily News*, February. 6, 1913.

19. *Lone Rock Journal*, February. 23, 1933.

20. *Richland Center Rustic* , 1918.

21. Lone Rock, Wisconsin, http://www.tustison.com/hometown/history.shtml

22. Fults, criminal complaint.

23. Ibid.

24. Ibid.

25. Ibid.

26. ed, "Body May Be Missing Woman," *Milwaukee Sentinel*, June 16, 1987.

27. Fults, criminal complaint.

28. Gribble, James, "Officers Intensify Search for Teacher," *Milwaukee Journal*, July 31, 1987.

29. Gribble, "Officers Intensify Search for Teacher."

30. Balousek, Marv. *101 Wisconsin Unsolved Mysteries*. Oregon, Wis.: Badger Books. 2000, 135-136.

31. Gribble, "Officers Intensify Search for Teacher." "Nude Body Found in Lafayette County," *Milwaukee Sentinel*, August 6, 1987.

32. Bergquist, Lee, "Body in Lafayette County Is Blackstone," *Milwaukee Sentinel*, August 7, 1987.

33. ed, "Woman's X-rays Taken for Body ID." *Milwaukee Journal*, August 7, 1987.

34. "Did Teacher Know Her Slayer?" *Milwaukee Journal*, August 7, 1987.

35. Bergquist, Lee, "Body in Lafayette County Is Blackstone," *Milwaukee Sentinel*, August 7, 1987.

36. Balousek, *101 Wisconsin Unsolved Mysteries*, 65-66.

37. *Milwaukee Journal*, "Did Teacher Know Her Slayer?"

38. Ibid.

39. Fults, criminal complaint.

40. Jaeger, Richard W., "Man Held in Murder of Hackl," *Wisconsin State Journal*, Feb. 14, 1989.

41. Fults, criminal complaint.

42. Fults, criminal complaint; Jaeger, "Man Held in Murder of Hackl."

43. Fults, criminal complaint.

44. Jaeger, "Man Held in Murder of Hackl."

45. Jaeger, Richard W., "Suspect Charged in Hackl Rape-Murder," *Wisconsin State Journal*, February. 15, 1989.

46. Rinard, Amy, "Man Guilty of Assaulting, Killing Hackl," *Milwaukee Sentinel*, October 4, 1989.

47. Rinard, "Man Guilty of Assaulting, Killing Hackl"; "Man Guilty in Hackl Slaying," *Milwaukee Journal*, October 5, 1989.

48. Ibid.

49. Ibid.

50. Rinard, Amy, "Life Term Ordered in '87 Killing." *Milwaukee Sentinel*, December 4, 1989.

51. Jaeger, Richard W., "He Will Be Back," *Wisconsin State Journal,* December 2, 1989.

52. Jaeger, "He Will Be Back."

53. Jones, Richard P., and Gordon, Bill, "Everything But Love," *Milwaukee Journal*, October 4, 1989.

54. Maller, Peter, "Friends Say They 'Hurt' for Dairy Princess," *Milwaukee Sentinel*, October 4,1989; Jones and Gordon, "Everything But Love."

55. Maller, "Friends Say They 'Hurt' for Dairy Princess"; Jones and Gordon, "Everything But Love."

56. Maller, "Friends Say They 'Hurt' for Dairy Princess"; Jones and Gordon, "Everything But Love."

57. Stone, Andrea. "Midwest Murder: A Love Gone Awry," *USA Today*, June 18, 1990; "Former Dairy Princess Gets Life Term for Strangling Rival," *Minneapolis Star Tribune*, August 25, 1990.

58. "Court Upholds Conviction," *Las Vegas Review - Journal*, May 28, 1992.

59. Weintraub, Joanne." Forthcoming TV Movie Takes Its Cue from Dairy Princess Saga." *Milwaukee Journal Sentinel*, July 14, 1995.

60. Balousek, *101 Wisconsin Unsolved Mysteries*, 135-136.

Chapter 7: Slaughter House on 25th Street

1. Comments to author, Limerick, 1993.

2. De Sousa, Christopher, *State of Milwaukee's Environment, Preliminary Report*, UWM Center for Economic Development, September 13, 2004.

3. Schwartz, Anne E., and Cuprisin, "Grisly Discovery Is Shocking to Neighborhood Used to Crime," *Milwaukee Journal*, July 23, 1991.

4. Lisheron, Mark, "Satanic Elements Found in Slaying," *Milwaukee Journal*, July 22, 1991.

5. US Census, 1990, http://www.ams.usda.gov/statesummaries/WI/MSA/MSA.pdf/Milwaukee.pdf. City of Milwaukee, http://www.thecityofmilwaukee.com.

6. Schwartz, Anne E. *The Man Who Could Not Kill Enough*. New York: Birch Lane Press. 1992, 2; http://en.wikipedia.org/wiki/Jeffrey_Dahmer; "Man Held in Grisly Slayings," *Milwaukee Journal*, July 23, 1991.

7. "Man Held in Grisly Slayings," *Milwaukee Journal*, July 23, 1991; "Horror Unfolds," *Milwaukee Sentinel*, July 24, 1991; Dahmer Neighbor Was Killed in May," *Milwaukee Journal*, July 28, 1991.

Notes

8. Schwartz, *The Man Who Could Not Kill Enough*, 4; *Crime Case Closed: Jeffrey Dahmer,* http://www.bbc.co.uk/crime/caseclosed/dahmer1.shtml; *Milwaukee Journal*, "Man Held in Grisly Slayings."

9. *Milwaukee Journal*, "Man Held in Grisly Slayings"; ed, "Dahmer Implicates Himself," *Milwaukee Journal*, July 24, 1991.

10. Schwartz, *The Man Who Could Not Kill Enough*, 4-5.

11. Schwartz, *The Man Who Could Not Kill Enough*; *Milwaukee Journal*, "Man Held in Grisly Slayings."

12. *Crime Case Closed: Jeffrey Dahmer,* http://www.bbc.co.uk/crime/caseclosed/dahmer1.shtml.

13. Schwartz, Anne, and Cuprisin, Tim, "Grisly Discovery Is Shocking to Neighborhood Used to Crime," *Milwaukee Journal*, July 23, 1991; Stephenson, Crocker, "Other Residents of Building Cannot Sleep, Plan to Move," *Milwaukee Sentinel*, July 25, 1991; interview, Barry Slagle, Milwaukee County Circuit Court commissioner, December 27, 2006.

14. Burnside, Tina, "Body Parts Found Inside Apartment," *Milwaukee Sentinel*, July 23, 1991.

15. Schwartz, *The Man Who Could Not Kill Enough*, 7-10.

16. http://www.bbc.co.uk/crime/caseclosed/dahmer1.shtml; *Milwaukee Journal*, "Man Held in Grisly Slayings";*Milwaukee Sentinel*, "Horror Unfolds"; Wilkerson, Isabel, "Parts of Many Bodies Found in a Milwaukee Apartment," *New York Times*, July 24, 1991; interview, Barry Slagle, Milwaukee County Circuit Court commissioner, December 27, 2006.

17. ed, "Dressler's Attorneys Seek Link to Multiple Slayings," *Milwaukee Sentinel*, July 25, 1991.

18. "'Homosexual Overkill' Meaning Is Discussed," *Milwaukee Journal*, July 23, 1991.

19. Ibid.

20. "First Charges Filed," *Milwaukee Sentinel*, July 26, 1991.

21. Vanden Brook, Tom, "Gay Response: Linking Deaths to Homosexuality Is Unfair," *Milwaukee Journal,* July 24, 1991.

22. Murphy, Mary Beth, "Street Priest Claims Dahmer Was Homophobic," *Milwaukee Sentinel*, July 26, 1991.

23. Cuprisin, Tim, "News Media, Residents Lured by the Lurid," *Milwaukee Journal,* July 24, 1991; Schwartz, Anne E., "Neighbor Decided Not to Have a Beer," *Milwaukee Journal*, July 25, 1991.

24. Cole, Jeff, "Author and Movie-Makers Seek to Capitalize on Story," *Milwaukee Sentinel*, July 27, 1991.

25. Vanden Brook, Tom, "Rumors of Stalker Were Heard at Gay Clubs in Chicago," *Milwaukee Journal*, July 25, 1991; Affidavit Tells of Deadly Visits," *Milwaukee Journal,* July 25, 1991.

26. Dresang, Joel, "Man Who Ran Gives Thanks for Escape," *Milwaukee Journal*, July 25, 1991; Held, Tom, and Stephenson, Crocker, "Man Who Fled Describes Four Hours of 'Hell,'" *Milwaukee Sentinel*, July 26, 1991; Schwartz, *The Man Who Could Not Kill Enough*, 111.

27. Schwartz, *The Man Who Could Not Kill Enough*, 112-114; Edwards, Tracy, case # 20706, Lee County Circuit Court, Tupelo, Miss., October, 1990.

28. Bothwell, Anne, "Medical Examiner Playing a Pivotal Role," *Milwaukee Journal*, July 24, 1991.

29. ed, "Authorities Identify 11 Victims," *Milwaukee Sentinel*, July 27, 1991.

30. Hanley, Daniel P, Jr., "Jentzen Declared Emergency to Cover Expenses," *Milwaukee Journal*, July 29, 1991.

31. Reuter, Heidi, "Hearing Has Air of Film Premiere," *Milwaukee Sentinel*, July 26, 1991.

32. *Portrait of a Serial Killer: Wis. v. Dahmer,* http://www.courttv.com/trials/taped/dahmer.html;

Got Murder?

Crime Case Closed: Jeffrey Dahmer.

33. Schwartz, *The Man Who Could Not Kill Enough*, 113-114.

34. "Seven Victims Identified So Far," *Milwaukee Sentinel*, July 26, 1991; "Victim in Slayings Leaves Behind Wife, 3 Children," *Milwaukee Journal*, July 26, 1991; Dresang, Joel, "Family of Victim Struggling to Cope," *Milwaukee Journal*, July 27, 1991; "Slaying Victim Was Trying to Turn His Life Around, Friends Say," *Milwaukee Journal*, July 28, 1991.

35. Johnson-Elie, Tannette, "Slayings of Minorities Disturb Black Leaders," *Milwaukee Sentinel*, July 27, 1991.

36. Herzog, Karen, and Poda, Paula A., "Report on Police Compounds Family's Grief," *Milwaukee Sentinel*, July 27, 1991.

37. Johnson-Elie, "Slayings of Minorities Disturb Black Leaders."

38. Brook, Tom Vanden, "Rally Leaves No Doubt of Anger at Police," *Milwaukee Journal*, July 31, 1991.

39. Sandin, Jo, "Why Wasn't Stench Reported by Residents?" *Milwaukee Journal*, July 26, 1991.

40. Schwartz, Anne E., "Fleeing in Terror: Woman Says Police Gave Boy Back to Dahmer," *Milwaukee Journal*, July 26, 1991.

41. *John Balcerzak*, http://en.wikipedia.org/wiki/John_Balcerzak; http://www.mpl.org/file/readyref_d.htm; Held, Tom, "Boy Reportedly Left by Officers," *Milwaukee Sentinel*, July 27, 1991; United States District Court for the Eastern District of Wisconsin; The Estate of Konerak Sinthasomphone, et al, v. City of Milwaukee, et al; Civil Action No. 91-C-1121, Civil Action No. 91-C-942, Civil Action No. 91-C-985, Civil Action No. 91-C-1337; 785 F. Supp. 1343; 1992 U.S. Dist. LEXIS 2653; Decided March 5, 1992; Filed March 5, 1992.

42. Skiba, Katherine M., Marchione, Marilyn, and Chin, Tyler, "The Man Who Hated Other Men," *Milwaukee Journal*, July 28, 1991; *Dahmer*, http://www.criminalprofiling.com/Dahmer_s128.html; Schwartz, *The Man Who Could Not Kill Enough*, 40-44; Mendoza, Manuel, and Dresang, Joel, "'Everybody Knew He Was Strange,'" *Milwaukee Journal*, July 24, 1991.

43. Dahmer, http://www.criminalprofiling.com/Dahmer_s128.html; Schwartz, *The Man Who Could Not Kill Enough*, 42; "Mother of Accused Mass Murderer Lived Here," *Chippewa Herald Tribune*, July 25, 1991; Skiba, Marchione, and Chin, "The Man Who Hated Other Men."

44. Skiba, Marchione, and Chin, "The Man Who Hated Other Men."

45. "Jeffrey Dahmer," http://en.wikipedia.org/wiki/Jeffrey_Dahmer.

46. *Crime Case Closed: Jeffrey Dahmer*; Schwartz, *The Man Who Could Not Kill Enough*, 44; Nelson, James B., "Dahmer Admits to 1978 Killing," *Milwaukee Sentinel*, July 27, 1991; Helbig, Bob, "Dahmer May Have Killed in Ohio and West Allis," *Milwaukee Journal*, July 27, 1991; "Bone Found in Ohio: Remains Retrieved at Ex-Dahmer Home," *Milwaukee Sentinel*, July 29, 1991. Marchione, Marilynn and Bothwell, Anne, "Search Uncovers Parts of Rib, Spine," *Milwaukee Journal*, July 30, 1991.

47. Mendoza, Manuel, "Dahmer's Statement Denies Links to Out-of-State Killings," *Milwaukee Journal*, July 28, 1991.

48. Schwartz, *The Man Who Could Not Kill Enough*, 44-45.

49. *Dahmer*, http://www.criminalprofiling.com/Dahmer_s128.html; ed, "Carnage May Extend to Slayings in Germany," *Milwaukee Journal*, July 25, 1991.

50. Schwartz, *The Man Who Could Not Kill Enough*, 50.

51. *Dahme*r, http://www.criminalprofiling.com/Dahmer_s128.htm.

52. Ibid.

53. *Dahme*r, http://www.criminalprofiling.com/Dahmer_s128.html; Schwartz, *The Man Who Could Not Kill Enough*, 50.

Notes

54. Schwartz, *The Man Who Could Not Kill Enough*, 51.

55. Ibid., 51-53.

56. Ibid., 54.

57. Ibid., 55.

58. Dahmer, http://www.criminalprofiling.com/Dahmer_s128.html; Schwartz, Anne E. *The Man Who Could Not Kill Enough*. New York: Birch Lane Press. 1992, 55.

59. Dahmer, http://www.criminalprofiling.com/Dahmer_s128.html; Christopolus, Mike, "Earlier Prosecutor Urged Prison for Dahmer," *Milwaukee Sentinel*, July 26, 1991.

60. ed, Dahmer, http://www.criminalprofiling.com/Dahmer_s128.html; "Letter To Judge in '89 Pleaded for Leniency," *Milwaukee Sentinel*, July 24, 1991; Mendoza, Manuel, "89 Transcripts of Dahmer Case Hint at Trouble," *Milwaukee Journal*, July 26, 1991.

61. "Letter to Judge in '89 Pleaded for Leniency," *Milwaukee Sentinel*, July 24, 1991.

62. Johnson-Elie, Tannette, "Dahmer Was Run-of-Mill Prisoner," *Milwaukee Sentinel*, July 26, 1991.

63. Ward, Mark, "Probation Visits Were Dropped," *Milwaukee Journal*, July 24, 1991; Ward, Mark, "Probation Agents Defend Handling of Case," *Milwaukee Journal*, July 28, 1991.

64. "Grisly Case for Better Probation," *Milwaukee Journal*, July 25, 1991.

65. Hanley, Daniel P., Jr., "Dahmer Had Talked of Suicide, Reports Say," *Milwaukee Journal*, July 26, 1991; Christopolus, Mike, "Dahmer Tried to Get Treatment," *Milwaukee Sentinel*, July 27, 1991.

66. ed, Dahmer, http://www.criminalprofiling.com/Dahmer_s128.html ; Helbig, Bob, "Authorities Have Identified All 11 Victims in Apartment," *Milwaukee Journal*, July 28, 1991; Schwartz, *The Man Who Could Not Kill Enough*, 195; interview, Milwaukee County District Attorney E. Michael McCann, September 25, 2006.

67. Helbig, "Authorities Have Identified All 11 Victims in Apartment,"; "Slaying Victim Was Trying to Turn His Life Around, Friends Say," *Milwaukee Journal*, July 28, 1991.

68. Helbig, "Authorities Have Identified All 11 Victims in Apartment."

69. Ibid.

70. Williams, Celeste, "Mother Identifies 'Baby' As Victim," *Milwaukee Journal*, July 25, 1991; Helbig, "Authorities Have Identified All 11 Victims in Apartment."

71. "Victim in Slayings Leaves Wife, 3 Children," *Milwaukee Journal*, July 26, 1991; Stingl, Jim, "Gruesome Pattern Emerges," *Milwaukee Journal,* July 26, 1991; Helbig, "Authorities Have Identified All 11 Victims in Apartment."

72. ed, Wisconsin Death Penalty Advisory Referendum, National Coalition to Abolish the Death Penalty, http://www.democracyinaction.org/dia/organizations/ncadp/news.jsp?key=2811&t; Kane, Eugene, "In My Opinion; Death Penalty Turns Clock Way Back," *Milwaukee Journal Sentinel*, March 9, 2006.

73. "Thompson Backs a Death Penalty," *Milwaukee Journal*, July 26, 1991.

74. Schwartz, *The Man Who Could Not Kill Enough*, 148-151; ed, "Dahmer Killed in Prison Attack," *Cincinnati Post*, November 28, 1994.

75. *Portrait of a Serial Killer: Wis. v. Dahmer*, http://www.courttv.com/trials/taped/dahmer.html.

76. Schwartz, *The Man Who Could Not Kill Enough*, 192.

77. Schwartz, *The Man Who Could Not Kill Enough*, 192; *Portrait of a Serial Killer: Wis. v. Dahmer*.

78. *Portrait of a Serial Killer: Wis. v. Dahmer.*

79. Schwartz, *The Man Who Could Not Kill Enough*, 193-199.

80. Dresang, Joel, "McCann Getting Advice from Man Who Prosecuted Gacy," *Milwaukee Journal*, July 28, 1991; interview, Milwaukee County District Atty. E. Michael McCann, September 25, 2006.

81. Ward, Mark, "Mental State Likely to Be Key to Case," *Milwaukee Journal*, July 26, 1991.

82. Douglas, John, and Mark Okshaker. *Mindhunter*. New York, N.Y.: Scribner. 1995. 256; Keige, Dale, "The Dark World of Park Dietz," *Johns Hopkins Magazine*, November, 1994 (electronic edition, http://www.jhu.edu/~jhumag/1194web/index.html).

83. Douglas and Okshaker, *Mind Hunter*, 348.

84. Schwartz, *The Man Who Could Not Kill Enough*, 211.

85. Schwartz, *The Man Who Could Not Kill Enough*, 213; McCann interview.

86. McCann interview.

87. ed, "Dahmer Is Killed; Left Unguarded in Wisconsin Prison," *Chicago Tribune*, November 28, 1994; Steinberg, Neil, "Dahmer Slain Serial Killer Attacked By Inmate," *Chicago Sun-Times*, November 28, 1994; "Dahmer," http://www.criminalprofiling.com/Dahmer_s128.html; McCann interview.

88. Moe, Doug, "Secrets of Dahmer Brain Will Continue," *Madison Capital Times*, June 21, 1999.

89. Ibid.

90. Janz, Bill, "A Plea to Draw a Speck of Light From a Horror," *Milwaukee Journal Sentinel*, September 1, 1995; Moe, Doug, "On the Matter of Gray Matter," *Madison Capital Times*, October 27, 2005.

91. Ferguson, Paul, "Judge Had to Decide What to Do with Dahmer's Brain," *Portage Daily Register/Wisconsin State Journal*, November 28, 2004.

92. McCann interview.

93. "Dahmer Building Razed," *Chicago Sun-Times*, November 16, 1992; ed, "Serial Killer's Possessions to Be Destroyed," *New York Times*, June 15, 1996; ed, "Group Destroys Serial Killer's Possessions," New York Times, June 28, 1996; Stingl, Jim, "Only Weeds Grow at Unwanted Site of Dahmer Deaths," *Milwaukee Journal Sentinel*, July 23, 1998; McCann interview.

94. *New York Times*, "Serial Killer's Possessions to Be Destroyed"; *New York Times*, "Group Destroys Serial Killer's Possessions."

95. Wilson, Colin, and Wilson, Damon. *The Killers Among Us, Book II*. New York, N.Y.: Warner Books. 1995, 309.

96. Boyle interview.

97. Stingel, Jim, "Good Heavens! Dahmer? Up There?" *Milwaukee Journal Sentinel*, October 20, 2006.

Chapter 8: Unlocked Doors

1. Jaeger, Richard W., "Link to Bondage Books Cited in Sex Killing," *Wisconsin State Journal*, October 1, 1987.

2. Serial Killer Central, http://www.skcentral.com/readarticle.php?article_id=449.

3. Jaeger, Richard W., "Man Held in Sex Killing," *Wisconsin State Journal*, September 12, 1987.

4. Jaeger, Richard W. "Lawyer: Nachreiner Suspect Innocent," *Wisconsin State Journal*, October 20, 1987.

5. 888 Knives R US, http://www.888knivesrus.com/category/butterfly_knives.

6. Death Tied to Search for Woman, *Milwaukee Journal*, July 30, 1987; Bergquist, Lee, "3 Cases

Notes

Put a Scare into Dells Area," *Milwaukee Sentinel*, July 31, 1987; Serial Killer Central, http://www. skcentral.com/readarticle.php?article_id=449; Gribble, James, "Officers Intensify Search for Teacher," *Milwaukee Journal*, July 31, 1987; Bergquist, Lee, "Oxford Man Charged in Nachreiner Slaying," September 5, 1987.

7. *Milwaukee Journal,* "Death Tied to Search for Woman"; "Nude Body Found in Lafayette County," *Milwaukee Sentinel*, August 6, 1987; "Oxford Man Questioned in Dells-Area Homicide," *Milwaukee Sentinel*, September 4, 1987.

8. Bergquist, Lee. "3 Cases Put a Scare into Dells Area," *Milwaukee Sentinel*, July 31, 1987.

9. "Angels Announce Plans for Branch in Madison," *Milwaukee Journal*, June 18, 1986; Weintraub, Joanne, "Angels Are a Big Draw in Dells," *Milwaukee Journal*, August 6, 1987; Rivedal, Karen, "Guardian Angels to Train Locals," *Wisconsin State Journal,* August 26, 2006.

10. Gribble, James, "Search for Teacher Continues; Father Seeks Governor's Help," *Milwaukee Journal*, August 1, 1987.

11. "Good 'Police Work' Evident in Case," *Capital Times*, September 5, 1987.

12. Correspondence, Adams County District Attorney Mark Thibodeau, March 31, 2006.

13. Moe, Doug, "The Haunting of Adams County," *Madison Magazine*, February, 1983.

14. Interview, Adams County District Attorney Mark D. Thibodeau, March 26, 2006; Thibodeau correspondence; interview, Doug Moe, *Capital Times*, April 4, 2006.

15. Thibodeau interview.

16. Ibid.

17. Jaeger, Richard W., "Murder Evidence Against Brown Was Overwhelming," *Wisconsin State Journal*, May, 18, 1988; Thibodeau interview; Jaeger, Richard W., "Several People Vie for Reward Money in Murder," *Wisconsin State Journal*, June 1, 1988.

18. Jaeger, "Man Held in Sex Killing"; Thibodeau correspondence.

19. Jaeger "Link to Bondage Books Cited in Sex Killing."

20. *Milwaukee Sentinel,* "Oxford Man Questioned in Dells-Area Homicide"; Bergquist, "Oxford Man Charged in Nachreiner Slaying"; Jaeger, "Link to Bondage Books Cited in Sex Killing"; Jaeger, "Oxford Man to Stand Trial for Sex Killing."

21. Serial Killer Central

22. Jaeger, "Man Held in Sex Killing."

23. Thibodeau correspondence.

24. *Milwaukee Sentinel,* "Oxford Man Questioned in Dells-Area Homicide"; Bergquist, "Oxford Man Charged in Nachreiner Slaying."

25. McCann, Dennis, "Man to Face Charges in Murder," *Milwaukee Journal,* September 4, 1987; Balousek, Marv, Accused Murderer An 'Ordinary Guy,' *Capital Times*, September 5, 1987; Maller, Peter, "Defendant in Slaying Called Loner," *Milwaukee Sentinel*, September 30, 1987.

26. Jaeger, "Man Held in Sex Killing."

27. Balousek, "Accused Murderer An 'Ordinary Guy'"; Maller, "Defendant in Slaying Called Loner"; "Good 'Police Work' Evident in Case," *Capital Times*, September 5, 1987.

28. Butler, Niquita, "Man's Arrest Surprises Neighbors," *Milwaukee Journal*, September 6, 1987.

29. Balousek, "Accused Murderer An 'Ordinary Guy.'"

30. Ibid.

31. Balousek, "Accused Murderer An 'Ordinary Guy'"; Butler, "Man's Arrest Surprises Neighbors."

32. Balousek, "Accused Murder An 'Ordinary Guy.'"

33. Ibid.

34. Serial Killer Central.

35. Jaeger, "Man Held in Sex Killing."

36. Schultze, Steve, "Authorities Discard Notion of Serial Murderer," *Milwaukee Journal*, September 11, 1987.

37. McCann, "Man to Face Charges in Murder"; Bergquist, "Oxford Man Charged in Nachreiner Slaying."

38. Thibodeau correspondence.

39. Jaeger, "Man Held in Sex Killing."

40. Jaeger,"Link to Bondage Books Cited in Sex Killing."

41. Documents provided by Adams County clerk of courts, March, 2006.

42. Interview, Atty. Gerald Boyle, interview, April 6, 2006.

43. Jaeger, Richard W., "Murder Suspect's Hearing Delayed," *Wisconsin State Journal*, September 15, 1987.

44. Jaeger,"Link to Bondage Books Cited in Sex Killing."

45. Jaeger, "Oxford Man to Stand Trial for Sex Killing."

46. Jaeger, Richard W., "Lawyer: Nachreiner Suspect Innocent," *Wisconsin State Journal*, October 20, 1987. "Judge Zappen to Hear Murder Trial," *Wisconsin State Journal*, October 25, 1987.

47. Jaeger, Richard W., "Nachreiner Suspect's Rights Plea Denied," *Wisconsin State Journal*, Feb. 11, 1988.

48. Jaeger, Richard W., "Brown's Murder Trial Moved," *Wisconsin State Journal*, November 13, 1987.

49. Ibid.

50. Jaeger, Richard W., "Nachreiner Suspect's Rights Plea Denied," *The Wisconsin State Journal*, Feb. 11, 1988.

51. Boyle interview.

53. Ibid.

54. Jaeger, Mark W., "Man Will Admit Torture-Killing," *Wisconsin State Journal*, May 14, 1988.

55. Jaeger, Richard W., "Fingerprint Links Suspect, Slaying," *Wisconsin State Journal*, May 14, 1988.

56. Thibodeau correspondence.

57. Adams County documents.

58, Jaeger, "Murder Evidence Against Brown Was Overwhelming."

59. Ibid.

60. Jaeger, Richard W., "Brown Confesses, Gets Life Term," *Wisconsin State Journal*, May 18, 1988.

61. Ibid.

62. Jaeger "Brown Confesses, Gets Life Term"; Boyle interview.

63. Jaeger, "Brown Confesses, Gets Life Term."

64. Jaeger, Richard W., "Several People Vie for Reward Money in Murder," *Wisconsin State Journal*, June 1, 1988.

65. Ibid.

66. Jaeger, Richard, "Torture-Killer Gets 120 More Years," *Wisconsin State Journal*, November 3, 1998.

67. Ibid.

68. Wisconsin Department of Justice, Division of Corrections, www.wi-doc.com/columbia.htm.

69. Adams County documents.

70. Documents provided by the Wisconsin Department of Corrections.

71. "Dahmer Murdered," *Capital Times*, December 15, 1994.

72. Whiteville Correctional Facility, www.state.tn.us/correction/institutions/wcfa.html; correspondence, John Dipko, Wisconsin Department of Justice, Division of Corrections, March 25 and 28, 2006.

73. Interview, Assistant Warden Steven Beck, Redgranite Correctional Institution, March 10, 2006.

74. Wisconsin Department of Justice, Division of Corrections, www.wi-doc.com/Redgranite. htm; interview, Assistant Warden Steven Beck, Redgranite Correctional Institution, March 10, 2006; correspondence, Assistant Warden Steven Beck, March 16 and 17, 2006; correspondence, John Dipko, Wisconsin Department of Justice, Division of Corrections, March 25 and 28, 2006.

Chapter 9: Deep, Deadly Waters

1. Larimer, Sarah, "'Disbelief' Reigns After Student's Body Recovered," *Milwaukee Journal Sentinel*, October. 3, 2006.

2. "Drowning is Coincidence Midwest Missing Student Mystery." http://www.vanceholmes. com/court/trial_missing_students.html.

3. "Half Moon Lake Study," University of Wisconsin-Eau Claire, http://www.uwec.edu/jolhm/ Halfmoon/Titlepage.htm; "Historic Randall Park Neighborhoods; http://www.randallpark. com/parksrec.html.

4. Daglas, Christine, "UW-Eau Claire Student Found Dead," *The Badger Herald*, March 27, 2003.

5. Centers for Disease Control and Prevention.

6. "Cerebral Hypoxia," wikipedia.org/wiki/Cerebral_hypoxia.

7. "Hypoxia," http://www.thefreedictionary.com/hypoxemia.

8. "The Physiology and Pathology of Drowning," *The Forensic Examiner, Journal of The American College of Forensic Examiners,* Volume 15, Number 3, Fall, 2006, 10-12.

9. Ibid.

10. "Explore Wisconsin's La Crosse County, http://www.explorewisconsin.com/countypages/ la_crosse.html; "La Crosse Bars," http://www.10best.com/La_Crosse/Nightlife/Bars/index.html; James, Matt, "Despite the Facts, the Urban Legend Won't Go Away," *La Crosse Tribune*, April 16, 2004.

11. Otto, Dick, operations director, United States Army Corps of Engineers, Natural Resources Office, La Crescent, Minnesota, interview, October 17, 2006.

12. Jones, Meg, "UW-La Crosse Student Missing," *Milwaukee Journal-Sentinel*, October 2, 2006; Schott, Kate, "UW-L Student missing; River Search Under Way," *La Crosse Tribune*, October 2, 2006.

13. Jones, "UW-La Crosse Student Missing."

14. "Homan's Death Ruled Drowning," *La Crosse Tribune*, October 3, 2006; Jungen, Anne and Springer, Dan, "Officials Say Student Drowned," *La Crosse Tribune*, October 4, 2006; Jungen, Anne and Springer, Dan, "Drowned Student's Alcohol Level Four Times Legal Limit," *La Crosse Tribune*, October 5, 2006.

15. Jones, "UW-La Crosse Student Missing"; Larimer, "'Disbelief' Reigns After Student's Body Recovered."

16. Jones, "UW-La Crosse Student Missing."

17. Larimer, "'Disbelief' Reigns After Student's Body Recovered."

18. Ibid.

19. ed, "Readers' Comments," *La Crosse Tribune* web site, October 3, 2006. http://www.lacrossetribune.com/articles/2006/10/03/editors_note/00lead.txt.

20. "River Drowning: Serial Killer or Urban Legend" http://co.la-crosse.wi.us/Departments/Medical%20Examiner/docs/River%20Drowning.ppt.

21. Rindfleisch, Terry R., "Police Say Facts Point Not to a Serial killer But to Fatal Cocktail of Alcohol, Water," *La Crosse Tribune*, April 18, 2004; Mercer, Anastasia, " Father Wants Regional Task Force to Look into River Deaths; Offers $175,000 Reward for Information Leading to a Conviction," *La Crosse Tribune*, April 30, 2004; "Jared Dion," Missing and Murdered Persons Message Forum, http://findcarrie.conforums.com/index.cgi?board=crimes&action=display&num=1095856564; Walker, Laurel, "In My Opinion; When Will Tragedy Spark Real Change?" *Milwaukee Journal Sentinel*, October 3, 2006; Larimer, "'Disbelief' Reigns After Student's Body Recovered"; "River Drowning: Serial Killer or Urban Legend," La Crosse County Medical Examiner's office, http://co.la-crosse.wi.us/Departments/Medical%20Examiner/docs/River%20Drowning.ppt.

22. Springer, Dan, "Body Identified as Missing La Crosse Man," *La Crosse Tribune*, June 8, 2004.

23. Springer, "Body Identified as Missing La Crosse Man"; "The Body of Gordon Stumlin Jr. Is Pulled from the River," *La Crosse Tribune*, June 5, 2004.

24. Rindfleisch, "Police Say Facts Point Not to a Serial killer But to Fatal Cocktail of Alcohol, Water"; La Crosse County Medical Examiner, "River Drowning: Serial Killer or Urban Legend."

25. Rindfleisch, "Police Say Facts Point Not to a Serial killer But to Fatal Cocktail of Alcohol, Water"; "Past River Tragedies," *La Cross Tribune*, October, 2006, http://www.lacrossetribune.com/rivertragedies; La Crosse County Medical Examiner, "River Drowning: Serial Killer or Urban Legend."

26. Hoskin, Ed, "Mother of Victim Has Warnings for Downtown Tavern-goers," *La Crosse Tribune*, October 6, 1999.

27. Rindfleisch, "Police Say Facts Point Not to a Serial killer But to Fatal Cocktail of Alcohol, Water"; *La Cross Tribune*, "Past River Tragedies"; La Crosse County Medical Examiner, "River Drowning: Serial Killer or Urban Legend."

28. Rindfleisch, "Police Say Facts Point Not to a Serial killer But to Fatal Cocktail of Alcohol, Water"; *La Cross Tribune*, "Past River Tragedies,"; "Explore Wisconsin's La Crosse County, http://www.explorewisconsin.com/countypages/la_crosse.html.

29. "Gallery of Huge Beings," http://www.wlra.us/hb/hbhiawa.html; "Explore Wisconsin's La Crosse County"; Hammes, Stephannie, and Crocker, Dr. Leslie T., "Forms and Spaces: Sculpture in La Crosse, Wisconsin," http://murphylibrary.uwlax.edu/digital/lacrosse/FormsSpaces.

30. La Crosse County Medical Examiner, "River Drowning: Serial Killer or Urban Legend."

31. Kapfer, Doris and Mark, "Realize the Danger of Underage Drinking," *La Crosse Tribune*, Feb. 24, 1999.

32. Rindfleisch, "Police Say Facts Point Not to a Serial killer But to Fatal Cocktail of Alcohol, Water"; La Crosse County Medical Examiner, "River Drowning: Serial Killer or Urban Legend."

33. Geesey, Laurie, "Let's Make Future Safer for Our Kids," *La Crosse Tribune*, July 25, 1999.

34. Rindfleisch, "Police Say Facts Point Not to a Serial killer But to Fatal Cocktail of Alcohol, Water"; La Crosse County Medical Examiner, "River Drowning: Serial Killer or Urban Legend."

35. "Black River Victim Presumed Drunk," *Milwaukee Journal Sentinel*, March 12, 2001; La Crosse County Medical Examiner, "River Drowning: Serial Killer or Urban Legend."

36. James, Matt, "Despite the Facts, the Urban Legend Won't Go Away," *La Crosse Tribune*, April 16, 2004.

37. Rindfleisch, "Police Say Facts Point Not to a Serial Killer But to Fatal Cocktail of Alcohol, Water."

38. Springer, Dan, "Chief Sets Meeting on River Deaths," *La Crosse Tribune*, April 20, 2004; Springer, Dan, "Community Discusses River Deaths," *La Crosse Tribune*, April 23, 2004; Epstein, Reid J., "Crowd Heckles La Crosse police for Blaming Drownings on Drinking," *Milwaukee Journal Sentinel*, April 23, 2004.

39. Interview, Dale G. Burke, assistant chief, University of Wisconsin-Madison police, October 13, 2006.

40. Kent, Joan, "Alcohol Task Force Prepares its Ideas," *La Crosse Tribune*, January 6, 2005; Kent, Joan, "City's Alcohol Task Force Makes Final Recommendations," *La Crosse Tribune*, February 11, 2005; Kent, Joan, "City Council Accepts Alcohol Task Torce's Report," *La Crosse Tribune*, March 11, 2005; ed, "The List of 19 Recommendations by the Alcohol Task Force," *La Crosse Tribune*, September 25, 2006.

41. Jungen, Anne, "Student in Riverside Park Taken to Detox," *La Crosse Tribune*, October 17, 2006.

Chapter 10: Death Stalks the Blue Hills

1. Nimm, Eileen, "Veteran Officer Calls Killings Unimaginable," *Rice Lake Chronotype*, December 1, 2004.

2. Jones, Meg, "Rise in Hunting Accidents Has Game Wardens Concerned; Officials Worry," *The Milwaukee Journal Sentinel*, November 19, 2004; Riepenhoff, Bob, "2004 Deer Hunting Season Opportunity Knocks," *The Milwaukee Journal Sentinel*, November 21, 2004; ed., "2004 Wisconsin Whitetailed Deer Harvest Summary," Wisconsin Department of Natural Resources, http://www.dnr.state.wi.us/org/land/wildlife/HUNT/deer/harvest04.htm

3. "Hunters Register Over 140,000 Opening Weekend of 2004 Wisconsin Deer Hunt," *Outdoors Weekly*, November 26, 2004; http://www.outdoorsweekly.com/news_archive/04_1126_news.html#1126wisconsi.

4. Jones, Riepenhoff, Wisconsin Department of Natural Resources

5. Jones, Meg, Boxrud, Gail and Barrett, Rick, "5 killed, 3 hurt in hunting rampage," *Milwaukee Journal Sentinel*, November 21, 2004; Associated Press, "Hunting Rage: Wis. Dispute Leaves 5 Dead," *Chicago Sun-Times*, November 22, 2004; Diedrich, John and Bergquist, Lee, "6th Victim Dies from Sunday's Shooting," *Milwaukee Journal Sentinel*, November 22, 2004; Freed, Joshua, "'We Are So Devastated Right Now'," *Chicago Sun-Times*, November 23, 2004; Bergquist, Lee, "Accused Shooter says Other Hunters Fired First," *Milwaukee Journal Sentinel*, November 23, 2004.

6. Jones, Boxrud and Barrett, "5 Killed, 3 Hurt in Hunting Rampage."

7. Diedrich and Bergquist, "6th Victim Dies from Sunday's Shooting"; Nimm, Eileen, "Rampage in the Woods Takes Six Lives," *Rice Lake Chronotype*, November 24, 2004.

8. Jones, Boxrud and Barrett, "5 Killed, 3 Hurt in Hunting Rampage"; "Birchwood," http://72.14.203.104/search?q=cache:kD66sLy3hzUJ:www.haywardlakes.com/visitorguide.

9. Jones, Boxrud and Barrett, "5 Killed, 3 Hurt in Hunting Rampage"; Held, Tom, "Disbelief Faded as Officers Saw Body After Body of Hunters in Woods," *Milwaukee Journal Sentinel*, December 12, 2004.

10. Diedrich and Bergquist, "6th Victim Dies from Sunday's Shooting"; Bergquist, "Accused Shooter Says Other Hunters Fired First."

11. Diedrich and Bergquist, "6th Victim Dies from Sunday's Shooting."

12. Diedrich and Bergquist, "6th Victim Dies from Sunday's Shooting"; Forster, Stacy, Boxrud, Gail and Barrett, Rick, "Alleged shooter was avid hunter," *Milwaukee Journal Sentinel*, November 22, 2004; Freed, Joshua, "Killing of 6 Hunters Stuns Wisconsin," *Deseret News*, November 23, 2004.

13. Forster, Stacy, Boxrud, Gail and Barrett, Rick, "Alleged Shooter Was Avid Hunter," *Milwaukee Journal Sentinel*, November 22, 2004; Helms, Marisa, "Chai Soua Vang," Minnesota Public Radio, November 24, 2004; Bergquist, Lee, "Accused shooter Says Other Hunters Fired First," *Milwaukee Journal Sentinel*, November 23, 2004; Forster, Stacy, "Hmong Leaders Decry Shooting," *Milwaukee Journal Sentinel*, November 23, 2004.

14. Forster, Boxrud and Barrett, "Alleged Shooter Was Avid Hunter"; Helms, Marisa, "Chai Soua Vang," Minnesota Public Radio, November 24, 2004; Bergquist, "Accused Shooter Says Other Hunters Fired First"; Ortiz, Vikki and Toosi, Nahal, "A Spiritual Leader, Jailed in Killings," *Milwaukee Journal Sentinel*, November 25, 2004.

15. Forster, Boxrud and Barrett, "Alleged Shooter Was Avid Hunter"; Helms, Marisa, "Chai Soua Vang," Minnesota Public Radio, November 24, 2004; Bergquist, "Accused Shooter Says Other Hunters Fired First."

16. Freed, "'We Are So Devastated Right Now'"; Forster, "Hmong Leaders Decry Shooting"; Ortiz, Vikki, "Cultural Gap Puts Wedge Between Hunters," *Milwaukee Journal Sentinel*, November 27, 2004.

17. Diedrich, John, "Vang Had Previous Trespass Offense," *Milwaukee Journal Sentinel*, November 24, 2004; Ortiz and Toosi, "A Spiritual Leader, Jailed in Killings."

18. Bergquist, "Accused Shooter Says Other Hunters Fired First."

19. Bergquist, "Accused shooter Says Other Hunters Fired First"; "Probable Cause Statement and Judicial Determination, State of Wisconsin Circuit Court, Sawyer County, State vs Chai Soua Vang, November 23, 2004.

20. Bergquist, "Accused Shooter Says Other Hunters Fired First"; Probable Cause Statement, State vs Chai Soua Vang.

21. Bergquist, "Accused Shooter Says Other Hunters Fired First."

22. Nimm, "Rampage in the Woods Takes Six Lives."

23. Forster, "Hmong Leaders Decry Shooting." Emerson, Tracy, "Hunter to Hmong: Stay Away," *Eau Claire Leader Telegram*, December 17, 2004.

24. Held, Tom, "Family, Friends Bury First of Slain Hunters," *Milwaukee Journal Sentinel*, November 27, 2004.

25. Held, Tom, "Charges Say 4 Were Shot in Back," *Milwaukee Journal Sentinel*, November 29, 2004; Antlfinger, Carrie, "Minnesota Man to be Charged Today in Killings of 6 Hunters," *Chicago Sun-Times*, November 29, 2004; Criminal complaint, Wisconsin v. Chai Soua Vang, Circuit Court, Sawyer County, undated November, 2006.

26. Held, Tom and Johnson, Mark, "Vang Appears in Court for First Time Since Shootings," *Milwaukee Journal Sentinel*, November 30, 2004; Imrie, Robert, "Hunter Accused of Killing 6 Gets High-Security Hearing," *Chicago Sun-Times*, December 1, 2004; "Hunter Faces Multiple Homicide Charges," *Rice Lake Chronotype*, December 1, 2004.

27. Nimm, Eileen and Finazzo, Sam, "Vang enters Not Guilty Pleas to Nine Counts," *Rice Lake Chronotype*, December 29, 2004; Held, Tom, "Psychologists Meet With Hunter Shooting Suspect," *Milwaukee Journal Sentinel*, December 29, 2004; Associated Press, "Minn. Man Pleads Not Guilty in Murders of Six Hunters," *Chicago Sun-Times*, December 30, 2004; Jones, Meg, "Defense Attorneys Ask That Trial in Slayings of Deer Hunters Be Moved," *Milwaukee Journal Sentinel*, March 2, 2005.

28. Nimm, Eileen, "Lawyers Seek Change of Venue in Hunter Shooting," *Rice Lake Chronotype*, March 2, 2005; Jones, "Defense Attorneys Ask That Trial in Slayings of Deer Hunters Be Moved"; Nimm, Eileen, "Lawyers Seek Change of Venue in Hunter Shooting," *Rice Lake Chronotype*, March 2, 2005.

29. Held, Tom. "Prosecutors Want Vang Tried in Sawyer County," *Milwaukee Journal Sentinel*, March 12, 2005.

30. Held, Tom, "Outside Jury Allowed for Hunter Trial," *Milwaukee Journal Sentinel*, June 17, 2005; "Judge Says Vang Jury to Come from Dane County," *Rice Lake Chronotype*, June 22, 2005.

31. "No Plea Bargain Pursued in Vang Trial Set to Begin Next Month," *Hmong Today*, August 25, 2005.

32. Held, Tom, "Jury Picked Quickly in Hunter Killings," *Milwaukee Journal Sentinel*, Sept. 8, 2005; Moua, Wameng, "Quest to Find Justice Underway," *Hmong Today*, September 8, 2005.

33. Zielinski, Graeme, "Was It Rage? Or Race? Vang Trial Begins," *Milwaukee Journal Sentinel*, September 10, 2005; Associated Press, "Several Witnesses Lined Up for Hunter Killings Trial," *Milwaukee Journal Sentinel*, September 11, 2005.

34. Held, Tom, "Survivor Denies Threatening Vang," *Milwaukee Journal Sentinel*, September 12, 2005.

35. Held, Tom, "Exchange Was Hostile, Second Survivor Says," *Milwaukee Journal Sentinel*, Sept. 13, 2005; Imrie, Robert, "Hunter Said Accused Man Fired First," *Chicago Sun-Times*, September 13, 2005.

36. Held, Tom, "Vang Killed to Save Own Life, He Says," *Milwaukee Journal Sentinel*, September 15, 2005; Harter, Kevin, "Vang Tells His Story to Jury," *Pioneer Press*, September 16, 2005; Imrie, Robert, "Hunter Recounts Confrontation Turned Deadly," *Chicago Sun-Times*, September 16, 2005.

37. Held, Tom, "Guilty on All Charges," *Milwaukee Journal Sentinel*, September 16, 2005; Imrie, Robert, "Asian Immigrant Convicted of Murdering 6 Deer Hunters," *Deseret News*, September 17, 2005; Associated Press, "Immigrant Guilty of Murdering Six Hunters," *Chicago Sun-Times*, September 17, 2005.

38. Imrie, Robert, "Man Gets Life Without Parole for Killing 6 Hunters," *Chicago Sun-Times*, November 9, 2005; Associated Press, "Man Who Killed 6 Hunters Gets Life With No Parole," *Deseret News*, November 9, 2005; Nimm, Eileen, "Vang Sentenced to Life x 6," *Rice Lake Chronotype*, November 10, 2005.

39. Associated Press, "Vang Sent to Iowa Prison Out of Safety Concerns," *Chicago Tribune*, April 7, 2006; "Vang Moved to Iowa Prison," *Rice Lake Chronotype*, April 19, 2006.

40. Held, Tom, "Hunters' Memorial Funds Redirected," *Milwaukee Journal Sentinel*, May 29, 2005.

41. Associated Press, "Rice Lake Dedicates Park to Slain Hunters," *Minneapolis Star Tribune*, August 7, 2006.

42. Wisconsin Department of Natural Resources, "2004 Wisconsin White-tailed Deer Harvest Summary"; Outdoors Weekly, "Hunters register over 140,000 opening weekend of 2004 Wisconsin deer hunt"; "Outdoors: Wisconsin Gun Deer Hunting History," *Wisconsin State Journal*, November 19, 2006.

43. Gutsche, Robert Jr., "In Northern Wisconsin, Death of Immigrant Fuels Tensions," *Washington Post*, January 16, 2007.

Chapter 11: Church of the Living Horror

1. Stephenson, Crocker, "It's Human Carnage," *Milwaukee Journal Sentinel*, March 12, 2005.

2. Coen, Jeff, and Heinzmann, David, "Police: DNA Matches," *The Chicago Tribune*, March 11,

Got Murder?

2005.

3. Brian Nichols, http://en.wikipedia.org/wiki/Brian_Nichols.

4. Dorfman, Daniel I., and Wilgoren, Jodi, "Gunman Kills 7 in Church Group Near Milwaukee," *The New York Times*, March 13, 2005; Living Church of God, http://www.livingcog.org.

5. Living Church of God. http://www.livingcog.org

6. Umhoefer, Dave, "Tragedy Puts Spotlight on Small, Obscure Church," *Milwaukee Journal Sentinel*, March 13, 2005; Sink, Lisa, and Seibel, Jacqueline, "Gunman Went to Church to 'Even the Score,' But No One Knows Why," *Milwaukee Journal-Sentinel*, September 9, 2005.

7. Stephenson, "It's Human Carnage"; Barton, Gina, and Sink, Lisa, "22 Shots Launched Hellish Day," *Milwaukee Journal Sentinel*, March 20, 2005.

8. Barton and Sink, "22 Shots Launched Hellish Day."

9. Diedrich, John, "Pastor, Family Called Targets," *Milwaukee Journal Sentinel*, March 15, 2005.

10. Twohey, Megan, "22 shots; One Minute of Terror," *Milwaukee Journal Sentinel*, March 14, 2005; Seibel and Sink, "Gunman Went to Church to 'Even the Score,' But No One Knows Why."

11. Stephenson, "It's Human Carnage"; Towhey, "22 shots; One Minute of Terror"; Johnson, Mike, "Harold L. Diekmeier: 'Gentle' Father Dies as Son Gives Sermon," *Milwaukee Journal Sentinel*, March 14, 2005.

12. Tunkieicz, Jennie, "Gloria Critari: Cudahy Family Sits Together in Back," *Milwaukee Journal Sentinel*, March 14, 2005.

13. Towhey, "22 shots; One Minute of Terror"; Diedrich, "Pastor, Family Called Targets"; Seibel, Jacqueline, and Sink, Lisa, "Gunman Went to Church to 'Even the Score,' But No One Knows Why," *Milwaukee Journal Sentinel*, September 3, 2005.

14. Stephenson, Crocker, "It's Human Carnage," *Milwaukee Journal Sentinel*, March 12, 2005; Seibel and Sink, "Gunman Went to Church to 'Even the Score,' But No One Knows Why."

15. Benson, Dan, "Bart Oliver: 'Any Parent Would be Proud' of Boy, 15," *Milwaukee Journal Sentinel*, March 14, 2005.

16. Seibel and Sink, "Gunman Went to Church to 'Even the Score,' But No One Knows Why."

17. Dorfman and Wilgoren, "Gunman Kills 7 in Church Group Near Milwaukee"; Diedrich, "Pastor, Family Called Targets"; Seibel and Sink, "Gunman Went to Church to 'Even the Score,' But No One Knows Why."

18. Towhey, "22 shots; One Minute of Terror"; Rabideau Silvers, Amy, "Gerald Miller: Hero to Friends May Have Shielded Woman From Bullets," *Milwaukee Journal Sentinel*, March 14, 2005; Diedrich, "Pastor, Family Called Targets."

19. Barton and Sink, "22 Shots Launched Hellish Day."

20. Ibid.

21. Ibid.

22. Ibid.

23. Stephenson, "It's Human Carnage"; Tunkieicz, Jennie, "Richard W. Reeves: Devout Nature Obvious to Family, Friends," *Milwaukee Journal Sentinel*, March 14, 2005; Tunkieicz, "Gloria Critari: Cudahy Family Sits Together in Back."

24. Stephenson, "It's Human Carnage."

25. Sink, Lisa, "Victims of Shooting Remembered at Vigil," *Milwaukee Journal Sentinel*, March 15, 2005; Umhoefer, Dave, "Church Announces Services for Six Shooting Victims," *Milwaukee Journal Sentinel*, March 16, 2005; Schultze, Steve, "Funerals Bring Grace, Peace," *Milwaukee Journal Sentinel*, March 19, 2005; Sink, Lisa, "Still Healing, a Year After Shooting," *Milwaukee Journal Sentinel*, March 9, 2006.

Notes

26. Seibel, Jacqueline, "Woman Crashes into Church," *Milwaukee Journal Sentinel*, March 15, 2005.

27. Seibel and Sink, "Gunman Went to Church to 'Even the Score,' But No One Knows Why."; Seibel, Jacqueline, "Response to Killings Criticized in Detail," *Milwaukee Journal Sentinel*, September 13, 2005.

28. Romell, Rick, "Quiet Man Gave No Hint of Violence," *Milwaukee Journal Sentinel*, March 13, 2005; Benson, Dan, "Ratzmann Called Smart But Angry," *Milwaukee Journal Sentinel*, March 14, 2005; Schultze, Steve, "Search For Wife Pained Shooter," *Milwaukee Journal Sentinel*, March 16, 2005.

29. Dorfman and Wilgoren, "Gunman Kills 7 in Church Group Near Milwaukee"; Diedrich, "Pastor, Family Called Targets."

30. Dorfman, Daniel I., and Wilgoren, Jodi, "Gunman Kills 7 in Church Group Near Milwaukee," *The New York Times*, March 13, 2005; Romell, Rick, "Quiet Man Gave No Hint of Violence," *The Milwaukee Journal Sentinel*, March 13, 2005.

31. Williams, Scott, "'Hapless Victim' or Murderous Gunman?" *Milwaukee Journal Sentinel*, August 28, 2006; http://www.thomasmgeiger.com/index.html; http://martyrdominmilwaukee.com.

Index

Got Murder?

Index

Got Murder?

Index